LAROUSSE

Los verbos ingleses

2

LAROUSSE

Los verbos ingleses

MANUAL PRÁCTICO

LAROUSSE

Publicado en Francia en 2004 por Chambers Harrap Publishers Ltd con el título
Verbes Anglais.

© Chambers Harrap Publishers Ltd 2004
7 Houpetoun Crescent, Edinburgh EH7 4AY

De la presente edición:
© Larousse Editorial, S.L., 2012
Mallorca, 45, 3ª planta
08029 Barcelona
larousse@larousse.es
www.larousse.es

Dirección editorial: Jordi Induráin
Coordinación editorial: María José Simón

Realización y preimpresión: La Cifra
Coordinación de la obra: Sergio Aguilar

Diseño de cubierta: Isaac Gimeno

ISBN: 978-84-15411-23-9
Depósito legal: B.4616-2012
2E1I

Prólogo

Este manual se centra en uno de los aspectos esenciales de la gramática inglesa: la forma y el uso de los verbos. Los primeros capítulos pretenden profundizar en el estudio de la estructura verbal a través de la aclaración de aquellos casos específicos del inglés, haciendo hincapié en la forma de los tiempos verbales, el uso de los auxiliares, del gerundio, de los verbos modales, etc. Estos términos gramaticales se explican de forma clara y precisa a lo largo de todo el libro.

En la segunda parte, el manual profundiza en unas estructuras verbales que se suelen considerar más difíciles, los *phrasal verbs* (verbos con partícula o compuestos), los cuales resultan esenciales en la lengua inglesa, al tiempo que la hacen muy dinámica y versátil. Tras un capítulo completo dedicado al uso de dichas estructuras, ilustrado con ejemplos traducidos, encontrará un diccionario con más de 1.000 verbos con partícula analizados y contextualizados.

Las abreviaturas usadas en el texto figuran en la página 109.

ÍNDICE

1 LAS FORMAS VERBALES: CONCEPTOS BÁSICOS

Los conceptos básicos descritos en este apartado hacen referencia al infinitivo, el participio presente y el participio pasado.

a) El **infinitivo** es la forma básica del verbo. No lleva indicativo de persona y, en inglés, puede ir precedido o no de la partícula to. En el «Diccionario de *phrasal verbs*» y el «Índice de verbos ingleses» de este manual (al final del libro), los verbos que aparecen se recogen en esta forma verbal. El verbo en infinitivo utilizado sin to recibe el nombre de **radical**. En los siguientes ejemplos, watch aparece en infinitivo:

do you want to watch TV?
¿quieres ver la televisión?

I can't watch
no puedo verla

Los diferentes usos del infinitivo aparecen en el capítulo 13.

b) El **participio presente** es la forma verbal acabada en -ing:

is anyone watching TV?
¿hay alguien viendo la televisión?

they were watching us
nos miraban o *estaban mirándonos*

El participio presente se utiliza para formar los tiempos continuos. Tal y como muestra el segundo ejemplo (were watching), se puede emplear para formar otros tiempos que no sean el presente.

El gerundio se forma como el participio presente (supposing you're right... *suponiendo que tengas razón...*).

Los detalles sobre la formación del participio presente y del gerundio aparecen en los capítulos 4 y 13, respectivamente.

c) El **participio pasado** inglés es la forma verbal utilizada sobre todo después del auxiliar have para formar el *present perfect* o pretérito perfecto compuesto (**it has rained** *ha llovido*, **you have tried** *has probado*, etc.). En los verbos regulares, el participio pasado tiene la misma forma que el *simple past* o pretérito perfecto simple, es decir, radical + **-(e)d**:

watch - watched
dance - danced

Los detalles que hacen referencia a los cambios ortográficos del participio pasado aparecen en el capítulo 4.

El participio pasado de los verbos irregulares aparece en el capítulo 6. He aquí algunos ejemplos:

go - gone
teach - taught
stand - stood

2 LOS AUXILIARES

El verbo auxiliar modifica al verbo principal de la frase. Los verbos **be**, **do** y **have** reciben el nombre de *auxiliares ordinarios*. También se utilizan como verbos con sentido propio, en cuyo caso significan: **ser** o **estar** *(be)*, **hacer** *(do)*, **tener** *(have)*.

Los auxiliares se utilizan para formar los tiempos compuestos de los verbos:

> what are you doing?
> *¿qué estás haciendo? (ahora)*

> what do you do?
> *¿qué haces? (en general, normalmente)*

> what have you done?
> *¿qué has hecho?*

Las formas de estos auxiliares en presente y pasado son:

BE

	SINGULAR	PLURAL
PRESENTE		
1.ª persona	I am	we are
2.ª persona	you are	you are
3.ª persona	he/she/it is	they are
PRETÉRITO		
1.ª persona	I was	we were
2.ª persona	you were	you were
3.ª persona	he/she/it was	they were

LOS AUXILIARES

DO

	SINGULAR	PLURAL
PRESENTE		
1.ª *persona*	I do	we do
2.ª *persona*	you do	you do
3.ª *persona*	he/she/it does	they do
PRETÉRITO		
1.ª *persona*	I did	we did
2.ª *persona*	you did	you did
3.ª *persona*	he/she/it did	they did

HAVE

	SINGULAR	PLURAL
PRESENTE		
1.ª *persona*	I have	we have
2.ª *persona*	you have	you have
3.ª *persona*	he/she/it has	they have
PRÉTÉRIT		
1.ª *persona*	I had	we had
2.ª *persona*	you had	you had
3.ª *persona*	he/she/it had	they had

3 LOS MODOS Y LOS TIEMPOS

Los modos

El modo es una categoría verbal que indica la actitud del hablante con respecto a la acción expresada por el verbo. Los modos principales que se distinguen en inglés son:

- **indicativo**: expresa una acción, un proceso o un estado como algo real y objetivo; es el modo más utilizado.
- **subjuntivo**: expresa una acción, un proceso o un estado como algo hipotético, dudoso, posible o deseado.
- **condicional**: expresa una acción, un proceso o un estado como algo eventual.
- **imperativo**: expresa ruego, orden o mandato.

La formación y el uso del imperativo, el condicional y el subjuntivo aparecen en los capítulos 14, 15 y 16, respectivamente.

El tiempo y el aspecto

a) El **tiempo** verbal indica el momento en que se realiza la acción. Los principales tiempos verbales son: el presente, el pasado y el futuro, y su uso aparece en los capítulos 10, 11 y 12, respectivamente.

En inglés, la mayoría de los verbos tienen la misma terminación en todas las personas de un mismo tiempo. Por ejemplo, en el pretérito:

I/you/he/she/it/we/they went

La excepción principal aparece en la tercera persona del singular del presente de indicativo, que acaba en **-s** o **-es** (véanse los modelos de verbos en la página 16). Por ejemplo:

	SINGULAR	PLURAL
1.ª persona	I watch	we watch
2.ª persona	you watch	you watch
3.ª persona	he/she/it watches	they watch

b) La mayoría de los verbos pueden tener diferentes aspectos. El aspecto hace referencia al momento en que se ve el transcurso de la acción: en su duración, su desarrollo, cuando ya está terminada, etc. En inglés se distinguen el aspecto simple, el continuo y el *perfect* (o pasado).

La forma continua, que expresa la acción durante su desarrollo, se forma con to be + participio presente (terminación -ing).

El *perfect*, que presenta una acción terminada o una acción del pasado que tiene consecuencias en el momento en que se enuncia, se forma con to have + participio pasado.

c) Los tiempos verbales se forman de la siguiente manera:

infinitivo	(to) watch *(mirar)*
infinitivo continuo	(to) be watching *(estar mirando)*
infinitivo pasado	(to)have watched *(haber mirado)*
infinitivo pasado continuo	(to) have been watching *(haber estado mirando)*
presente simple	(I/you/he, etc.) watch(es) *(miro, miras,etc.)*
presente continuo	" am/are/is watching *(estoy, estás, está mirando)*
futuro simple	" will watch *(miraré, mirárás, mirará)*
futuro continuo	" will be watching *(estaré, estarás, estará mirando)*
pretérito perfecto simple	" watched *(miré, miraste, miró)*
pretérito perfecto continuo	" was/were watching *(estaba, estabas, estaba mirando)*

pretérito perfecto compuesto	" have/has watched *(he, has, ha mirado)*
pretérito perfecto compuesto continuo	" have/has been watching *(he, has, ha estado mirando)*
pretérito pluscuamperfecto	" had watched *(había, habías, había mirado)*
pretérito pluscuamperfecto continuo	" had been watching *(había, habías, había estado mirando)*
futuro compuesto	" will have watched *(habré, habrás, habrá mirado)*
futuro compuesto continuo	" will have been watching *(habré, habrás, habrá estado mirando)*
condicional simple	" would watch *(miraría, mirarías, miraría)*
condicional simple continuo	" would be watching *(estaría, estarías, estaría mirando)*
condicional compuesto	" would have watched *(habría, habrías, habría mirado)*
condicional compuesto continuo	" would have been watching *(habría, habrías, habría estado mirando)*

La voz pasiva aparece en el capítulo 5.

4 MODELOS DE VERBO

En este capítulo aparecen diferentes modelos de verbo según los cambios ortográficos que experimentan. Los verbos que figuran en el índice de este manual aparecen con un código y remiten a un modelo de verbo.

M1

	añadir
he/she/it **en presente**	-s
participio presente	-ing
participio pasado	-ed

Por ejemplo: look: looks - looking - looked

M2

	añadir
he/she/it **en presente**	-es
participio presente	-ing
participio pasado	-ed

Por ejemplo: watch: watches - watching - watched

Nota:

Se añade -es a los verbos que acaban en -s, -z, -ch y -sh.

M3

	añadir
he/she/it **en presente**	-s
participio presente	-ing
participio pasado	-d

Por ejemplo: agree: agrees - agreeing - agreed

M4

	quitar	añadir
he/she/it **en presente**		-s
participio presente	-e final	-ing
participio pasado		-d

Por ejemplo: hate: hates - hating - hated

M5

	cambiar	añadir
he/she/it **en presente**		-s
participio presente	repetir la consonante final	-ing
participio pasado	repetir la consonante final	-ed

Por ejemplo: grab: grabs - grabbing - grabbed
                 occur: occurs - occurring - occurred

Nota:

La consonante final se repite cuando hay una vocal corta sobre la que recae el acento tónico, como en los ejemplos anteriores. Esto no sucede en el caso siguiente:

    keep: keeps - keeping

donde la vocal es larga. Tampoco ocurre en:

    vomit: vomits - vomiting - vomited

donde la vocal anterior a la consonante final no es tónica (el acento recae en la primera vocal).

En **inglés británico**, a veces se repite la consonante después de una vocal corta átona, como por ejemplo:

    kidnap: kidnaps - kidnapping - kidnapped
    travel: travels - travelling - travelled

Pero, en inglés americano, estas formas verbales se escriben con una sola consonante:

    kidnap - kidnaping - kidnaped
    travel - traveling - traveled

En el índice, los verbos que se conjugan siguiendo el modelo americano van acompañados de la abreviatura (*U.S.*).

M6

	cambiar	*añadir*
he/she/it **en presente**	la -y final por -ies	
participio presente		-ing
participio pasado	la -y por -ied	

Por ejemplo: accompany: accompanies - accompanying
                              - accompanied
                      cry: cries - crying - cried

M7

	cambiar	*añadir*
he/she/it **en presente**		-s
participio presente	la -ie final por -y	-ing
participio pasado		-d

Por ejemplo: die: dies - dying - died

M8

	cambiar	*añadir*
he/she/it **en presente**		-s
participio presente	la -c final por -ck	-ing
participio pasado	la -c final por -ck	-ed

Por ejemplo: plcnic: picnics - picnicking - picnicked

M9

Este código se utiliza para indicar los verbos cuyo participio pasado es **irregular** (véase p. 22):

choose: chooses - choosing - chosen

Estos verbos llevan dos códigos. En el caso de choose, aparecerán los códigos M4 y M9. El código M9 indica que el verbo es irregular y que las formas irregulares, como son fijas, no sufren ningún cambio ortográfico. Para el resto de las formas, el verbo sigue el modelo M4.

5 LA VOZ PASIVA

En la frase **our new partner signed the contract** (*nuestro nuevo socio firmó el contrato*), el verbo **signed** está en voz activa: el sujeto realiza la acción. Pero en la frase **the contract was signed by our new partner** (*el contrato fue firmado por nuestro nuevo socio*), el verbo **was signed** tiene un sentido pasivo: el sujeto recibe la acción. El uso de la voz pasiva es mucho más frecuente en inglés que en español.

a) La voz pasiva se forma con el auxiliar **be** + participio pasado. Tomemos, por ejemplo, el verbo **watch** (las traducciones aparecen a título indicativo):

infinitivo	(to) be watched *(ser mirado)*
infinitivo pasado	(to) have been watched *(haber sido mirado)*
infinitivo continuo	(to) be being watched *(estar siendo mirado)*
presente simple	am/are/is watched *(soy/eres/es, etc. mirado)*
presente continuo	am/are/is being watched *(estoy/estás/está siendo mirado)*
futuro simple	will be watched *(seré/serás, etc. mirado)*
futuro continuo	will be being watched *(estaré/estarás, etc. siendo mirado)*
pretérito perfecto simple	was/were watched *(fui, fuiste, etc. mirado)*
pretérito perfecto continuo	was/were being watched *(estaba/estabas siendo mirado)*
pretérito perfecto compuesto	have/has been watched *(he/ha sido mirado)*
pretérito perfecto compuesto continuo	have/has been being watched *(he/ha estado siendo mirado)*
pretérito pluscuamperfecto	had been watched *(había sido mirado)*

pretérito pluscuamperfecto continuo	had been being watched *(había estado siendo mirado)*
futuro compuesto	will have been watched *(habré sido mirado)*
condicional simple	would be watched *(sería mirado)*
condicional simple continuo	would be being watched *(estaría siendo mirado)*
condicional compuesto	would have been watched *(habría sido mirado)*

He aquí algunos ejemplos con diferentes verbos:

it was hidden under some old papers
estaba escondido debajo de unos periódicos viejos

it had deliberately been hidden by his assistant
había sido escondido a propósito por su ayudante

it was thought to have been hidden by the Romans
se pensaba que había sido escondido por los romanos

he objected to this information being hidden away at the bottom of the form
se quejó de que la información estaba oculta al final del formulario

you'll be closely watched
serás vigilado de cerca

the programme will have been watched by ten million viewers in total
el programa habrá sido visto por un total de diez millones de teles-pectadores

if he were a suspect, he would be being asked a lot of questions by now
si fuera sospechoso, ya estaría siendo interrogado

if he had made any comment, it would have been ignored
si hubiera hecho algún comentario, habría sido ignorado

b) La frase activa:

they sent him the wrong letter
le enviaron la carta equivocada

en inglés puede decirse de dos formas distintas en voz pasiva:

the wrong letter was sent to him
le fue enviada la carta equivocada

he was sent the wrong letter
se le envió la carta equivocada

c) Los verbos intransitivos pueden asimismo ser empleados con un sentido de pasivo:

it opens at the front
se abre por delante

her article reads well
su artículo está bien escrito

this material won't wash very well
este tejido no se lava demasiado bien

6 LISTA DE VERBOS IRREGULARES

Las formas en inglés americano se indican con un asterisco (*), mientras que las formas poco corrientes, arcaicas o literarias aparecen entre paréntesis. Las traducciones no son restrictivas (sólo se ofrecen los significados más comunes).

INFINITIVO		PASADO	PARTICIPIO PASADO
abide	soportar	(abode) [1]	abided
arise	surgir	arose	arisen
awake	despertarse	awoke, awaked	awoken, (awaked)
bear	llevar	bore	borne [2]
beat	golpear	beat	beaten [3]
become	convertirse en	became	become
befall	acontecer	befell	befallen
beget	engendrar	begot	begotten
begin	comenzar	began	begun
behold	contemplar	beheld	beheld
bend	doblar	bent	bent [4]
bereave	privar	bereaved	bereft [5]
beseech	implorar	besought	besought
bestride	cabalgar	bestrode	bestridden
bet	apostar	bet, betted	bet, betted
bid	ofrecer	bid	bid
bid	ordenar, mandar	bade	bidden

[1] Regular en la construcción abide by «atenerse a, obrar de acuerdo con»: they abided by the rules.

[2] Pero born en la pasiva = «nato», en la acepción de «parir» (un hijo), o como adjetivo: he was born in Spain; a born gentleman.

[3] Nótese la forma coloquial this has me beat/you have me beat there *eso me supera/me dejas perplejo* y beat con el significado de «hecho polvo»: I'm (dead) beat.

[4] Obsérvese la oración on one's bended knees *de rodillas*.

[5] Pero bereaved, con el significado de «afligido», como en the bereaved received no compensation *la desconsolada familia no recibió compensación alguna*. Compárese: he was bereft of speech *se le negó la palabra*.

INFINITIVO		PASADO	PARTICIPIO PASADO
bind	atar, unir	bound	bound
bite	morder	bit	bitten
bleed	sangrar	bled	bled
blow	soplar	blew	blown
break	romper	broke	broken [6]
breed	criar (animales)	bred	bred
bring	traer	brought	brought
broadcast	retransmitir	broadcast	broadcast
build	construir	built	built
burn	quemar	burnt, burned	burnt, burned
burst	explotar	burst	burst
buy	comprar	bought	bought
cast	tirar	cast	cast
catch	coger, atrapar	caught	caught
chide	regañar	chid, chided	chid, (chidden), chided
choose	elegir, escoger	chose	chosen
cleave	partir	clove, cleft	cloven, cleft [7]
cleave	adherirse	cleaved, (clave)	cleaved
cling	agarrarse	clung	clung
clothe	vestir	clothed, (clad)	clothed, (clad)
come	venir	came	come
cost	costar	cost	cost
creep	deslizarse	crept	crept
crow	cacarear	crowed, (crew)	crowed
cut	cortar	cut	cut
dare	atreverse	dared, (durst)	dared, (durst)
deal	comerciar	dealt	dealt
dig	cavar	dug	dug
dive	bucear, zambullirse	dived, dove*	dived
draw	dibujar	drew	drawn
dream	soñar	dreamt, dreamed	dreamt, dreamed

---

[6] Pero broke cuando funciona como adjetivo = «sin blanca»: I'm broke.

[7] Cleft únicamente se utiliza con el significado de «cortar en dos». Obsérvese cleft palate *paladar hendido* y to be caught in a cleft stick *encontrarse en un callejón sin salida*, pero cloven foot/hoof *pata hendida*.

INFINITIVO		PASADO	PARTICIPIO PASADO
drink	*beber*	drank	drunk [8]
drive	*conducir*	drove	driven
dwell	*habitar*	dwelt, dwelled	dwelt, dwelled
eat	*comer*	ate	eaten
fall	*caer*	fell	fallen
feed	*alimentar*	fed	fed
feel	*sentir*	felt	felt
fight	*luchar*	fought	fought
find	*encontrar*	found	found
fit	*ajustarse*	fit*, fitted	fit*, fitted
flee	*esfumarse*	fled	fled
fling	*lanzar*	flung	flung
fly	*volar*	flew	flown
forbear	*abstenerse*	forbore	forborne
forbid	*prohibir*	forbad(e)	forbidden
forget	*olvidar*	forgot	forgotten
forgive	*perdonar*	forgave	forgiven
forsake	*abandonar*	forsook	forsaken
freeze	*helar*	froze	frozen
get	*obtener*	got	got, gotten* [9]
gild	*dorar*	gilt, gilded	gilt, gilded [10]
gird	*rodear*	girt, girded	girt, girded [10]
give	*dar*	gave	given
go	*ir*	went	gone
grind	*moler*	ground	ground
grow	*crecer, cultivar*	grew	grown

[8] Cuando se trata de un epíteto (un adjetivo delante de un nombre) que designa a una persona, se puede utilizar drunken (a lot of drunk(en) people *mucha gente borracha*). Sin embargo, siempre debe utilizarse delante de los nombres de cosas, de los objetos inanimados, etc. (drunken parties *fiestas de borrachera*).

[9] Sin embargo, have got to también se emplea en inglés americano con el significado de «tener que, estar obligado a»: I've got to go *tengo que irme*. Compárese con: she has gotten into a bit of a mess *se metió en un berenjenal*.

[10] Las formas de participio pasado gilt y girt se utilizan como epítetos: gilt mirrors *espejos dorados*, a flower-girt grave *una tumba rodeada de flores* (pero siempre gilded youth *juventud dorada*, donde gilded se utiliza en sentido figurado).

INFINITIVO		PASADO	PARTICIPIO PASADO
hang	colgar, suspender	hung, hanged [11]	hung, hanged [11]
hear	oír	heard	heard
heave	levantar	hove, heaved [12]	hove, heaved [12]
hew	tallar	hewed	hewn, hewed
hide	esconder	hid	hidden
hit	pegar	hit	hit
hold	sostener	held	held
hurt	doler	hurt	hurt
keep	conservar	kept	kept
kneel	arrodillarse	knelt, kneeled	knelt, kneeled
knit	tejer	knit, knitted [13]	knit, knitted [13]
know	saber, conocer	knew	known
lay	poner	laid	laid
lead	dirigir	led	led
lean	apoyarse	leant, leaned	leant, leaned
leap	saltar	leapt, leaped	leapt, leaped
learn	aprender	learnt, learned	learnt, learned
leave	dejar	left	left
lend	prestar	lent	lent
let	dejar	let	let
lie	echarse	lay	lain
light	encender	lit, lighted	lit, lighted [14]

[11] Regular cuando significa «ahorcar».

[12] **Hove** se utiliza en el ámbito náutico, como en la expresión **heave into sight** (*aparecer en el horizonte),* aunque también se utiliza en sentido figurado: and suddenly, she **hove** into sight *y de repente, apareció.*

[13] Irregular cuando significa «unir» (a **close-knit** family *una familia unida*), pero regular cuando significa «de punto» y cuando hace referencia a los huesos = «soldarse».

[14] Cuando el participio pasado se utiliza como epíteto, a menudo se prefiere el uso de **lighted** al de **lit**: a **lighted** candle *una vela encendida* (pero: the candle is **lit** *la vela está encendida*, she has **lit** a candle *ha encendido una vela*). En los nombres compuestos, generalmente se utiliza **lit**: well-**lit** streets *calles bien iluminadas.* En sentido figurado (con **up**), se usa únicamente **lit** en el pasado o el participio pasado: her face **lit** up when she saw me *se le iluminó la cara cuando me vio.*

Infinitivo		Pasado	Participio pasado
lose	*perder*	lost	lost
make	*hacer*	made	made
mean	*significar*	meant	meant
meet	*conocer*	met	met
melt	*fundir*	melted	melted, molten [15]
mow	*cortar*	mowed	mown, mowed
pay	*pagar*	paid	paid
plead	*rogar*	pled,* pleaded	pled,* pleaded [16]
put	*poner*	put	put
quit	*dejar*	quit, (quitted)	quit, (quitted) [17]
read	*leer*	read	read
rend	*desgarrar*	rent	rent
rid	*deshacerse de*	rid (ridded)	rid
ride	*montar*	rode	ridden
ring	*sonar*	rang	rung
rise	*subir*	rose	risen
run	*correr*	ran	run
saw	*serrar*	sawed	sawn, sawed
say	*decir*	said	said
see	*ver*	saw	seen
seek	*buscar*	sought	sought
sell	*vender*	sold	sold
send	*enviar*	sent	sent
set	*poner*	set	set
sew	*coser*	sewed	sewn, sewed
shake	*temblar*	shook	shaken
shear	*esquilar*	sheared	shorn, sheared [18]

[15] Se utiliza **molten** sólo como epíteto y únicamente cuando significa «fundido a alta temperatura», por ejemplo: **molten** lead *plomo fundido* (pero **melted** butter *mantequilla derretida*).

[16] En el inglés de Escocia y en el americano se utiliza **pled** en el pasado y en el participio pasado.

[17] En inglés americano, las formas regulares no se utilizan; en inglés británico, cada vez se utilizan con menor frecuencia.

[18] Normalmente, delante de un nombre, el participio pasado es **shorn** (newly-shorn lambs *corderos recién esquilados*) y siempre en la expresión **to be shorn of** *ser desprovisto de*: **shorn** of his riches he was nothing *desprovisto de sus riquezas, no era nada*.

INFINITIVO		PASADO	PARTICIPIO PASADO
shed	perder	shed	shed
shine	brillar	shone [19]	shone [19]
shoe	calzar	shod, shoed	shod, shoed [20]
shoot	disparar	shot	shot
show	mostrar	showed	shown, showed
shrink	encoger	shrank, shrunk	shrunk, shrunken [21]
shut	cerrar	shut	shut
sing	cantar	sang	sung
sink	hundir	sank	sunk, sunken [22]
sit	sentarse	sat	sat
slay	asesinar	slew	slain
sleep	dormir	slept	slept
slide	deslizar	slid	slid
sling	tirar	slung	slung
slink	escabullirse	slunk	slunk
slit	cortar	slit	slit
smell	oler	smelt, smelled	smelt, smelled
smite	golpear	smote	smitten [23]
sneak	soplar, chivarse	snuck,* sneaked	snuck,* sneaked
sow	sembrar	sowed	sown, sowed
speak	hablar	spoke	spoken
speed	apresurarse	sped, speeded	sped, speeded
spell	deletrear	spelt, spelled	spelt, spelled
spend	gastar	spent	spent
spill	derramar	spilt, spilled	spilt, spilled

[19] Es regular cuando significa «encerar, sacar brillo», en inglés americano.

[20] Cuando es adjetivo, únicamente se utiliza **shod**: a well-**shod** foot *un pie bien calzado.*

[21] **Shrunken** sólo se utiliza cuando es adjetivo: **shrunken** limbs *miembros contraídos,* her face was **shrunken** *frunció el ceño.*

[22] **Sunken** sólo se emplea como adjetivo: **sunken** eyes *ojos hundidos.*

[23] Verbo arcaico cuyo participio pasado **smitten** todavía se emplea como adjetivo: he's completely **smitten** with her *está completamente enamorado de ella.*

INFINITIVO		PASADO	PARTICIPIO PASADO
spin	*hilar*	spun	spun
spit	*escupir*	spat, spit*	spat, spit*
split	*partir, dividir*	split	split
spoil	*estropear*	spoilt, spoiled	spoilt, spoiled
spread	*extender*	spread	spread
spring	*saltar*	sprang	sprung
stand	*estar de pie*	stood	stood
steal	*robar*	stole	stolen
stick	*clavar, pegar*	stuck	stuck
sting	*picar*	stung	stung
stink	*apestar*	stank	stunk
strew	*esparcir*	strewed	strewn, strewed
stride	*andar a zancadas*	strode	stridden
strike	*pegar*	struck	struck, stricken [24]
string	*encordar*	strung	strung
strive	*esforzarse*	strove	striven
swear	*jurar*	swore	sworn
sweat	*sudar*	sweat,* sweated	sweat,* sweated
sweep	*barrer*	swept	swept
swell	*hinchar*	swelled	swollen, swelled [25]
swim	*nadar*	swam	swum
swing	*balancear(se)*	swung	swung
take	*tomar*	*took*	taken
teach	*enseñar*	taught	taught
tear	*arrancar*	tore	torn
tell	*decir*	told	told

[24] **Stricken** únicamente se utiliza en sentido figurado (**stricken with grief** *afligido por la pena*). Su uso es muy corriente en los nombres compuestos (*afligido por/abrumado por*): **poverty-stricken**, **fever-stricken**, **grief-stricken**, **horror-stricken** (también **horror-struck**), **terror-stricken** (también **terror-struck**), pero siempre se dice **thunderstruck** *atónito*. También se trata de un uso americano: the remark was **stricken** from the record *el comentario se borró del documento*.

[25] **Swollen** es más común que **swelled** como verbo (her face has **swollen** *se le ha hinchado la cara*) y como adjetivo (her face is **swollen**/a **swollen** face). To have a **swollen** head (*ser un sabelotodo*) pasa a ser to have a **swelled** head en inglés americano.

INFINITIVO		PASADO	PARTICIPIO PASADO
think	*pensar*	thought	thought
thrive	*prosperar*	thrived, (throve)	thrived, (thriven)
throw	*tirar*	threw	thrown
thrust	*empujar*	thrust	thrust
tread	*pisar*	trod	trodden
understand	*entender*	understood	understood
undertake	*emprender*	undertook	undertaken
wake	*despertar(se)*	woke, waked	woken, waked
wear	*llevar (puesto)*	wore	worn
weave	*tejer*	wove [26]	woven [26]
weep	*llorar*	wept	wept
wet	*mojar*	wet,* wetted [27]	wet,* wetted [27]
win	*ganar*	won	won
wind	*envolver*	wound	wound
wring	*torcer*	wrung	wrung
write	*escribir*	wrote	written

[26] Pero es regular cuando significa «serpentear/zigzaguear»: the motorbike **weaved** through the traffic *la moto serpenteaba entre el tráfico.*

[27] Pero también es irregular en inglés británico cuando significa lo siguiente: he **wet** his bed *se orinó en la cama.*

7 LAS CONTRACCIONES

Las contracciones (o formas contractas) son muy corrientes en la lengua inglesa estándar, tanto oral como escrita:

BE

I am	I'm
you are	you're
he/she/it is	he's/she's/it's
we/they are	we're/they're
I am not	I'm not
you are not	you're not, you aren't
he/she/it is not	he's/she's/it's not, he/she/it isn't
we/they are not	we/they aren't
am I not?	aren't I?
are you not?	aren't you?
is he/she/it not?	isn't he/she/it?
are we/they not?	aren't we/they?

DO

I/you/we/they do not	I/you/we/they don't
he/she/it does not	he/she/it doesn't
do I/you/we/they not?	don't I/you/we/they?
does he/she/it not?	doesn't he/she/it?

HAVE

I have	I've
you/we/they have	you've/we've/ they've
he/she/it has	he's/she's/it's
	(más usual con el pretérito perfecto compuesto, como en: **I've seen**, etc.)
I/you/we/they have not	I/you/we/they haven't
he/she/it/has not	he/she/it hasn't
have I/you/we/they not?	haven't I/you/we/they?
has he/she/it not?	hasn't he/she/it?
I/he/she/it was not	I/he/she/it wasn't
you/we/they were not	you/we/they weren't
I, *etc.* did not	I, etc. didn't
I/you, *etc.* will	I'll/you'll, etc.
I/he, *etc.* will not	I/he, etc. won't
I shall	I'll
I shall not	I shan't
I/you, *etc.* would	I'd/you'd, etc.
I/you, *etc.* would not	I/you, etc. wouldn't
I/he, *etc.* would have	I'd've/ he'd've, etc.
I/he, *etc.* would not have	I/he, etc. wouldn't have

Las contracciones no se utilizan sólo con los pronombres personales:

that'll be the day!
Mummy's just gone out

Véase también el capítulo «Los auxiliares modales», en p. 63.

8 LA FORMA INTERROGATIVA

1 Cuando no hay verbo auxiliar, la forma interrogativa se construye con **do**:

do you like whisky?
¿te gusta el whisky?

how do you spell it?
¿cómo se deletrea?

doesn't she expect you home?
¿no te espera en casa?

did you talk to him?
¿has hablado con él?

didn't I tell you so?
¿no os lo había dicho?

2 Si se utiliza otro auxiliar (**be, have, will**, etc.), se invierte el orden del sujeto y del verbo. Atención al orden de las palabras:

he is Welsh	**is he Welsh?**
él es galés	*¿es galés?*
they're going home tomorrow	**are they going home tomorrow?**
mañana vuelven a casa	*¿vuelven mañana a casa?*
Daphne will be there too	**will Daphne be there too?**
Daphne también estará allí	*¿Daphne también estará allí?*
I can't understand	**why can't I understand?**
no puedo entenderlo	*¿por qué no puedo entenderlo?*

En las oraciones interrogativas indirectas, el orden de las palabras es igual que en las oraciones afirmativas:

when is she leaving?	**she is leaving tomorrow**
¿cuándo se va?	*se va mañana*
he asked me when she was leaving	
¡me preguntó cuándo se iba (ella)	

3 Si el sujeto es un pronombre interrogativo no hay verbo auxiliar:

who made that noise?   what happened?
¿quién hizo ese ruido?   *¿qué pasó?*

4 Las *question-tags:*

Las *question-tags:* suelen traducirse por «¿no?» o «¿verdad?» en español. Se trata de un giro interrogativo muy utilizado en inglés que se coloca al final de la frase y que permite, en general, confirmar lo que se pregunta. Están compuestas por un pronombre personal y un verbo auxiliar.

a) Una frase afirmativa va seguida de una *question-tag* negativa, y viceversa:

you **can** see it, **can't** you?
lo puedes ver, ¿no?

you **can't** see it, **can** you?
no puedes verlo, ¿verdad?

Si la *question-tag* no se utiliza para formular una pregunta sino que sirve para reforzar el sentido de la frase principal, ambas serán afirmativas:

so **you've** seen a ghost, **have you**? *(incredulidad, sarcasmo)*
¿así que habéis visto un fantasma?

he's got married again, **has he**? *(sorpresa, interés)*
¿de verdad que se ha vuelto a casar?

En este último ejemplo, es importante distinguir entre las formas contractas de **be** y **have** para poder formar la *question-tag.*

b) La *question-tag* se conjuga en el mismo tiempo en el que aparece el verbo de la frase principal. Si la oración anterior está en presente o en pretérito perfecto simple y, por lo tanto, carece de auxiliar, se utilizará **do** en la *question-tag:*

you want to meet him, **don't you**?
quieres verlo, ¿no?

you wanted to meet him, **didn't you**?
querías verlo, ¿no?

c) Si la oración anterior está regida por un auxiliar, es decir, si el verbo está en un tiempo compuesto, dicho auxiliar se repetirá en la *question-tag:*

you'll want to meet him, won't you?
querrás verlo, ¿no?

Peter has been here before, hasn't he?
Peter ya ha estado aquí, ¿verdad?

they aren't stopping, are they?
no van a parar, ¿verdad?

you will sign it, won't you?
lo firmarás (tú), ¿no?

d) Si la *question-tag* va detrás de un imperativo, a menudo se utiliza **will/would**. Estas *question-tags* permiten suavizar la orden, evitando un tono demasiado seco:

leave the cat alone, will you?
deja tranquilo al gato, ¿no?

take this to Mrs Brown, would you?
lleva esto a la señora Brown, ¿quieres?

En el ejemplo siguiente, la forma negativa **won't** indica una invitación:

help yourselves to drinks, won't you?
sírvanse algo para beber, por favor:

you want to meet him, don't you?
quieres verlo, ¿no?

you wanted to meet him, didn't you?
querías verlo, ¿no?

you'll want to meet him, won't you?
querrás verlo, ¿no?

9 LA FORMA NEGATIVA

1 Cuando no hay verbo auxiliar (**be, will**, etc.), se utiliza **do** seguido de **not** para construir la negación (véase también el capítulo «Las contracciones», en p. 30):

I like it
me gusta

I do not (don't) like it
no me gusta

she agrees with them
está de acuerdo con ellos

she does not (doesn't) agree
with them
no está de acuerdo con ellos

I expected him to say that
esperaba que dijera eso

I did not (didn't) expect him to
say that
no me esperaba que dijera eso

2 Si hay un verbo auxiliar sólo se añade **not**:

I will (I'll) take them with me
me los llevaré/los cogeré

I will not (I won't) take them *me
me
no me los llevaré/no los cogeré*

they are just what I'm looking for
son exactamente los que buscaba

they are not (they aren't/they're
not) really what I'm looking for
*no son exactamente los que
buscaba*

3 **Not** se utiliza también con el infinitivo y el gerundio:

to be or not to be
ser o no ser

try not to think about it
intenta no pensar en ello

it would have been better not to have mentioned it at all
habría sido mejor no haberlo mencionado

he's worried about not having enough money
tiene miedo de no tener suficiente dinero

Véase también el capítulo «El imperativo», en p. 55.

10 EL PRESENTE

En inglés existen dos maneras diferentes de expresar el presente: el presente simple y el presente continuo.

Uso del presente simple

a) Para expresar acontecimientos generales, o habituales, o verdades universales:

I **get up** at seven o'clock every morning
me levanto todas las mañanas a las siete en punto

she **works** for an insurance company
trabaja en una compañía de seguros

where **do** you buy your shoes?
¿dónde te compras los zapatos?

where **do** you come from?
¿de dónde vienes?/¿de dónde eres?

the earth **revolves** round the sun
la Tierra gira alrededor del Sol

b) Con los verbos que expresan un estado de ánimo, una opinión, etc., o verbos que hacen referencia a los sentidos (vista, oído, olfato, gusto y tacto):

I **(dis)like/love** that girl
me gusta (no me gusta)/me encanta esa chica

I **hate/want** that girl
odio/quiero a esa chica

I **believe/suppose/think/imagine** he's right
creo/supongo/pienso/imagino que tiene razón

we **hear/see/feel/perceive** the world around us
oímos/vemos/sentimos/percibimos el mundo que nos rodea

it **tastes** good/it **smells** good
sabe bien/huele bien

Uso del presente continuo

a) Para expresar acontecimientos o estados que tienen lugar en el momento en que se habla:

what are you doing up there?
¿qué haces/estás haciendo ahí arriba?

I'm trying to find my old passport
intento encontrar mi viejo pasaporte

at the moment it's being used as a bedroom
en este momento lo utilizamos como habitación

what are you thinking about?
¿en qué estás pensando?

b) Con adverbios de frecuencia (normalmente utilizados con el presente simple), para expresar una acción o un hecho que se produce a menudo de una forma inesperada o no intencionada:

he's always mixing our names up
siempre confunde nuestros nombres

he's forever forgetting his car keys
siempre se olvida las llaves del coche

Diferencias entre el presente simple y el presente continuo

I live in London *(presente simple)*
vivo en Londres

I'm living in London *(presente continuo)*
(actualmente) vivo en Londres

La segunda frase implica que el hablante no vive de una forma permanente o definitiva en Londres, sino que está instalado allí temporalmente. La primera frase indica un estado de cosas.

I have a shower every morning *(presente simple)*
me ducho cada mañana

I'm having a shower every morning (these days) *(presente continuo)*
me estoy duchando cada mañana (en la actualidad)

La segunda frase implica que ducharse regularmente por la mañana es tan solo un hecho temporal, una cosa que se hace en un momento determinado (y que puede no durar). La primera frase, en presente simple, no conlleva estas restricciones temporales.

she works for an insurance company
trabaja en una compañía de seguros

she's working for an insurance company
(actualmente) trabaja en una compañía de seguros

En este segundo ejemplo, la diferencia no es tan clara. Pero la primera frase nunca haría referencia a una situación temporal. La segunda frase puede hacer referencia tanto a una situación temporal como definitiva.

En algunos casos no existe ninguna diferencia entre el presente simple y el presente continuo:

how are you feeling this morning?
how do you feel this morning?
¿cómo te encuentras esta mañana?

11 EL PASADO

El pretérito perfecto simple

Se utiliza para expresar toda clase de acontecimientos pasados y acciones acabadas, aunque sean muy recientes:

> he got up and left the room
> *se levantó y abandonó la sala*

> he caught the train yesterday
> *cogió el tren ayer*

> in what year did the Rolling Stones have their first hit?
> *¿en qué año lograron los Rolling Stones su primer éxito?*

Used to/would

Estas dos formas se utilizan para hacer referencia a acontecimientos habituales o regulares del pasado:

> on Fridays we always used to have fish
> on Fridays we would have fish
> *los viernes, siempre comíamos pescado*

El pretérito perfecto continuo

Este tiempo se forma con el auxiliar be en pasado + verbo que se conjuga acabado en -ing. Permite insistir en la continuidad, la duración de una acción o situación:

> I was living in Germany when that happened
> *vivía en Alemania cuando sucedió aquello*

> sorry, could you say that again? I wasn't listening
> *perdón, ¿puedes repetirlo? No estaba escuchando*

> what were you doing out in the garden last night?
> *¿qué estabais haciendo anoche en el jardín?*

> I **was having** dinner when he came home
> *estaba cenando cuando él llegó*

El pretérito perfecto simple y el pretérito perfecto continuo suelen emplearse para resaltar la relación existente entre dos hechos del pasado o la forma en que el hablante quiere presentarlos. En este último ejemplo, una acción puntual (**he came home**) se contrapone a una acción que dura (**I was having dinner**). Compárese dicho ejemplo con el siguiente:

> I **had** dinner when he **was coming** home
> *cené mientras (él) volvía a casa*

El sentido de esta frase es muy diferente. La acción que dura se encuentra en una oración subordinada (**he was coming home**). La oración principal (**I had dinner**) hace referencia a una cosa que tiene lugar en un momento preciso, pero durante el desarrollo de una acción más larga (**was coming home**). Compárese también con:

> I **was having** dinner while he **was coming** home
> *estaba cenando mientra él volvía a casa*

En este caso, las dos acciones se desarrollan paralelamente.

El pretérito perfecto compuesto («present perfect»)

a) Este tiempo se utiliza para hacer referencia a situaciones o acciones del pasado pero que tienen conexión con el presente:

> I **have read** nearly all of Somerset Maugham's books
> *he leído casi todos los libros de Somerset Maugham*

> I **have** never **read** any of Somerset Maugham's books
> *nunca he leído ningún libro de Somerset Maugham*

En estos dos ejemplos se hace referencia a aquello que se ha leído hasta ahora de la obra de Somerset Maugham.

Podemos comparar estos ejemplos con el siguiente:

> I **read** one of Maugham's novels on holiday last year
> *leí una novela de Maugham cuando estaba de vacaciones el año pasado*

Esta frase describe una acción acabada en el pasado, de ahí el uso del pretérito perfecto simple.

O estos otros dos ejemplos:

have you seen him this morning?
 (*la pregunta se hace cuando la mañana todavía no ha terminado*)
did you see him this morning?
 (*la pregunta se hace por la tarde o por la noche*)
¿lo has visto esta mañana?

b) La forma continua del pretérito perfecto compuesto se emplea
 para insistir en la duración:

what have you been reading recently?
¿qué has leído recientemente?

we haven't seen you for ages, what have you been doing with yourself?
hace muchísimo tiempo que no nos veíamos, ¿qué es de vuestra
 vida?

what have you been saying to him to make him cry?
¿qué le has dicho para hacerlo llorar?

I've been meaning to ask you something, doctor
hace tiempo que quiero preguntarle una cosa, doctor

A veces el sentido puede variar un poco entre la forma simple y
la forma continua del pretérito perfecto compuesto:

I've been living here for 15 years (*continuo*)
I've lived here for 15 years *(simple)*
vivo aquí desde hace 15 años/llevo viviendo aquí 15 años

«Desde» se traduce por for cuando va seguido de un nombre y
por since cuando va seguido de una fecha, es decir, cuando se
hace referencia a un momento concreto del pasado:

I've been living here since 1972
I've lived here since 1972
vivo aquí desde 1972/llevo viviendo aquí desde 1972

El pretérito pluscuamperfecto («past perfect»)

a) Este tiempo se forma con el auxiliar have + participio del verbo que
 se conjuga. Se utiliza para describir acciones o hechos acaecidos
 con anterioridad a otros sucesos del pasado. Así, hace referencia a
 un momento del pasado relacionado con otro momento del pasado:

the fire had already been put out when they got there *(pasiva)*
el incendio ya había sido extinguido cuando llegaron al lugar

he searched the directory but the file had been erased the day before
(pasiva)
buscó el directorio pero el fichero había sido borrado el día anterior

had you heard of him before you came here?
¿habías oído hablar de él antes de venir aquí?

they hadn't left anything in the fridge so I went out to eat
no habían dejado nada en la nevera, así es que me fui a comer a un restaurante

También puede utilizarse para indicar el fin de una situación o un estado de cosas (un estado de ánimo, etc.):

I had hoped to speak to him this morning
esperaba hablar con él esta mañana

Esta frase implica que las probabilidades de hablar con esa persona son ahora mínimas.

b) El pretérito pluscuamperfecto continuo se emplea para hacer hincapié en la duración:

I'd been wanting to ask that question myself
yo también quería hacer esta pregunta

had you been waiting long before they arrived?
¿has estado esperando mucho tiempo a que llegaran?

Para los casos en que el pretérito pluscuamperfecto indica condición, véase p. 59.

12 EL FUTURO

Will et shall

a) Para expresar el futuro en la primera persona del singular o del plural se utiliza will o shall (la forma shall es mucho más frecuente en inglés británico), que pueden aparecer en la forma contracta 'll. La contracción de will not es won't y la de shall not es shan't:

I will/I'll/I shall let you know as soon as I can
os lo haré saber en cuanto pueda

we won't/shan't need that many
no necesitaremos tanto

b) Para las demás personas se utiliza will:

will you be there?
¿estarás allí?

lunch will take about another ten minutes
la comida estará lista en unos diez minutos

they'll just have to wait
solo tendrán que esperar

c) Si el hablante expresa una promesa o una amenaza dirigidas a la 2.ª o la 3.ª persona se utiliza shall, aunque cada vez es más habitual emplear will:

you shall be treated just like the others
serás tratado como el resto

they shall pay for this!
¡me las pagarán!

Si la intención o la voluntad no dependen del hablante se emplea will ('ll):

he will/he'll do it, I'm sure
lo hará, estoy seguro

d) **Shall** se utiliza para proponer o sugerir algo :

shall we go?
¿vamos?

e) **Will** se emplea para pedir a alguien que haga algo:

will you come with me, please?
venga conmigo, por favor

f) Para exresar el futuro inmediato:

En los ejemplos siguientes, **will** se emplea más que **shall** (siendo la forma contracta **'ll** la más frecuente):

leave it, I'll do it myself
deja, lo haré yo

I'll have a beer, please
tomaré una cerveza, por favor

that's the doorbell – ok, I'll get it
llaman al timbre – vale, ya voy

El futuro simple y el futuro continuo

a) **Will** y **shall** seguidos de una forma continua se emplean para insistir en la continuidad de la acción:

what will you be doing this time next year?
¿qué harás el año que viene por estas fechas?

b) Compárense los ejemplos siguientes:

will you speak to him about it? *(simple)*
¿le hablarás de eso?

will you be speaking to him about it? *(continuo)*
¿piensas hablarle de eso?

El uso de la forma continua en el segundo ejemplo indica que el hablante no hace una pregunta directa (como en el primer ejemplo), sino que pregunta simplemente y de forma objetiva si la persona a quien se dirige tiene la intención de «hablarle de eso».

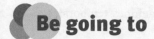

Be going to

a) Esta forma suele emplearse de la misma manera que **will**:

will it ever stop raining?
is it ever going to stop raining?
¿dejará de llover algún día?

b) Para expresar una intención es más usual emplear **be going to** que **will** o **shall**:

I'm going to take them to court
los voy a llevar a los tribunales

they're going to buy a new car
van a comprarse un coche nuevo

c) Es preferible usar **be going to** en lugar de **will** cuando las razones que justifican las previsiones están directamente relacionadas con el presente:

it's going to rain (look at those clouds)
va a llover (¿has visto qué nubes?)

I know what he's going to say (it's written all over his face)
sé lo que va a decir (se lee en su cara)

El presente simple

a) Este tiempo puede expresar el futuro cuando se hace referencia a algo establecido, un horario, etc.:

when does the race start?
¿a qué hora empieza la carrera?

the match kicks off at 2 o'clock
el partido empieza a las dos en punto

Tal y como muestra este último ejemplo, el uso del presente simple es muy habitual cuando se precisa el tiempo o la hora con un adverbio u otra expresión temporal:

we go on holiday tomorrow
nos vamos mañana de vacaciones

the plane leaves at 7 a.m.
el avión despega a las siete en punto

b) El presente simple suele emplearse en oraciones temporales o condicionales:

you'll be surprised when you see her
os sorprenderéis cuando la veáis

if he turns up, will you speak to him?
si viene, ¿hablarás con él?

Nota:

Las oraciones que empieza por **when** o **if** no deben confundirse con las oraciones interrogativas indirectas:

does he know when they'll arrive? (when will they arrive?)
¿sabe cuando llegarán? (¿cuando llegarán?)

I don't know if he'll agree (will he agree?)
no sé si estará de acuerdo (¿estará de acuerdo?)

El presente continuo

a) El presente continuo se utiliza a menudo de forma parecida a **be going to** para expresar intención:

I'm putting you in charge of the investigation (= I'm going to put you in charge of...)
te confío la responsabilidad de la investigación (= te voy a confiar...)

what are you doing over Christmas? (= what are you going to do...?)
¿qué haces por Navidad? (= ¿qué vas a hacer...?)

Pero hay una diferencia sutil entre los dos ejemplos siguientes:

I'm taking him to court
lo voy a demandar

I'm going to take him to court
lo voy a demandar

La intención es más fuerte en el primer ejemplo y menos definitiva en el segundo.

b) El presente continuo también puede utilizarse para hacer referencia a un acontecimiento organizado o previsto para el futuro.
   En este caso su empleo sería similar al del futuro continuo o al
   del presente simple:

he's giving a concert tomorrow
da un concierto mañana

when are they coming?
¿cuándo vienen?

they're arriving at Heathrow at midnight
llegan a Heathrow a medianoche

 Be to

Be to suele emplearse en un registro culto para hacer referencia a
proyectos futuros específicos, concretamente a proyectos que dependen de la decisión de otras personas:

we are to be there by ten o'clock
debemos estar allí a las diez en punto

I'm to report to a Mr Glover on Tuesday
debo presentarme el martes ante un tal señor Glover

 **Be about to**

Esta forma se emplea para expresar el futuro inmediato:

please take your seats, the play is about to begin
siéntense, por favor, la obra está a punto de empezar

you are about to meet a great artist
estás a punto de conocer a un gran artista

Esta forma también puede utilizarse para expresar las intenciones
futuras de una persona:

I'm not about to sign a contract like that!
¡no firmaré un contrato como éste!

En inglés británico se tiende a utilizar **be going to**.

El futuro compuesto

a) El futuro compuesto, es decir **will have** + participio, se utiliza para hacer referencia a una acción que se acabará antes que otra en el futuro:

by the time you get there we **will have finished** dinner
cuando lleguéis, ya habremos acabado de cenar

b) También se emplea para hacer suposiciones, hipótesis sobre el presente o el pasado, como en el siguiente ejemplo, donde aparece la forma continua:

I expect you'll **have been wondering** why I asked you here
supongo que se ha preguntado por qué lo he convocado

13 EL INFINITIVO Y EL GERUNDIO

El infinitivo

1 Se utiliza sin **to**

a) Después de **do** (I don't know), después de los auxiliares modales como **might**, **must**, etc. (véase capítulo 17) y después de **dare** y **need** cuando éstos se utilizan como auxiliares (véase página 74).

b) Después de **had better**:

you'd better apologize
deberías disculparte

c) Después de **why** o **why not**:

why stay indoors in this lovely weather?
¿por qué quedarnos dentro con el tiempo que hace?

d) En la construcción de complemento de objeto directo: nombre/pronombre + infinitivo (compárase con el punto 2.b, más abajo):

- después de **let** (*dejar*), **make** (*hacer*) y **have** (*hacer*):

we let him smoke   I made him turn round
le dejamos fumar   *lo hice darse la vuelta*

we had him say a few words
le hemos hecho decir algunas palabras

- detrás de los verbos de percepción **feel** (*sentir*), **hear** (*oír*), **see** (*ver*), **watch** (*mirar*):

I felt the woman touch my back
sentí cómo la mujer me tocaba la espalda

Estos verbos también pueden ir seguidos del participio para resaltar la duración de la acción:

I felt her creeping up behind me
noté que se me acercaba de puntillas

- Después de **help** se pueden encontrar las dos formas del infinitivo (con o sin **to**):

  we helped him (to) move house
  le ayudamos a hacer la mudanza

2 Se utiliza con **to**

a) Como sujeto, como atributo o como complemento directo. La frase siguiente contiene los tres usos (en este orden):

  to die is to cease to exist
  morir es dejar de existir

b) Como complemento directo (compárese con el punto 1.d anterior):

  - después de verbos que expresan un deseo o una antipatía, en particular, como **want** (*querer*), **wish** (*desear*), **like** (*gustar*), **prefer** (*preferir*), **hate** (*odiar*):

    I want you to remember this
    quiero que recuerdes esto

  - en un registro de lenguaje bastante culto, tras verbos que expresan un punto de vista, una opinión, una suposición o una afirmación:

    we believe this to be a mistake
    creemos que se trata de un error

    En un lenguaje más coloquial, se utiliza una proposición introducida por **that**:

    we believe (that) this is a mistake
    creemos que se trata de un errror

  - en la forma pasiva correspondiente se conserva **to**:

    this was believed to be a mistake
    pensábamos que se trataba de un error

  - la forma **to** + infinitivo también debe emplearse en construcciones pasivas con los verbos mencionados en el apartado 1.d anterior:

    she was made to do it
    la obligamos a hacerlo

c) Detrás de nombres, pronombres y adjetivos:

  there are things to be done
  hay cosas que hacer

glad to meet you!
¡encantado de conocerlo!

d) Cuando se encuentra en una proposición subordinada:

- para expresar un fin o una consecuencia, a veces acompañado de **in order** o **so as** (objetivo) u **only** (consecuencia):

    he left early to/in order to/so as to get a good seat for the performance
    se fue pronto para conseguir un buen sitio para el espectáculo

    they arrived (only) to find an empty house
    cuando llegaron se encontraron con una casa vacía

- en oraciones interrogativas indirectas:

    we didn't know who to ask
    no supimos a quién preguntar

- para expresar tiempo, en cuyo caso la proposición que contiene el infinitivo equivale a un complemento circunstancial que empieza con **when** (**when one hears him speak...**):

    to hear him speak, one would think he positively hates women
    oyéndolo hablar, cualquiera pensaría que realmente odia a las mujeres

e) En la construcción **for** + nombre/pronombre + infinitivo:

    he waited for her to finish
    esperó a que ella acabara

f) La cesura del infinitivo:

    Se dice que el infinitivo «se corta» cuando entre el **to** y el radical aparece un adverbio:

    they then decided to definitely leave
    entonces decidieron marcharse definitivamente

    Esta forma se usa con relativa frecuencia, si bien se prefiere esta otra:

    they then decided definitely to leave

El gerundio

El gerundio, también llamado «verbo sustantivado», posee características propias tanto de los sustantivos como de los verbos. Tiene la misma forma que el participio presente (terminación en **-ing**), pero se aplica en otro tipo de situaciones.

1 Características nominales

a) Un gerundio puede ser sujeto, atributo o complemento:

smoking is not good for you (*sujeto*)
fumar no es bueno para la salud

that's **cheating** (*atributo*)
eso es trampa

I love **reading** (*complemento*)
me encanta leer

b) Puede colocarse detras de una preposición:

he's thought of **leaving**
ha pensado en irse

c) Puede ser modificado por un artículo, un adjetivo o un posesivo:

the **timing** of his remarks was unfortunate
escogió un mal momento para hacer sus comentarios

careless **writing** leaves a bad impression
una escritura descuidada causa una mala impresión

do you remember his **trying** to persuade her?
¿recuerdas que intentó convencerla?

Nota:

En este último ejemplo, se podría haber utilizado el pronombre **him** en lugar del adjetivo posesivo **his**. Se pueden emplear ambas formas cuando el gerundio es complemento del verbo o cuando aparece detrás de una preposición. El uso del adjetivo posesivo es más habitual en la lengua escrita (estilo más culto) que en la oral:

we were surprised about **you/your** not being chosen
nos sorprendió que no fuerais seleccionados

2 Características verbales

a) Un gerundio puede tener un sujeto:

the thought of **Douglas doing** that is absurd
pensar que Douglas ha podido hacer eso es absurdo

b) Puede ir seguido de un complemento de objeto o de un atributo:

writing this letter took me ages
escribir esta carta me ha costado siglos

being left-handed has never been a problem
ser zurdo nunca ha sido un problema

c) Puede ser modificado por un adverbio:

it's a question of precisely defining our needs
se trata de definir con precisión cuáles son nuestras necesidades

Comparación entre el infinitivo y el gerundio

Cuando funcionan como complemento directo, pueden utilizarse indistintamente detrás del verbo:

I can't stand seeing him like this
I can't stand to see him like this
no soporto verlo así

Pero a veces hay una diferencia de sentido importante:

we stopped smoking	we stopped to smoke
dejamos de fumar	*nos paramos para fumar*
he was too busy talking to her	he was too busy to talk to her
estaba demasiado ocupado	*estaba demasiado ocupado para*
hablando con ella	*hablar con ella*

En estos ejemplos, el gerundio se utiliza como complemento directo mientras que el infinitivo funciona como un complemento circunstancial de finalidad, lo que explica la diferencia de sentido.

Otros verbos habituales que siempre van seguidos de **infinitivo** son:

demand	*exigir*
deserve	*merecer*
expect	*esperar (figurarse algo, contar con)*
hope	*esperar (tener esperanza)*
want	*querer*
wish	*desear*

En cambio, otros verbos solo van seguidos del **gerundio**:

avoid	*evitar*
consider	*considerar*
dislike	*no gustar*
enjoy	*apreciar, disfrutar*
finish	*acabar*
keep	*guardar, mantener*
practise	*practicar, hacer*
risk	*arriesgar*

14 EL IMPERATIVO

El modo imperativo se utiliza para dar órdenes o rogar algo. En la forma negativa expresa prohibición.

1 Para expresar la forma imperativa se utiliza el verbo en infinitivo (sin to):

stop that!
¡para eso!

have another
tómese otra

well, just look at him!
desde luego... ¡fíjate en aquel!

try mine
prueba el mío

somebody do something!
¡que alguien haga algo!

2 Para sugerir algo o hacer una frase en 1.ª persona del plural se emplea **let's** + infinitivo sin **to**:

let's leave it at that for today
dejémoslo aquí por hoy

let's just agree to differ
aceptemos simplemente que no opinamos lo mismo

3 La prohibición o la petición negativa:

Para expresar prohibición o una petición negativa se utiliza **do not** o **don't** delante del infinitivo. En inglés oral estándar, **don't** es la forma más frecuente, a no ser que se quiera dar más énfasis a la frase:

don't listen to what he says
no escuches lo que dice

please don't feel you have to accept
por favor, no te sientas obligado a aceptar

look, I've told you before, do not put your hands near the hotplate!
¡mira, ya te lo he dicho, no pongas las manos cerca de la placa!

Con la forma **let's**, se coloca **not** entre **let's** y el verbo. También se puede utilizar **don't let's**, aunque es menos frecuente:

let's not go just yet
don't let's go just yet
no nos vayamos todavía

4 **Do not** se utiliza mucho en los paneles indicativos:

please do not feed the animals
prohibido dar de comer a los animales

5 Para reforzar un imperativo también es posible utilizar el auxiliar **do**:

oh, do be quiet!
¡cállate!

15 EL CONDICIONAL

El ejemplo:

> if you don't hurry, you'll miss your train
> *si no te das prisa, perderás el tren*

es una oración condicional. La condición se expresa en la oración subordinada (que empieza por **if**), la cual puede colocarse delante o detrás de la oración principal (**you'll miss your train**).

La forma de los verbos varía según el tiempo al que hacen referencia y según el grado de probabilidad de la condición.

Para hacer referencia al presente/futuro

a) Posibilidad probable:

El verbo de la oración que empieza por **if** está en presente o en pretérito perfecto compuesto y el verbo de la oración principal es **will** + infinitivo (a veces **shall** + infinitivo en 1.ª persona):

> if I **see** her, **I'll tell** her
> *si la veo, se lo diré*

> if you **have completed** the forms, **I will send** them off
> *si ya han rellenado los formularios, los enviaré*

Hay tres excepciones importantes:

- Si el verbo de la oración principal también está en presente, se espera una consecuencia lógica, por automatismo o costumbre. En este caso, **if** tiene el sentido de **when(ever)** (*cada vez, cuando*):

> if the sun shines, people **look** happier
> *cuando brilla el sol, la gente parece más feliz*

> if you're happy, then **I'm** happy
> *si tú eres feliz, yo también lo soy*

- Cuando will se utiliza en la oración que empieza por if, el hablante hace alusión a la voluntad o intención de alguien de hacer algo:

  if you will kindly look this way, I'll try to explain the painter's method
  si hace el favor de mirar por aquí, intentaré explicarle el método que utiliza el pintor

  well if you will mix your drinks, what can you expect!
  si continúas mezclando el alcohol/las bebidas alcohólicas, ¿qué esperas?

  Cuando se emplea esta forma para pedir algo, se puede utilizar would para que la frase sea más formal:

  if you would be kind enough to look this way...
  si fuera tan amable de mirar por aquí...

- Cuando se utiliza should en la oración que empieza por if (no importa en qué persona), la condición parece tener menos probabilidades de realizarse. Estas oraciones con should suelen ir seguidas del imperativo, como en el primer ejemplo:

  if you should see him, please ask him to ring me
  si lo viera, ¿podría decirle que me telefonee?

  if they should not be there, you will have to manage by yourself
  si no estuvieran allí, tendrás que arreglártelas tú solo

  En un registro más formal, se puede omitir if y la frase puede empezar con una oración subordinada en la que aparezca should:

  should the matter arise again, telephone me at once
  si se presentara nuevamente el problema, llámame inmediatamente por teléfono

b) Posibilidad poco probable o irreal:

  Si la condición tiene pocas probabilidades de realizarse, si presenta un carácter de duda o si se opone a hechos ya conocidos, el verbo de la oración que empieza por if se colocará en pasado, mientras que el verbo de la oración principal será would (o también should en 1.ª persona) + infinitivo:

  if I saw her, I would (I'd) tell her
  si la viera, se lo diría

if she had a car, she would visit you more often
si tuviera coche, vendría a verte más a menudo

Nota:

Este tipo de frase no expresa necesariamente una posibilidad poco probable o irreal. Muchas veces la diferencia entre este tipo de frase y el descrito en el punto a es mínima:

if you worked harder, you would pass the exam
if you work harder, you will pass the exam
si trabajaras más, aprobarías el examen

El empleo del pasado puede dar a la frase un tono más amistoso o educado.

Para hacer referencia al pasado

a) Cuando la condición no se ha realizado, el verbo de la oración subordinada se coloca en pretérito pluscuamperfecto. Se utilizará would (o should en 1.ª persona) + infinitivo pasado en la oración principal:

if I had seen her, I would have told her
si la hubiera visto, se lo habría dicho

if you had finished that one, I would have given you another one
si te hubieras acabado éste, te habría dado otro

En un estilo un poco más formal, se puede omitir if y utilizar had al principio de la oración subordinada. En este caso se invierte el orden del pronombre personal y had:

had I seen her, I would/should have told her
si la hubiera visto, se lo habría dicho

b) Excepciones:

- Si la oración principal hace referencia a la no realización en el presente de una condición pasada, también se puede utilizar would + infinitivo (presente):

if I had studied harder, I would be an engineer today (= if I had studied harder, I would have been an engineer today)
si hubiera estudiado más, hoy día sería ingeniero

- El pasado se emplea en las dos proposiciones si, como hemos visto en la página 57, se sobrentiende una consecuencia automática o habitual (**if** = **when(ever)**, *cada vez, cuando*):

if people got ill in those days, they often died
en aquella época, si una persona enfermaba, solía morir

- Si la condición se ha realizado, las restriciones de las formas verbales no son válidas. En este caso, **if** suele significar «ya que» o «puesto que»:

if he **was** rude to you, why **did** you not **walk** out?
si (= ya que/puesto que) te faltó al respeto, ¿por qué no te marchaste?

if he **was** rude to you, why **have** you still **kept** in touch?
si (= ya que/puesto que) te faltó al respeto, ¿por qué has mantenido el contacto con él?

if he **was** rude to you, why **do** you still **keep** in touch?
si (= ya que/puesto que) te faltó al respeto, ¿por qué mantienes el contacto con él?

16 EL SUBJUNTIVO

El indicativo es el modo de lo real, mientras que el subjuntivo es el modo de lo irreal. Expresa deseo, esperanza, posibilidad, etc.

El subjuntivo se reconoce por la omión de la **-s** en la 3.ª persona del singular y en el uso de **be** en lugar de **is**, en presente, y de **were** en lugar de **was**, en el pasado. El modo subjuntivo es menos frecuente en inglés que en español. Usos principales:

1 En las locuciones fijas que expresan deseo:

long **live** the King!
¡viva el Rey!

God **rest** his soul
Dios lo tenga en su gloria

Heaven **be praised**
alabado sea Dios

2 En la expresión **if need be** (*si se necesita, si es necesario*):

well, **if need be**, you could always hire a car
bueno, si es necesario, siempre puedes alquilar un coche

3 En oraciones como:

it is vital that he **understand** this
es de vital importancia que lo entienda

they recommended she **sell** the house
le aconsejaron que vendiera la casa

we propose that this new ruling **be adopted**
proponemos que se apruebe esta nueva ley

El subjuntivo se utiliza en un registro más culto. En la lengua oral, su uso es más frecuente en inglés americano que en inglés británico.

4 Después de **if only** y en las proposiciones que aparecen detrás de **wish** y **had rather**:

if only we **had** a bigger house...
si tuviéramos una casa más grande...

where's your passport? – I wish I knew!
¿dónde está tu pasaporte? – ojalá lo supiera

do you want me to tell you? – I'd rather you didn't
¿quieres que te lo diga? – prefiero que no lo hagas

Nota:

En estas oraciones que expresan deseo siempre se utiliza el pretérito de subjuntivo. Este tiempo se construye como el pretérito perfecto simple de indicativo, excepto en el caso de **to be,** en el que se coloca **were** en todas las personas del pasado.

5 Después de **it's time** (uso del pretérito de subjuntivo):

it's (high) time we spoke to him
ya es hora de que hablemos con él

Compárese con el empleo del infinitivo, que únicamente expresa la oportunidad del momento:

it's time to speak to him about it
ha llegado la hora de hablar con él

6 if I was/if I were :

Compárese:

(a)   if I was in the wrong, it wasn't intentional
       si me he equivocado, no lo he hecho a propósito

(b)   if I were in the wrong, I would admit it
       si me hubiera equivocado, lo admitiría

En el ejemplo (a), el hablante no dice que no se haya equivocado, pero precisa la ausencia de mala inteción. En el ejemplo (b), por el contrario, el hablante no reconoce que se ha equivocado; para él, hay una duda sobre este hecho. De ahí el uso de **were**.

En la frase (b), también se podría utilizar **was** y se conservaría el mismo sentido. **Was** sería más coloquial que **were**.

17 LOS AUXILIARES MODALES

Los auxiliares modales o de modo, que, como todo auxiliar, modifican el verbo principal de la frase, se llaman así porque en numerosas ocasiones sustituyen al modo subjuntivo. Una de sus características es que se construyen sin **do** en las formas interrogativa y negativa.

Can-Could

Las formas contractas negativas son **can't-couldn't**. La forma negativa sin contracción del presente es **cannot**. Se utiliza:

a) para expresar la **capacidad**, el hecho de poder o saber hacer alguna cosa:

I can't afford it
no puedo permitírmelo

I can swim
sé nadar

when I was a student, I could explain this theory easily
cuando era estudiante, podía explicar esta teoría fácilmente

En este último ejemplo en pasado, también se puede utilizar **be able to** (*poder, ser capaz de*). Este giro permite expresar la capacidad en los demás tiempos:

I used to be able to explain this theory easily
antes podía explicar esta teoría fácilmente

I'll be able to tell you the answer tomorrow
podré darte la respuesta mañana

I've never been able to understand her
nunca he podido comprenderla

Nota:

> En una oración condicional, **could** + infinitivo hace referencia
> al presente o al futuro (compárese con **would** en el capítulo «El
> condicional», en p. 58):
>
> you **could** do a lot better if you'd only try
> *podrías hacerlo mucho mejor si tan sólo lo intentaras*

b) para expresar **permiso**:

can/could I have a look at your photos?
¿puedo/podría ver tus fotos?

Nota:

> **Could** hace referencia al presente y al futuro de la misma man-
> era que **can.** La única diferencia reside en el hecho de que
> **could** es un poco más culto o menos afirmativo. Por jemplo,
> un niño no dirá:
>
> **could** I go out to play?
> *¿puedo ir a jugar?*

A veces, también se puede emplear **could** para expresar permiso
en el pasado, cuando es evidente que se trata de un contexto en
pasado:

for some reason we **couldn't** smoke in the lounge before; but now we
  can
*por alguna razón, antes no podíamos fumar en el salón, pero ahora
  podemos*

En este último ejemplo es posible utilizar **be allowed to** (*poder,
tener autorización para*). Este giro permite expresar permirso en el
resto de los tiempos:

we **weren't allowed to** see him, he was so ill
no pudimos verlo, estaba demasiado indispuesto

will they **be allowed to** change the rules?
¿tendrán autorización para cambiar las reglas?

c) para expresar posibilidad:

that can't be right
no puede ser

what shall I do? – you can always talk to a lawyer/you could talk to a
lawyer
¿qué voy a hacer? – siempre puedes consultar a un abogado/podrías
consultar a un abogado

Aquí could tampoco hace referencia al pasado, sino al presente o
al futuro. Si se desea hacer referencia al pasado, could debe ir
seguido del infinitivo pasado:

you could have talked to a lawyer
podrías haber consultado a un abogado

I know I could have, but I didn't want to
sé que habría podido, pero no quise

Could y may se pueden usar indistintamente cuando expresan
posibilidad o eventualidad:

you could/may be right
quizá tengas razón

Pero, a veces, existe una diferencia importante entre can y may
en relación con la posibilidad o la eventualidad:

(a)   your comments can be overheard
      pueden oírse tus comentarios/tus comentarios pueden ser oídos

(b)   your comments may be overheard
      podrían oírse tus comentarios/tus comentarios podrían ser oídos

El ejemplo (a) significa que se pueden oír sus comentarios
(porque los hace en voz alta, por ejemplo) sin especificar si
alguien los oirá o no. El ejemplo (b) significa que existe la posibilidad de que los comentarios se puedan oír de verdad.

La diferencia también existe en la forma negativa:

don't worry, he can't have heard us
no te preocupes, no puede habernos oído (es imposible que nos haya
oído)

because of all the noise, he may not have heard us
con este ruido, es posible que no nos haya oído

d) Para expresar **sugerencia** (únicamente **could**):

you **could** try a supermarket
puedes intentar buscarlo en un supermercado

they **could** always sell their second house if they need money
siempre pueden vender su segunda residencia si necesitan dinero

e) Para expresar **reproche, molestia, irritación** (únicamente **could**):

you **could** have told me I had paint on my face!
¡podrías haberme dicho que tenía pintura en la cara!

May-Might

La forma contracta **mayn't** no es habitual en el sentido de «permiso» que tiene **may**. En su lugar se utiliza **may not** o **must not/mustn't**. La forma negativa contracta de **might** es **mightn't**, pero ésta no se emplea para expresar prohibición.

a) Para expresar **permiso** o **prohibición**:

may I open a window? – no, you **may not**!
¿puedo abrir la ventana? – ¡no, ni hablar!

El uso de **may** es una forma un poco más culta que **can**. Un hablante que utiliza **might** para pedir permiso se mostraría igualmente educado:

I wonder if I **might** have another of those cakes
¿podría tomar otro pastel?

might I suggest we stop there for today?
¿puedo sugerir que lo dejemos aquí por hoy?

Nota:

Might expresa presente o futuro. En muy raras ocasiones hace referencia al pasado cuando se utiliza en una oración principal. Compárese:

he then asked if he might smoke *(might en la oración subordinada)*

he then asked if he was allowed to smoke
entonces preguntó si podía fumar

y

he wasn't allowed to smoke
no podía fumar/no le estaba permitido fumar

No se puede utilizar might en el último ejemplo; en su lugar se recurre a las formas de be allowed to.

b) Para expresar **posibilidad**:

it may/might still be possible
puede que todavía sea posible

they may/might change their minds
es posible que cambien de parecer

it may not/mightn't be necessary after all
quizá no será necesario, después de todo

she may/might have left a note upstairs
quizá ha dejado una nota arriba

c) Para expresar **sorpresa, irritación** (habitualmente might):

and who may/might you be to give out orders?
¿quién te crees que eres para dar órdenes?

and what might that be supposed to mean?
¿y qué se supone que quiere decir?

d) Para expresar **sugerencia** (únicamente might):

they might at least apologize
por lo menos podrían pedir disculpas

you might like to try one of these cigars
quizá quieras probar uno de estos puros

Nota:

> Obsérvese que en esta frase constituye casi una orden:
>
> you might take this down the road to your Gran
> *¿quieres hacer el favor de llevarle esto a tu abuela?*
>
> you might like to read the next chapter for Monday
> *¿me harán el favor de leer el próximo capítulo para el lunes?*

e) Para expresar **reproche** (únicamente might):

you might have told me he was deaf!
¡podrías haberme dicho que era sordo!

they might have written back to us at least!
¡al menos podrían habernos contestado!

f) Para expresar **deseo** (atención al orden de las palabras):

may you have a very happy retirement
le deseo una feliz jubilación

may all your dreams come true!
¡deseo que todos vuestros sueños se hagan realidad!

may/might you be forgiven for telling such lies!
¡que Dios te perdone por decir tales mentiras!

Por lo general, este uso se limita a locuciones fijas o a un estilo retórico o literario.

 Must-Had to

La forma contracta negativa de must es mustn't (para have, véase la página 31).

a) Para expresar **obligación**:

you have no choice, you must do what he wants
no tienes más remedio que hacer lo que él quiere

must you go already?
¿ya tienes que irte?

El estilo de este último ejemplo es muy culto. También se puede utilizar have to en presente o, en un registro más coloquial, have got to:

you have no choice, you have (got) to do what he says
no tienes más remedio que hacer lo que él dice

do you have to go already/have you got to go already?
¿ya tienes que irte?

El sentido a menudo es el mismo, pero a veces hay una ligera diferencia. Must expresa sentimientos personales de obligación o coacción, mientras que have to suele emplearse cuando se sobrentiende una obligación exterior (cuando alguien nos ha pedido hacer algo). Compárese:

I must go to the dentist (= I have toothache, etc.)
he de ir al dentista (= me duelen las muelas, etc.)

I have (got) to go to the dentist (= I have an appointement)
he de ir al dentista (= tengo cita con él)

Para el pasado y el futuro, se utiliza have to:

we had to do what he wanted
tuvimos que hacer lo que él quería

I'll have to finish it tomorrow
tendré que acabarlo mañana

b) Para expresar **prohibición** o **ausencia de obligación** (forma negativa):

- Must not se utiliza para expresar prohibición:

  you mustn't drink and drive
  si bebes no conduzcas

  En el pasado, se utiliza not to be allowed to:

  when we were children we weren't allowed to...
  cuando éramos pequeños no teníamos permiso para...

- Don't have to o haven't got to se utilizan para expresar ausencia de obligación:

  we don't have to drive all night, we could always stop at a hotel
  no estamos obligados a conducir toda la noche, siempre podemos pararnos en un hotel

  La forma del pasado se conjuga igual que have:

  you didn't have to buy one, you could have used mine
  no tenías necesidad de comprarte uno, podías haber utilizado el mío

c) Para expresar **probabilidad, deducción**:

hello, you must be Susan
hola, usted debe de ser Susan

that must be my mistake
debe de tratarse de un error por mi parte

she must have been surprised to see you
ha debido de sorprenderse al verte

Have to también se utiliza a menudo en este sentido:

you have to be kidding!
¿bromeas?

de la misma manera que have got to, sobre todo en inglés británico:

well if she said so, it's got to be true (it's = it has)
si ella lo ha dicho, ha de ser verdad

Ought to

La forma contracta negativa es **oughtn't to**. El infinitivo después de ought va precedido de **to**, a diferencia de los demás auxiliares modales.

a) Para expresar **obligación**:

Ought to tiene el mismo sentido que **should** cuando expresa obligación:

you oughtn't even to think things like that
ni siquiera tendrías que pensar en ese tipo de cosas

and he ought to know!
¡y él debe saberlo!

Pero **ought to** no es tan fuerte como **must** en este sentido. Compárense estos dos ejemplos:

I must/have to avoid fatty foods (*obligación firme o necesidad*)
debo evitar los alimentos grasos

I ought to avoid fatty foods (*obligación menos estricta*)
debería evitar los alimentos grasos

Normalmente, **must** o **have (got) to** sustituyen a **ought to** en las preguntas:

must you/do you have to/have you got to visit your mother every
Sunday?
¿debes ir a ver a tu madre todos los domingos?

b) Para expresar la **probabilidad**:

they ought to have reached the summit by now
a estas horas deberían de haber alcanzado la cumbre

£50, that ought to be enough
50 libras deberían de ser suficientes

Shall-Should

Las formas contractas negativas son **shan't-shouldn't**. Para el condicional, véase la página 57. Para expresar futuro, véase la página 43.

a) Para expresar **obligación**, a menudo moral (únicamente should):

you should take more exercise
deberías hacer más ejercicio

you shouldn't talk to her like that
no deberías hablarle así

what do you think I should do?
según tú, ¿qué debería hacer?

with a new fuse fitted it should work
con un fusible nuevo debería funcionar

b) Para expresar **probabilidad, deducción** (únicamente should):

it's after ten, they should be in Paris by now
son más de las diez, ya deben de estar en París

if doing one took you two hours, then three shouldn't take longer
than six hours, should it?
*si haces uno en dos horas, deberías de poder hacer tres en seis
horas, ¿no?*

is it there? – well, it should be because that's where I left it
¿está allí? – pues debería, porque es allí donde lo dejé

c) Para expresar su **opinión de forma vacilante**, siendo should
ligeramente más culto que would (únicamente should):

I should just like to say that...
simplemente me gustaría decir...

I should hardly call him a great intellectual but...
yo no diría de él que es un gran intelectual, pero...

d) Para expresar **sorpresa, irritación, molestia:**

there was a knock at the door, and who should it be but...
llaman a la puerta, y ¿quién es...?

where have I put my glasses? – how should I know?
¿dónde he puesto mis gafas? – ¿y cómo quieres que yo lo sepa?

e) **Shall** se utiliza en el lenguaje **jurídico u oficial:**

the committee shall consist of no more than six members
el comité estará constituido por no más de seis miembros

the contract shall be subject to English law
el contrato se regirá por las leyes inglesas

Will-Would

Las formas negativas contractas son won't-wouldn't. Para las frases en condicional, véase la página 57. Para expresar el futuro, véase la página 43.

a) **Will** se utiliza para insistir en las nociones de **capacidad, inclinación natural, costumbre** o **comportamiento característico:**

cork will float on water
el corcho flota en el agua

the car won't start
el coche no arranca

the tank will hold about 50 litres
el depósito tiene capacidad para unos 50 litros

he will sit playing quietly on his own for hours
puede quedarse tranquilamente sentado jugando solo durante horas

it's so annoying, he will keep interrupting!
¡me molesta tanto!, ¡no para de molestarme!

Se utiliza **would** para hacer referencia al pasado:

when he was little, he would sit playing quietly on his own for hours
cuando era pequeño se quedaba tranquilamente sentado jugando solo durantes horas

they would insist on calling me «Jacko»
no dejaban de insistir en llamarme «Jacko»

she created a scene in public – she would!
ha montado un número en público – ¡es propio de ella!/¡no me extraña de ella!

b) Para expresar **órdenes** o para reforzar una afirmación:

you will do as you are told!
¡harás lo que se te dice!

will you stop that right now!
¡para eso enseguida!/¡para inmediatamente!

I will not tolerate this!
¡no lo pienso tolerar!

c) Para hacer mención, en un tono más bien ceremonioso, a los recuerdos o a los conocimientos de alguien:

you will recall last week's discussion about the purchase of a computer
seguramente recordarán nuestra discusión de la semana pasada sobre la compra de un ordenador

as you will all know, there have been rumours recently about...
como todos ustedes sabrán, recientemente han circulado rumores sobre el tema...

d) Para hacer **suposiciones**:

there's someone at the door – that'll be Graham
hay alguien en la puerta – será Graham

how old is he now? – he'll be about 45
¿qué edad tiene? – rondará los 45

e) Para hacer **preguntas** o **proposiciones** en un registro formal:

will you have another cup of tea? – thank you, I will
¿quiere usted otra taza de té? – sí, por favor

won't you try one of these?
¿no desea probar uno?

did they ask you if you would like to try one?
¿le han preguntado si quería probar uno?

f) Para formular una **petición**:

will/would you move your car, please?
¿podría usted cambiar su coche de sitio, por favor?

La forma would es más formal, menos directa.

OTROS AUXILIARES

Used to

Used to (para expresar una acción habitual en el pasado) se puede considerar una especie de semiauxiliar, ya que el empleo de do es opcional en las frases interrogativas y negativas:

he used not to smoke so much
he didn't use to smoke so much
antes no solía fumar tanto

used you to know him?
did you use to know him?
¿lo conocías de antes?

No obstante, la forma sin do es poco usual y pertenece más a la lengua escrita.

Dare, need

Estos verbos pueden funcionar como verbos corrientes o como auxiliares modales. Cuando son auxiliares, no presentan la -s en la 3.ª persona del singular del presente; do no se utiliza en las frases interrogativas ni en las negativas, y si van seguidos de un infinitivo, no se coloca to delante del radical.

a) Como **verbos corrientes**:

I don't dare to say anything
no me atrevo a decir nada

does he dare talk openly about it?
*¿se atreve a hablar
 abiertamente sobre ello?*

you don't need to ask first
no necesitas preguntar primero

do I need to sign it?
¿tengo que firmarlo?

b) Como **auxiliares modales**:

I **daren't** say anything
no me atrevo a decir nada

dare he talk openly about it?
¿se atreve a hablar
abiertamente sobre ello?

you **needn't** ask first
no necesitas preguntar primero

need I sign it?
¿tengo que firmarlo?

El uso de **dare** y de **need** como auxiliares pertenece a un registro más formal.

- **Dare** también puede funcionar como un verbo corriente en las formas interrogativa y negativa (es decir con **do**) y, como los auxiliares, seguido de un infinitivo sin **to**:

I **don't dare say** anything
no me atrevo a decir nada

- En las oraciones principales que no son interrogativas ni negativas, **need** siempre se comporta como un verbo corriente:

I **need to go** to the toilet
necesito ir al lavabo

Have, get

Have o **get** pueden utilizarse en construcciones del tipo «hacer que alguien haga algo» (**have/get** + complemento de objeto directo + participio pasado):

we're going to **have/get** the car resprayed
vamos a pintar el coche de nuevo

I can't do it myself but I can **have/get** it done for you
no puedo hacerlo personalmente, pero puedo mandar que os lo
hagan

Cuando **have/get** van seguidos de un infinitivo en voz activa, **to** se omite después de **have**, pero se mantiene detrás de **get**:

I'll **have** the porter **bring** them up for you
I'll **get** the porter **to bring** them up for you
le pediré al portero que te los suba

18 LAS PARTÍCULAS DE LOS *PHRASAL VERBS*

Este apartado trata de las partículas de los *phrasal verbs* o verbos compuestos. El sentido de estos verbos no equivale obligatoriamente a la suma del significado de los dos elementos que los componen. Por ejemplo, run up puede tener el sentido de «subir corriendo» o de «acumular» (I've run up a huge overdraft *tengo un descubierto enorme*). Así pues, los *phrasal verbs* forman un todo; la partícula es indispensable, ya que permite modificar el sentido del verbo principal.

A continuación figura una lista de estas partículas con sus principales usos, así como algunos ejemplos que corresponden a sus respectivos significados.

Véase también el «Diccionario de *phrasal verbs*», en la p. 107, donde se ilustran estos verbos con numerosos ejemplos para cada acepción.

About

1 movimiento desordenado que va en todos los sentidos:

I felt about for the light switch
buscaba el interruptor a tientas

I was rushing about trying to get ready when the phone rang
iba de un lado para otro intentando estar arreglada cuando sonó el teléfono

people milled about in the streets
las calles son un hervidero de gente

2 inmovilidad, inacción, ociosidad:

I hate standing about at street corners, so make sure you're on time
odio estar plantada en una esquina esperando, así que intenta ser puntual

she always keeps me hanging about when we arrange to meet
siempre me hace esperar un montón cuando quedamos

3 alrededor, por los alrededores:

he looked about for a taxi
buscó un taxi por allí

4 acerca de:

what do you think about his latest film?
¿qué piensas (acerca) de su última película?

Across

comunicar, hacer entender algo:

he finds it hard to put his ideas across
le cuesta expresar sus ideas con claridad

how can I get it across to them that it's important to keep copies of all your files?
¿cómo puedo hacerles entender que es importante hacer una copia de todos los ficheros?

After

1 siguiendo, detrás, tras:

he was running after his ball and dashed out into the road
iba corriendo detrás de la pelota y de repente apareció en la carretera

she tore after him, determined to catch him
se lanzó tras él, dispuesta a atraparlo

2 a propósito de:

she always remembers to ask after them
nunca olvida preguntar por ellos

3 lazo o parecido familiar:

my niece takes after me
mi sobrina se parece a mí

he's called after his grandfather
se llama igual que su abuelo

Against

1 protección contra algo:

fluoride is said to guard against tooth decay
dicen que el flúor protege contra las caries

2 ser perjudicial para alguien:

will the fact that he has a previous conviction go against him?
¿el hecho de que haya sido condenado anteriormente puede jugar en su contra?

Ahead

1 enfrente, delante:

the favourite has got ahead now and looks likely to win
el favorito se encuentra ahora en cabeza y parece que va a ganar

2 noción de éxito, de progreso:

you will never get ahead unless you are conscientious
nunca conseguirás nada si no eres más concienzudo

3 en el futuro:

let's look ahead to the next month's meeting
pensemos en la reunión del próximo mes

it is essential to plan ahead for your retirement
es muy importante pensar en la jubilación

Along

1 acción en curso, progresión:

we were driving along when suddenly...
íbamos conduciendo tranquilamente cuando de repente...

they were tearing along, so that they would arrive first
corrían a toda velocidad para llegar los primeros

things are coming along nicely
las cosas se presentan bastante bien

2 ir o hacer ir:

I'll have to hurry along if I want to catch my train
tendré que darme prisa si no quiero perder el tren

it's time for me to be getting along
ha llegado la hora de irme

the police told the crowd to move along
la policía pidió a la mutiltud que se dispersara

3 con:

why not bring your sister along?
¿por qué no vienes con tu hermana?

4 hacia un lugar cercano, a menudo en una misma calle:

my mother sent me along to see how you were
mi madre me pidió que viniera para ver cómo estabas

Apart

1 separación:

the two fighters had to be pulled apart
tuvieron que separar a los dos boxeadores

I saw them draw apart as I entered the room
los vi separarse uno del otro cuando entré en la habitación

I can't get these two pieces apart
no consigo separar estos dos trozos

2 a trozos, en diferentes partes:

he says it just came apart in his hands
dijo que al cogerlo se rompió

3 diferenciarse de los demás:

her talent sets her apart from all the other children in my class
se distingue del resto de los niños de mi clase por su talento

Around (véase también round)

1 en diferentes lugares, en todas partes:

you have to search around for that kind of information
tendrás que buscar en diferentes lugares para obtener este tipo de información

I'm hunting around for a new flatmate
estoy buscando por todas partes un nuevo compañero de piso

2 alrededor:

where's that umbrella? – it must be lying around somewhere
¿dónde está aquel paraguas? – debe de estar por algún sitio

3 no tener nada que hacer:

how much longer do we have to wait around before he arrives?
¿cuánto tiempo vamos a tener que esperar hasta que llegue?

Aside

1 de lado, al lado:

please step aside and let us pass
por favor, póngase a un lado y déjenos pasar

2 separado de un grupo:

the teacher drew him aside to ask how his father was
el profesor lo llevó aparte para preguntarle cómo estaba su padre

3 dejar una cosa de lado para volver a ella o utilizarla más tarde:

leaving that question aside for the moment...
dejemos este tema de lado de momento...

could you put that aside and work on this instead?
¿puedes dejar eso por ahora y hacer esto otro?

I have some money set aside for emergencies
tengo algo de dinero aparte para imprevistos

At

hacia, en dirección a:

> the explorers worked their way through the jungle, chopping at the undergrowth with their machetes
> *los exploradores se abrieron camino a través de la selva a golpe de machete*

> the birds were picking at the crumbs
> *los pájaros picoteaban las migajas*

> he hinted at the possibility of my getting a promotion
> *dio a entender que yo podía obtener un ascenso*

Away

1 ausentarse o irse:

> I'm sorry but he has been called away on business
> *lo siento pero ha tenido que ausentarse por un asunto de negocios*

> he ran away into the crowd
> *se fue corriendo hacia la muchedumbre*

2 tomar distancia o alejarse:

> she backed away from the dog
> *retrocedió ante el perro*

> why do you move away whenever I approach you?
> *¿por qué te alejas cada vez que me acerco a ti?*

3 continuar algo durante algún tiempo:

> they just sat there giggling away
> *estaban allí sentados, riendo sin parar*

> she was in the bath, singing away to herself
> *estaba en el baño canturreando*

> he lay groaning away on the ground
> *estaba tendido en el suelo gimiendo*

> he's working away on his novel
> *trabaja sin descanso en su novela*

4 quitar algo o desembarazarse de ello:

maybe someone with a van could take the wardrobe away
podría llevarse el armario alguien que tuviera una camioneta

if you don't want it, throw it away
si no lo quieres, tíralo

5 guardar, en reserva:

lock it away where it'll be safe
ponlo bajo llave en un lugar seguro

he keeps it stored away in the attic
lo guarda en el desván

I wouldn't be surprised if he had salted away a lot of money
no me extrañaría que hubiera guardado aparte/apartado mucho dinero

6 hasta desaparecer:

the water has all boiled away
el agua se ha evaporado por completo

he is wasting away with grief
la pena lo corroe poco a poco

the water trickled away down the plughole
el agua desapareció por el desagüe

7 agotar algo:

he has drunk his entire inheritance away
gastó toda su herencia en alcohol

8 principio de una acción:

could I ask some questions? – sure, fire away
¿puedo hacerle algunas preguntas? – desde luego, adelante

Back

1 detrás, atrás, hacia atrás:

she flung back her hair
se echó el pelo hacia atrás

thinking back...
volviendo la vista atrás...

2 idea de vuelta, de volver:

flood waters are receding and people are beginning to filter back to their homes
las inundaciones están disminuyendo y la gente empieza a volver a sus hogares

it's so cold I think I'll head back
hace tanto frío que creo que voy a volver a casa

she's being moved back to the personnel department
la han vuelto a trasladar al departamento de personal

bring it back once you've finished with it
devuélvemelo una vez lo hayas terminado

3 de nuevo:

we've bought back our old house
hemos vuelto a comprar nuestra antigua casa

stop the tape and play the last ten frames back
para la cinta (de vídeo) y vuelve a pasar las últimas diez imágenes

4 retirarse, perder la vitalidad, etc.:

the intense heat forced them back
el intenso calor los obligó a volver

the plant will die back in autumn
la planta se marchitará en otoño

5 frenar, reducir:

rein your horse back
detenga su caballo

the pilot throttled the engines back and came in to land
el piloto redujo la velocidad y aterrizó

6 cortar o reducir algo:

this old rose bush needs to be cut back
este viejo rosal necesita una poda

we'll have to cut back on our expenses
tenemos que reducir gastos

7 contener, retener, esconder algo:

I forced back my tears
contuve las lágrimas

what are you keeping back from us?
¿qué nos escondes?

Behind

1 tarde, con retraso:

the landlady says we're getting behind with the rent
la propietaria dice que nos hemos retrasado con el alquiler

if you're slipping behind with your work...
si te retrasas con tu trabajo...

2 ser dejado atrás, quedarse atrás:

do you mind being left behind to look after the children?
¿te importa quedarte y cuidar de los niños?

you go on ahead, I'll stay behind
seguid, yo me quedo

By

1 movimiento, paso:

we had to push by a lot of people
tuvimos que empujar a mucha gente

the cars raced by
los coches pasaron a toda velocidad

time goes by so fast
el tiempo pasa deprisa

2 referirse a algo:

my mother swears by castor oil
mi madre confía ciegamente en el aceite de ricino

which theory do you go by?
¿en qué teoría se basa?

3 hacer una visita o una parada rápida:

we'll drop by to see you one day
pasaremos a visitaros un día de estos

I stopped by at the chemist's on the way home
me paré en la farmacia de camino a casa

Down

1 movimiento de arriba abajo, hacia el suelo:

call Tom down for tea
dile a Tom que baje a tomar el té

pass me down that big plate from the top shelf
pásame el plato grande que está en el estante de arriba

I bent down to pick up the old man's stick
me agaché para recoger el bastón del anciano

the hurricane blew down hundreds of mature trees
el huracán derribó centenares de árboles viejos

pull the blinds down
baja las persianas

2 tomar notas, para hacer referencia a algo más tarde:

could someone note down the main points?
¿alguien puede anotar los puntos principales?

I've written it down in my notebook
lo he anotado en mi cuaderno

I could see him scribbling something down
lo vi garabateando algo

3 rechazar o poner fin a algo:

the bill was voted down
el proyecto de ley fue rechazado

they all shouted the speaker down
todos abuchearon al orador

4 sujetar o apretar algo (con clavos, tornillos, etc.):

nail it down or the wind will blow it away
clávalo o el viento se lo llevará

screw the lid down properly
atornilla bien la tapa

glue it down
pégalo

5 parar un vehículo:

we flagged a taxi down
paramos un taxi

6 transmitir algo de una generación a otra:

the necklace came down to her from her great-aunt
heredó el collar de su tía abuela

the song was passed down from generation to generation
esta canción ha pasado de generación en generación

7 reducción, disminución:

everything in the shop has been marked down
todos los artículos de la tienda han sido rebajados

thin the sauce down with a little milk if necessary
si fuera necesario, reduzca la salsa con un poco de leche

you're going too fast, slow down
vas demasiado deprisa, reduce la velocidad

8 dejar de funcionar, no estar en forma, etc.:

the car has broken down
el coche se ha averiado

she broke down and wept
se vino abajo y se echó a llorar

9 acción punitiva impuesta por una autoridad:

the police are clamping down on illegal parking
la policía está tomando medidas drásticas contra el aparcamiento indebido

the teacher really came down on me for not having learnt the dates properly
el profesor me castigó severamente por no haberme aprendido bien las fechas

10 tragar, tomar alimentos, etc.:

if you don't force some food down you'll collapse
si no te esfuerzas en comer algo no resistirás

the dog gobbled it down in a second
el perro se lo engulló de un bocado

she absolutely wolfed her dinner down
prácticamente devoró la comida

For

1 el fin, el objetivo:

she felt in her bag for the keys
buscó las llaves en su bolso

stop fishing for compliments!
¡deja de buscar cumplidos!

the qualities looked for in candidates are...
las cualidades que se buscan en los candidatos son...

2 estar a favor de algo:

the points of view argued for in this paper...
los puntos de vista que se defienden en este artículo...

Forth

1 hacia delante, sobre todo para enfrentarse a un adversario:

the army went forth into battle *(en desuso o literario)*
el ejército se puso en marcha para la batalla

he sallied forth to face the waiting fans *(uso literario o humorístico)*
salió para enfrentarse a todos sus fans

2 idea de nacimiento o producción:

Mary brought forth a son *(empleo en desuso o registro culto)*
Mary ha traído un hijo al mundo

the tree puts forth the most gloriously scented blossom
este árbol da flores con un perfume de lo más exquisito

3 hablar mucho rato y, a veces, de forma pomposa:

he is always holding forth about something
siempre está disertando sobre cualquier cosa

she spouted forth about the benefits of free enterprise
soltó un discurso interminable sobre las ventajas de la libre empresa

Forward

1 adelante, hacia adelante:

please come forward one by one as I call your names
hagan el favor de avanzar de uno en uno a medida que diga sus nombres

she leaned forward to hear what they were talking about
se inclinó hacia delante para oír de qué estaban hablando

pull your chair forward
empuja tu silla hacia delante

2 hablar del futuro, anticipar:

we're really looking forward to seeing them again
tenemos muchas ganas de volverlos a ver

that's something I am definitely not looking forward to
es algo de lo que no tengo ningunas ganas

looking forward to hearing from you *(en una carta)*
a la espera de sus noticias

3 avanzar, adelantar un acontecimiento:

the board meeting has been brought forward a week
*la reunión del consejo de administración ha sido adelantada una
semana*

4 sugerir, proponer algo:

does anyone have any other suggestions they wish to bring forward?
¿alguien desea hacer alguna otra sugerencia?

the theory that he puts forward in his book...
la teoría que avanza en su libro...

Home

1 en casa, en el hogar:

who is taking you home?
¿quién te lleva a casa?

I'll see you home
te veré en casa

2 clavar o encajar algo correctamente:

make sure you hammer the nails home
comprobad que claváis bien los clavos

is the plug pushed home properly?
¿el tapón está bien encajado?

3 hacer comprender o hacer apreciar algo a alguien:

did you drive it home to them that they must be back by midnight?
¿les has dejado claro que deben estar de vuelta a medianoche?

the recent accident brought home to them the need for insurance
*después del accidente que acaban de tener se han dado cuenta de la
 necesidad de estar asegurado*

that comment really hit home
aquel comentario dio en el clavo

1 movimiento del exterior hacia el interior:

there's no need to burst in like that
no es necesario irrumpir de esa manera

we crept in so as not to disturb you
hemos entrado de puntillas para no molestarte

don't stand so close to the edge of the pool, you might fall in
no te pongas en el borde de la piscina, que te puedes caer

2 en algún sitio, en un lugar:

you shouldn't have left this paragraph in
no tendrías que haber conservado este párrafo

I'm going to the bank to pay in these cheques
voy al banco a ingresar estos cheques

fold in the flour
agregue la harina

the car's pretty full but we could squeeze one more in
el coche está casi lleno, pero todavía cabe una persona más

3 estar encerrado o no poder salir:

when the police arrived they found he had barricaded himself in
cuando llegó la policía, vieron que se había atrincherado

the man next door has blocked me in
el coche de mi vecino me impide salir

help, I'm locked in!
¡socorro, me he quedado encerrado!

4 entrar, acercarse en dirección a algo:

members of the orchestra began to filter in
los miembros de la orquesta empezaron a entrar uno tras otro

when the train pulled in...
cuando el tren entró en la estación...

as I looked out of the window I saw a car drive in
mientras miraba por la ventana vi entrar un coche

5 completar o rellenar algo:

fill in this form
rellene este impreso

the artist then drew in the remaining features
a continuación, el artista completó los rasgos del rostro

6 en casa de uno o en casa de alguien:

I'm staying in this evening to wash my hair
esta noche me quedo en casa para lavarme el pelo

let's invite the people next door in for a coffee
invitemos a los vecinos a tomar café

7 action de entregar o de entregarse:

the wanted man handed himself in to the police
el hombre que buscaban se entregó a la policía

hand your essays in tomorrow
entregadme las redacciones mañana

8 parar o pararse:

I've jacked my job in
he dejado el trabajo

pack that noise in!
¡deja de hacer ese ruido!

the engine's packed in
el motor se ha parado

9 ceder, hundirse, desplomarse, etc.:

they had to beat the door in since nobody had a key
tuvieron que echar la puerta abajo porque nadie tenía la llave

the roof fell in, showering the firemen with debris
*el techo se derrumbó y una lluvia de escombros cayó sobre los
  bomberos*

10 disminuir o acortar algo:

I asked the dressmaker to take in the sleeves
le he pedido a la modista que me acorte las mangas

pull the rope in a bit to get rid of the slack
tira un poco de la cuerda para que esté tensa

the nights are drawing in
las noches son más cortas

hold your stomach in
mete la tripa

Into

1 movimiento del exterior hacia el interior:

don't just barge into the room, knock first
no irrumpas así en la habitación, llama a la puerta primero

the operator cut into our conversation
la operadora interrumpió nuestra conversación

the Fraud Squad is looking into the affair
la brigada de delitos monetarios está investigando el asunto

2 utilizar una parte de algo, normalmente en contra de la voluntad:

we're going to have to break into our savings to pay for the repairs to
  the roof
*tendremos que echar mano de nuestros ahorros para pagar las obras
  del tejado*

it cuts into our free time too much
esto nos quita demasiado tiempo libre

3 contacto físico, chocar con alguien o algo:

if you looked where you were going, you wouldn't keep running into people
si mirases por donde vas, dejarías de chocar con la gente

some idiot running for a train barged into me
un imbécil que iba corriendo para coger el tren chocó contra mí

Off

1 quitar algo, llevarse a alguien:

don't bite it off, use the scissors
no lo arranques con los dientes, usa las tijeras

it took ages to scrape the paint off
ha llevado siglos quitar la pintura

he was taken off in a police car
se lo llevaron en un coche de policía

2 partir, irse:

the car slowly moved off
el coche se alejó lentamente

they rushed off when they saw the policeman approaching
se fueron como un rayo cuando vieron que la policía se acercaba

don't hurry off, stay and have some tea
no te vayas tan deprisa, quédate un poco más y toma una taza de té

3 empezar algo:

let me start off by saying...
permítanme comenzar diciendo...

who's going to lead off with the first question?
¿quién desea comenzar planteando la primera pregunta?

4 abandonar un medio de transporte:

as the bus slowed, he jumped off
cuando el autobús aminoró la velocidad, saltó de él

the doors opened and everyone got off
las puertas se abrieron y todo el mundo bajó

she doesn't like riding because she keeps falling off
no le gusta ir en bicicleta porque se cae todo el rato

5 apagar, parar algo:

turn the lights off, please
apaga las luces, por favor

he has sworn off alcohol
ha dejado el alcohol

6 cambio, degradación de algo:

the meat has gone off
la carne se ha echado a perder

attendances have fallen off
la asistencia ha bajado

7 para intensificar el sentido de un verbo:

the scriptwriters have decided to kill off this character
los guionistas han decidido matar a este personaje

the detective was bought off
el detective fue sobornado

most of the land has been sold off
se han vendido las mayoría de las tierras

8 licencia, permiso (para ausentarse):

take a few days off
tómate unos días de vacaciones

9 estar inutilizado, desahuciado o inaccesible:

for reasons of safety, that part of the road has been closed off
por razones de seguridad, este tramo de carretera ha sido cerrado al tráfico

this part has been partitioned off from the rest of the room
esta parte se ha separado del resto de la habitación con un tabique

On

1 continuar algo:

read on to the end of the chapter
continúa leyendo hasta el final del capítulo

they chatted on for hours
estuvieron charlando durante horas

she worked on into the night
trabajó hasta altas horas de la noche

2 poner o ponerse algo:

she threw a dressing gown on and went to answer the door
se puso una bata y fue a abrir la puerta

what did he have on?
¿qué llevaba puesto?

I couldn't get it on
no me cabía

3 encender (un aparato eléctrico, etc.):

turn the TV on, would you?
enciende la televisión, por favor

do you know that you've left the headlights on?
¿sabes que te has dejado los faros encendidos?

4 utilizar algo para funcionar, sobrevivir, etc.:

what do the animals feed on in winter?
¿de qué se alimentan estos animales en invierno?

all cars should run on unleaded petrol
todos los coches deberían funcionar con gasolina sin plomo

5 a bordo de un medio de transporte:

the train stopped and everybody got on
el tren se paró y todo el mundo subió

they couldn't get any more passengers on
no podían admitir más pasajeros

6 adaptarse a algo, encajar, etc.:

the lid bolts on
la tapa se fija con un perno

where does this bit fit on?
¿dónde va esta pieza?

7 aceptar algo:

it seemed like an excellent idea and we seized (up) on it immediately
nos pareció una idea excelente y la aceptamos inmediatamente

8 hacer avanzar:

the crowd is cheering her on as she reaches the last mile
cuando alcanza el último kilómetro, la multitud la aclama con aplausos y gritos de entusiasmo

he wanted to look in the car showroom but I hurried him on
quería mirar los coches de la exposición, pero le metí prisa

9 previsto, programado:

I've got something on every night next week
la próxima semana tengo algo previsto para cada noche

10 transmitir o pasar algo a alguien:

she passed your book on to me
me ha pasado tu libro

could you pass the news on?
¿puedes transmitir la noticia?

Out

1 salir de un sitio, irse:

they bolted out of the door
salieron de golpe

she drove out of the garage
salió con el coche del garaje

I'm popping out to the library
voy a hacer una escapada a la biblioteca

the train had only just pulled out of the station when...
el tren acababa de salir de la estación cuando...

he walked out on his wife and kids
abandonó a su mujer y a sus hijos

2 indica una privación o una exclusión:

that tree is blocking out all the sun
este árbol tapa el sol

heavy floods have driven thousands of people out of their homes
miles de personas han tenido que ser evacuadas de sus casas a causa de las grandes inundaciones

I've thrown out your old jacket
he tirado tu chaqueta vieja

I feel a bit left out
me siento un poco excluido

they have a habit of freezing out people they don't like
tienen la costumbre de desdeñar a la gente que no les gusta

3 repartir:

we need volunteers to hand out leaflets
necesitamos voluntarios para repartir folletos

4 tender, alargar algo:

he held out his hand in a pleading gesture
tendió la mano con un gesto suplicante

hold out your glass
acerca tu vaso

5 quitar o sacar:

it's time to take the cake out
es hora de sacar el pastel (del horno)

don't push me out of the way
no me saques a empujones

a lot of the pages have been ripped out
hay muchas páginas arrancadas

6 resolver un problema, solucionar una situación:

things just didn't work out between us
simplemente, las cosas no han funcionado entre nosotros

it all came out right in the end
al final todo se arregló

7 zafarse de una situación difícil o librarse de algo:

how did you get out of doing your maths homework?
¿cómo has conseguido librarte de hacer los deberes de matemáticas?

I wish I could wriggle out of this visit to my in-laws
¡si pudiera ingeniármelas para no ir a casa de mis suegros!

8 indica un ruido fuerte:

stop barking out orders like a sergeant-major
para de vociferar órdenes como si fueras un sargento

the loudspeakers were blaring out the candidate's message
los altavoces difundían a todo volumen el mensaje del candidato

she cried out in pain
lanzó un grito de dolor

9 apagarse:

the fire has gone out
el fuego se apagó

he stubbed his cigar out in the ashtray
apagó el puro en el cenicero

switch the garage light out
apaga la luz del garaje

the boxer was knocked out in the first round
el boxeador cayó K.O. en el primer asalto

10 en el exterior, fuera de casa:

the soldiers camped out in the fields
los soldados acamparon en los campos

I've been invited out for lunch
me han invitado a comer fuera

11 ensanchar o alargar algo:

my dress needs to be let out at the seams
mi vestido ha de ensancharse de las costuras

your essay needs to be fleshed out
has de añadir más detalles a tu redacción

Over

1 ir de un lado a otro, atravesar, cruzar:

she walked over the railway bridge
cruzó el puente ferroviario

he saw me on the other side of the road and hurried over
me vio al otro lado de la carretera y cruzó rápidamente

hey, move over, there's room for two in this bed!
¡oye, échate hacia un lado, que en esta cama caben dos!

2 recorriendo una distancia corta:

I'll drive over and see you soon
vendré pronto a verte (en coche)

our neighbours are having us over for dinner on Saturday night
nuestros vecinos nos han invitado a cenar en su casa el sábado por la noche

3 pasar de una cosa a otra:

I don't like this programme, could you change over?
no me gusta este programa, ¿puedes cambiar de cadena?

4 dar la vuelta a algo, remover algo:

he folded over the letter so that I couldn't see the signature
dobló la carta para que no pudiera ver la firma

fork the ground over thoroughly before planting
labra bien la tierra antes de plantar

5 transmitir un sentimiento, una intención, una impresión, etc.:

they need to find a better way of putting their company image over
necesitan encontrar un método mejor para transmitir la imagen de su empresa

they come over as being rather arrogant
dan la impresión de ser bastante arrogantes

6 por encima de, sobre:

he leaned over the balcony for a better look
se inclinó sobre la barandilla del balcón para ver mejor

with this threat hanging over him...
con esta amenaza que se cierne sobre él...

7 idea de cubrir:

skies are expected to cloud over in the afternoon
está previsto que el cielo se nuble por la tarde

the lake rarely freezes over
el lago casi nunca se hiela

the door was papered over many years ago
hace muchos años que se tapó la puerta con papel pintado

8 quedar, refiriéndose a algo:

there's quite a lot left over
queda bastante

9 acabar o hacer algo por completo:

be sure to read over your essay before handing it in
repasa bien la redacción antes de entregarla

10 desbordarse, derramarse:

the milk has boiled over
la leche se ha derramado del cazo

the river flooded over into the streets
el río se desbordó inundando las calles

11 ser atropellado, caer:

she was knocked over by a bus
la atropelló un autobús

she fell over
se cayó

Past

pasar:

he brushed past me in the street
pasó rozándome por la calle

we had just gone past the shop when...
acabábamos de pasar por delante de la tienda cuando...

cars raced past
pasaron unos coches a toda velocidad

he just casually strolled past
pasó tranquilamente, sin apresurarse

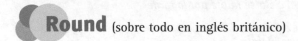

Round (sobre todo en inglés británico)

1 movimiento circular:

thoughts were spinning round in her head
los pensamientos le rondaban por la cabeza

pass your sweets round
ve pasando tus caramelos

2 haciendo un círculo:

a crowd gathered round to watch
una multitud se agolpó alrededor para mirar

they all crowded round
se agolparon alrededor

3 dar la vuelta a algo, visitar, mirar alrededor:

we went round the art gallery
hemos visitado el museo de bellas artes

would you like to see round the house?
¿les gustaría visitar la casa?

I'll phone round and see if anyone else knows about it
haré unas cuantas llamadas para ver si alguien más está al corriente

4 cambiar de sitio o de dirección:

I've been bumping into things ever since your mother changed all the
furniture round
*no he parado de darme golpes con las cosas desde que tu madre
cambió todos los muebles de sitio*

he turned the car round and went home
dio media vuelta con el coche y se fue a casa

5 acudir a casa de alguien que no vive muy lejos:

could you call round tomorrow morning, doctor?
doctor, ¿podría venir mañana por la mañana?

they always go out when their son has his friends round
siempre salen cuando su hijo invita a sus amigos a casa

drop round some time
pasa a vernos alguna vez

let's invite them round for dinner
invitémoslos a cenar

Through

1 a través, indica paso o tránsito:

we're not stopping here, just passing through
no paramos aquí, pasamos de largo

he looked through me as if I didn't exist
me miró como si no existiera

2 penetrar en el interior de algo:

the crowd broke through the barriers
la muchedumbre atravesó las barreras

the sun didn't break through until the afternoon
no penetró ni un rayo de sol hasta la tarde

the soles of my boots are almost worn through
las suelas de mis botas están casi agujereadas

3 indica éxito:

we'll just have to muddle through without her
tendremos que salir del paso sin ella

he was very ill but he's pulled through now
estaba muy enfermo pero ahora se está recuperando

4 hacer algo correctamente, de arriba abajo, del principio al fin:

they went through everyone's hand luggage
registraron a fondo todos los equipajes de mano

will you read through my speech and give me your opinion?
¿quieres leer mi discurso con atención y darme tu opinión?

the plan hasn't been properly thought through
el proyecto no fue pensado con todo detalle

1 llegar a algo (negativo):

it got to the point where she could no longer look after him
llegó un momento en que ya no pudo cuidar de él

I never thought it would come to this
nunca pensé que llegaríamos a esto

2 ponerse a, empezar a hacer algo:

we fell to work
nos pusimos manos a la obra

she took to wearing black every day
empezó a vestirse de negro a diario

3 ocuparse de algo o de alguien:

are you being attended to, madam?
¿se ocupan bien de usted, señora?

I'll see to the dinner
voy a ocuparme de la cena

it fell to me to break the bad news to everyone
me tocó a mí comunicar las malas noticias a todo el mundo

4 elevarse a:

profits amounted to several million dollars
los beneficios se elevan a varios millones de dólares

how much did the dinner come to?
¿cuánto costó la cena?

5 quedarse en un sitio:

he's taken to his bed with the flu
está en cama con gripe

you should keep to the main roads when it's icy
deberías continuar por las carreteras principales cuando hay hielo

6 recobrar la conciencia:

when he came to, he had no recollection of the accident
cuando recobró la conciencia, no recordaba nada del accidente

Together

conjunto, para formar un todo:

we always gathered together for morning prayers
siempe nos reuníamos para la plegaria de la mañana

you must keep the group together and not let people wander off on
their own
*debes mantener a todos juntos y no dejar que nadie se separe del
grupo*

what were just vague ideas are coming together into a definite proposal
*lo que empezó como una serie de vagas ideas está tomando forma
para acabar siendo un proyecto bien definido*

Under

1 debajo de, bajo:

when the sirens sounded, we always used to get under the table
*cuando sonaban las sirenas, siempre nos metíamos debajo de la
mesa*

fold the edges under
doblad los bordes por debajo

2 en virtud de, depender de algo:

that information comes under the Official Secrets Act
esta información compete a la ley sobre el Secreto de Estado

3 reprimir, contener:

a military government held the country under for many years
el país pasó muchos años bajo el dominio de un gobierno militar

the government is doing its best to keep the rebels under
el Gobierno hace todo lo que puede para contener a los rebeldes

4 designar cierta categoría:

I'm looking for books on landscape gardening; what subject do they
come under in the catalogue?
*busco libros sobre paisajismo, ¿bajo qué tema están clasificados en
el catálogo?*

what should I look under? vegetables or fruit?
¿bajo qué debería buscar?, ¿verduras o frutas? (p. ej., buscando en
 un libro)

Up

1 movimiento hacia arriba:

pass that hammer up so I don't have to get off the stepladder
pásame aquel martillo, así no tendré que bajar de la escalera

she hitched up her skirt and started to run
se alzó la falda y empezó a correr

I'll just finish pinning up the hem of this dress
voy a acabar de coger con alfileres el dobladillo de este vestido

hold your head up
mantén erguida la cabeza

2 planta superior, piso de arriba:

carry this tray up to your father
sube esta bandeja a tu padre

let's invite our neighbours up for coffee
invitemos a subir a nuestros vecinos a tomar café

3 levantarse o enderezarse, erguirse:

I jumped up to protest
me levanté de un salto para protestar

they all stood up
todos se levantaron

the old man sat up in bed with a start
el anciano se irguió en la cama sobresaltado

4 acercarse:

the dog ran up to me as soon as I went in
en cuanto entré, el perro corrió hacia mí

he wandered up to us
se acercó tranquilamente a nosotros

5 mejorar:

business is looking up
los negocios están mejorando

the weather has cleared up
el tiempo se ha despejado

6 aumentar, referido a un precio, una cantidad, un volumen, etc.:

this has forced prices up
esto ha hecho subir los precios

the fire blazed up
el fuego prendió rápidamente

turn the television up, I must be going deaf
sube el volumen del televisor, creo que me estoy volviendo sordo

let me plump up your pillows
déjame ahuecarte las almohadas

7 reunir, juntar o buscar algo:

she bundled up her clothes and left hurriedly
hizo un fardo con la ropa y salió apresuradamente

do you think you can rake up enough money for the deposit?
¿crees que podrás juntar suficiente dinero para la fianza?

where did you dig up that story?
¿de dónde has sacado semejante historia?

8 sostener:

it's held up by a central beam
se sostiene con una viga central

can anyone back your story up?
¿alguien puede confirmar tu relato?

9 el fin de una acción:

that wraps up our programme for today
y eso ha sido todo por hoy (p. ej., en un programa de televisión)

come on, drink up
vamos, acábate la copa

they ate up and left
acabaron de comer y se fueron

10 hacer algo a fondo o por completo:

she's in big trouble for smashing up the company car
se encuentra en un gran apuro por haber destrozado el coche de la compañía

you've messed our plans up
has echado a perder nuestros planes

tighten this screw up
aprieta bien este tornillo

11 acabar llegando a un sitio, tras una serie de acciones:

we ended up in the pub, of course
acabamos en el pub, evidentemente

we're going to land up in hospital if you don't slow down
vamos a acabar en el hospital si no disminuyes la velocidad

12 estar encerrado o retenido en el interior:

he'll be locked up for several years
pasará varios años entre rejas

why don't you talk about your problems instead of bottling things up?
¿por qué no hablas de tus problemas en lugar de guardártelos dentro?

they've bricked up the old doorway
han tapiado la vieja puerta

13 cortar en trozos:

chop the meat up
trocea la carne

break it up into four pieces
córtalo en cuatro trozos

14 sacar algo:

you owe me money, so pay up
me debes dinero, así que suéltalo

he has been coughing up blood
ha estado escupiendo sangre

Upon

a veces se puede intercambiar con on (véase On), pero, a menudo, con un uso más culto

With

utilizar algo:

you can have the ones I've finished with
puedes coger los que ya no necesito

Diccionario de
PHRASAL VERBS

En este «Diccionario de *phrasal verbs*» se usan las abreviaturas siguientes:

U.S.	inglés americano
BRIT.	ingles británico
FAM.	lenguaje familiar (coloquial)
FIG.	sentido figurado

Las abreviaturas de los tipos de verbo son:

VI	verbo intransitivo (1)
VT INSEP	verbo transitivo con partícula inseparable (2)
VT SEP	verbo transitivo con partícula separable (3)

1 **VI:** verbo intransitivo, es decir, un verbo que no lleva complemento directo.

get off: he got off at Victoria Station
se bajó en Victoria Station

listen in: do you mind if I listen in while you talk?
¿le molesta que escuche su conversación?

2 **VT INSEP:** verbo transitivo con partícula inseparable. El complemento directo va después de la partícula; el verbo nunca puede separarse de la partícula.

look after: she looks after children
cuida niños

3 **VT SEP:** verbo transitivo con partícula separable. El complemento directo puede colocarse entre el verbo y la partícula, o bien después de la partícula.

send back: he sent back the letter
devolvió la carta

o

he sent the letter back
devolvió la carta

A

abide by VT INSEP *(cumplir, acatar)* you'll have to abide by the rules

account for VT INSEP (a) *(explicar)* how did they account for their absence?; there's no accounting for taste, I suppose, but have you seen what they've done with their living room? (b) *(encontrar, localizar)* the firemen did not need to enter the building since all the occupants were accounted for (c) *(representar)* wine accounts for 5 % of all exports; *(ser el origen o la causa de)* shoplifting accounts for most of the store's losses (d) *(eliminar)* in recent action, the rebels have accounted for a great many government troops

act (up)on VT INSEP (a) *(actuar sobre)* rust is caused by salt acting on metal (b) *(seguir un consejo, etc.)* acting on her lawyer's advice, she has decided not to sue

act out VT SEP *(realizar)* he treats his patients for neuroses by having them act out their fantasies; *(representar)* local people act out scenes from the town's history

act up VI FAM. *(hacer de las suyas)* that child acts up every time her mother goes out without her; *(funcionar mal)* the photocopier is acting up again

add in VT SEP *(añadir)* add in a little salt and the mixture is complete

add on VT SEP *(añadir)* we're thinking about adding on a conservatory; should we add something on as a tip?

add up 1 VI (a) *(contar)* I'd have thought that at your age you could add up by now! (b) *(tener sentido, cuadrar)* it's all beginning to add up; it's a mystery, it just doesn't add up
2 VT SEP *(sumar)* if you add all the figures up the total is surprisingly large

add up to VT INSEP (a) *(sumar, ascender a)* how much does it all add up to? (b) *(venir a ser, dar como resultado)* is that all you've done? – it doesn't add up to much, does it?; if you put all the facts together it adds up to quite an interesting case

adhere to VT INSEP *(adherirse a)* I don't adhere to that philosophy at all

admit to VT INSEP *(reconocer, confesar)* he admitted to a slight feeling of apprehension

agree on VT INSEP *(ponerse de acuerdo en)* they cannot agree on a name for the baby

agree to VT INSEP *(acceder a, aceptar)* she felt she could not agree to my terms; they agreed to their son taking the job

agree with VT INSEP (a) *(estar de acuerdo con, aprobar)* I'm afraid I cannot agree with you; she doesn't agree with all this psychoanalytic treatment for paedophiles (b) *(sentar bien a)* seafood doesn't agree with me

allow for VT INSEP *(tener en cuenta)* when calculating how much material you'll need, always allow for some wastage; I suppose I should allow for his inexperience; has that been allowed for in your figures?

allow out VT SEP *(autorizar a salir)* the curfew meant that nobody was allowed out after dark; some prisoners are allowed out at weekends

angle for VT INSEP FIG. *(ir a la caza de)* he was angling for promotion so he developed a sudden interest in the boss's daughter; never angle for compliments

answer back 1 VI (a) *(contestar con insolencia)* don't answer back, young man! (b) *(replicar)* she's the boss, so I can't answer back
2 VT SEP *(contestar con insolencia)* that child will answer anyone back

answer for VT INSEP *(responder de)* if he keeps on at me like this, I won't answer for my actions; *(responder por)* the people who voted for him have a great deal to answer for

answer too VT INSEP (a) *(responder por)* who do you answer to in your job?; *(tener que vérselas con, rendir cuentas)* if you lay one finger on him you'll have me to answer to (b) *(corresponder a, responder a)* a woman answering to the description has been seen in the area

argue away 1 VT SEP *(negar la importancia de)* you cannot argue the facts away: ozone depletion is a serious problem
2 VI *(discutir)* they've been arguing away all morning

argue for/against VT INSEP *(estar a favor/en contra)* the speakers will argue for and against unilateral disarmament

argue out vt sep *(buscar una solución)* I'll leave you to argue it out between you

ask after vt insep *(preguntar por, interesarse por)* let your grandfather know I was asking after him

ask around vi *(preguntar)* I'll ask around at work and see if anyone else is interested

ask back vt sep *(invitar a alguien a casa a tomar algo)* do you want to ask them back for a drink after the theatre?

ask in vt sep *(invitar a pasar)* I would ask you in for tea but my husband's not very well

ask out vt sep *(invitar a salir)* he's asked her out so many times she must be running out of excuses by now; he's finally summoned up the courage to ask her out

ask round vt sep *(invitar a casa)* why don't we ask them round for dinner one night?

ask up vt sep *(invitar a subir a casa)* don't get too excited if she asks you up for coffee, her mother lives with her!

attend to vt insep (a) *(atender, ocuparse de)* are you being attended to?; I'll attend to this (b) *(prestar atención a, observar)* now attend to the experiment very closely, I'll be asking you questions later

auction off vt sep *(subastar)* they auctioned off all the family silver to raise some money

average out 1 vt sep *(calcular el término medio de)* I've averaged out how much I spend a week, and it's frightening
2 vi *(hacer una media)* over a full year it averages out quite differently

average out at vt insep *(hacer un promedio)* how much does that average out at a year?

B

babble away/on vi *(farfullar)* you were babbling away in your sleep last night; *(contar, explicar)* I have no idea what you're babbling on about

back down vi *(echarse atrás)* he takes pride in never backing down, however strong the opposition's case

back on to u onto vt insep *(dar por la parte de atrás a)* the house backs on to a lane

back out 1 vi (a) *(salir de espaldas, salir marcha atrás)* he backed out of the drive (b) fig. *(echarse)* they can't back out from the deal now!
2 vt sep *(salir marcha atrás)* I'm not very good at backing the car out, will you do it?

back up 1 vi (a) *(retroceder, dar marcha atrás)* all the cars had to back up to let the ambulance past (b) *Informática (hacer una copia de seguridad)* remember to back up regularly
2 vt sep (a) *(dar marcha atrás)* the driver had to back his lorry up all the way to the service station (b) *(apoyar, respaldar)* he'll need to back up his claim to the estate with something stronger than that; I doubt if the electors will back them up (c) *Informática (hacer una copia de seguridad de)* you should back up all your files at the end of the day (d) u.s. *(inmovilizar)* the accident backed traffic up all the way to the turnpike

bail out vt sep (a) *(obtener la libertad bajo fianza para)* their lawyer bailed them out (b) *(ayudar, sacar de un apuro)* I'm not bailing you out again, you're on your own this time

balance out 1 vi *(equilibrarse, compensar)* the figures don't balance out
2 vt sep *(complementarse)* he cooks and she knows a lot about wine, so they balance each other out very nicely

bale out 1 vi (a) *(lanzarse en paracaídas)* Dad never tires of telling how he had to bale out over the Channel during a dogfight (b) *(achicar agua)* she's taking on a lot of water, start baling out
2 vt sep *(achicar)* we'll have to bale the water out first

band together vi *(unirse)* if we band together we can do something about this problem

bandy about/around vt sep *(utilizar a menudo)* «decentralization» is a word the government bandies about a lot; *(rumorear)* the newspapers have been bandying that story around for weeks now

bank (up)on vᴛ ɪɴsᴇᴘ *(contar con)* him turn up on time? I wouldn't bank on it if I were you

bargain for vᴛ ɪɴsᴇᴘ *(esperar)* if she marries him she'll get more than she bargained for

bargain on vᴛ ɪɴsᴇᴘ *(contar con)* I'm bargaining on it; I didn't bargain on your kid brother coming as well

bash about/around vᴛ sᴇᴘ ғᴀᴍ. *(dar una paliza a)* her husband bashes her about something awful; *(tratar a patadas)* you can always rely on baggage handlers bashing your suitcases about

bash on vɪ Bʀɪᴛ. ғᴀᴍ. *(seguir)* the weather forecast was bad but they decided to bash on with their plans for a picnic

battle on vɪ *(seguir luchando)* he has fallen very far behind the other runners but he's still battling on; just battle on as best you can in the circumstances

bawl out vᴛ sᴇᴘ (a) *(gritar)* please don't bawl out my name in public like that (b) ғᴀᴍ. *(echar un rapapolvo, regañar)* the boss really bawled us out for that mistake

bear down 1 vɪ (a) *(empujar, hablando de una mujer en el parto)* if that midwife had said «bear down, dear» one more time, I would have screamed (b) *(abalanzarse sobre)* the crew of the fishing boat jumped overboard as they saw the liner bearing down on them; the boys scattered as the headmaster bore down on them
2 vᴛ sᴇᴘ *normalmente en voz pasiva (aplastar)* the Third World is borne down by the burden of poverty

bear out vᴛ sᴇᴘ *(corroborar, confirmar)* onlookers bore out her statement to the police; he feels that the report bears him out in his estimates of radiation levels in the area

bear up vɪ *(mantener el ánimo)* she found it difficult to bear up when there was still no news after the second day; bear up! just one more day to the weekend

bear (up)on vᴛ ɪɴsᴇᴘ *(tener relación con)* I don't see how that bears on what I am supposed to be doing

bear with vᴛ ɪɴsᴇᴘ *(tener paciencia con)* the old lady asked the salesman to bear with her while she looked for her glasses

beat back **vt sep** *(rechazar, repeler)* they beat back the attackers three times but were eventually overrun

beat down 1 **vi** *(caer con fuerza)* the rain was beating down so fast it was difficult to see the road; *(picar, calentar mucho)* the sun was beating down
2 **vt sep** (a) *(destruir, derribar)* the drunk threatened to beat the door down if they didn't open up; hailstorms have beaten down the county's entire barley crop (b) *(conseguir rebajar regateando)* I felt quite proud of myself for beating him down so much

beat off **vt sep** *(rechazar)* the tourists tried unsuccessfully to beat off all the people trying to sell them things

beat out **vt sep** (a) *(apagar)* desperate sheep-farmers were beating out the brush fires with their bare hands (b) *(tocar, marcar)* she beat out the rhythm on the table (c) *(desabollar)* the car door panel will have to be beaten out

beat up **vt sep** (a) **fam.** *(dar una paliza a)* he got beaten up on his way home last night (b) *(batir, hablando de la nata, los huevos, etc.)* just beat up a few eggs for an omelette

beaver away **vi fam.** *(afanarse en, aplicarse en)* he's still beavering away at his studies

belt out **vt sep fam.** *(cantar a grito pelado, berrear)* he really belted that song out

belt up **vi** (a) **Brit. fam.** *(cerrar el pico)* I wish you would belt up (b) *(abrocharse el cinturón de seguridad)* I'm not starting this car until you belt up

bind over **vt sep** *(poner en libertad con la condición de no alterar el órden público)* the drunk was bound over for three months to keep the peace

black out 1 **vi** *(desmayarse)* she was all right until she saw the blood and then she blacked out
2 **vt sep** (a) *(dejar a oscuras)* the impact of the scene is heightened when they black the stage out (b) *(suspender la programación)* we regret that industrial action has blacked out this evening's programmes

blast off **VI** *(despegar, hablando de un cohete, una nave espacial)* the latest space shuttle blasted off at 5 a.m. local time today

blaze away **VI** (a) *(arder, hablando de un fuego)* the fire is blazing away merrily in the grate (b) *(disparar continuamente)* the troops blazed away at the target

blink at **VT INSEP FIG.** *(hacer caso omiso de)* his wife blinks at his affairs

blink away **VT SEP** *(contener)* I blinked my tears away

block in **VT SEP** *(cerrar el paso a)* that man next door has blocked me in again

block off **VT SEP** *(bloquear, cortar)* the street will be blocked off until the wreckage is cleared

block up **VT SEP** (a) *(tapar)* don't throw the tea leaves down the sink or you'll block it up; the worst thing about a cold is that your nose gets all blocked up (b) *(atrancar)* they've blocked up the entry

blossom out **VI FIG.** *(transformarse en)* she's blossoming out into quite a beautiful young woman

blot out **VT SEP** *(borrar)* a word has been blotted out here; you must try to remember and come to terms with the past, not blot it out; *(ocultar, tapar)* the mist has blotted out the view

blow in 1 **VI** (a) *(romperse)* all the windows blew in because of the explosion (b) *(entrar, por la fuerza del viento)* shut the door, the dust is blowing in (c) **FAM.** *(llegar inesperadamente, aterrizar)* when did you blow in?
2 **VT SEP** *(romper)* the blast blew all the windows in

blow off 1 **VI** *(salir volando)* some of the roof tiles have blown off
2 **VT SEP** (a) *(llevarse el viento)* the high winds blew the tiles off the roof (b) *(volar de un disparo)* the gunman threatened to blow their heads off

blow out 1 **VI** *(apagarse)* the candles have blown out (b) *(reventarse)* the rear tyre blew out
2 **VT SEP** (a) *(apagar)* be sure to blow the match out properly (b) *(calmar)* the storm soon blew itself out (c) *(locución)* to blow someone's brain out *saltar la tapa de los sesos a alguien*

blow over 1 **vi** (a) *(caer, hundirse)* the garage must have blown over in the high winds last night (b) *(calmarse, amainar)* the storm will blow over soon; **FIG.** it will soon blow over and you'll be friends again

2 **VT SEP** *(hacer caer, volcar)* did the wind blow anything over?

blow up 1 **vi** (a) *(saltar por los aires, explotar)* the ammunitions depot blew up (b) **FAM.** *(explotar, ponerse hecho una furia)* do you often blow up like that? (c) *(estallar, desencadenarse)* the argument blew up out of nowhere

2 **VT SEP** (a) *(hacer saltar por los aires)* terrorists have blown up the presidential palace (b) *(hinchar, inflar)* do the tyres need blowing up? (c) *(ampliar)* I'd like this photograph blown up (d) *(exagerar)* you're blowing this up out of all proportion

bluff out **VT SEP** *(salir de un apuro)* she can bluff her way out of anything; when the police get here we'll just have to bluff it out

board in/up **VT SEP** *(tapar)* the windows and doors have all been boarded up to stop tramps getting in

bog down **VT SEP** *normalmente en voz pasiva (atascarse en el lodo, encenagarse)* the car is bogged down in the mud; **FIG.** *(perderse)* the important thing is not to get bogged down in details

boil down to **vi** *(reducirse a)* what his claim boils down to is...

boil up 1 **VT SEP** *(poner a hervir)* boil up some water for the pasta

2 **vi FAM.** *(aumentar)* I could feel the anger boiling up inside me

bolt down 1 **VT INSEP** *(bajar corriendo)* she bolted down the stairs and into the street

2 **VT SEP** *(tragar, engullir)* don't bolt your food down like that

bone up on **VT INSEP FAM.** *(empollar)* you'll have to bone up on your history if you want to pass that test next week

book in 1 **vi BRIT.** *(registrarse en la recepción de un hotel, etc.)* do we have to book in by a certain time?

2 **VT SEP** *(reservar una habitación para)* I've booked them in to the best hotel in town

book out 1 **vi** *(dejar la habitación del hotel)* when do we have to book out by?

2 **VT SEP** *(registrar la salida de un hotel, etc.)* the receptionist booked them out before noon

book up 1 **vi** *(reservar)* have you booked up for your holiday?
2 **vt sep** *normalmente en voz pasiva (estar al completo)* the hotel is all booked up

boot up *Informatica* 1 **vi** *(iniciarse, arrancar)* for some reason the computer is refusing to boot up
2 **vt sep** *(iniciar, arrancar)* use this disk to boot up the computer

bottle up **vt sep** *(reprimir, contener)* it does no good to bottle up your feelings

bottom out **vi** *(tocar fondo)* the government hopes that unemployment has finally bottomed out

bow out **vi** *(irse)* when the company brought in computers, old Mr Parsons decided the time had come to bow out

bowl out **vt sep** *(descalificar)* we bowled him out for ten

bowl over **vt sep** (a) *(derribar)* the old lady was bowled over by a boy on a bike (b) **fam.** *(dejar pasmado, dejar atónito)* I was bowled over when I won first prize

box in **vt sep** (a) *(acorralar, rodear)* the defence seem to have him boxed in (b) *(sentirse encajonado)* don't you feel boxed in in such a small room? (c) *(cubrir, tapar)* we're boxing in the sink

branch off **vi** *(bifurcarse)* the road branches off to the left

branch out **vi** *(diversificarse, extenderse)* the company intends to branch out into a new area of business

brazen out **vt sep** *(mostrarse insolente)* normalmente «to brazen it out» when they accused him of gatecrashing the party, he brazened it out and refused to admit he hadn't been invited

break away **vi** (a) *(escapar de)* she broke away from the guards who were escorting her to hospital (b) *(separarse de)* when did you break away from your family?; it was the year France broke away from NATO

break down 1 **vi** (a) *(averiarse)* the car broke down on the motorway (b) *(fracasar)* their marriage seems to be breaking down; talks between the two sides have broken down; *(no tenerse en pie)* that's where your argument breaks down (c) *(derrumbarse)* I broke down in tears (d) *(dividirse)* the report breaks down into three parts (e) *componerse)* the compound breaks down into a number of components

2 **VT SEP** (a) *(derribar, echar abajo)* the firemen had to break down the door to rescue the children (b) *(vencer)* she was unable to break down her parents' opposition to her plans (c) *(desglosar)* we really need to break the figures down a bit further

break in 1 **VI** (a) *(forzar la entrada)* when did you realize that someone had broken in? (b) *(interrumpir una conversación, etc.)* I really must break in at this point

2 **VT SEP** (a) *(forzar, romper)* the thieves broke the door in (b) *(domar) (un animal)* she's good at breaking in horses; *(una prenda de vestir)* I hate having to break new shoes in

break into **VT INSEP** (a) *(entrar)* thieves broke into a number of houses on the street last night (b) *(echar mano de)* I'll have to break into my holiday money to pay for the repairs to my car (c) *(interrumpir)* why did you break into the conversation like that? (d) *(ponerse a)* I broke into a cold sweat when I realized how high up I was; he often breaks into song in the shower

break off 1 **VI** (a) *(desprenderse, romperse)* it just broke off in my hand, honestly (b) *(interrumpirse)* he broke off when the chairman entered the room (c) *(parar)* can we break off for the rest of the day?

2 **VT SEP** (a) *(partir)* break off two pieces of chocolate for you and your brother (b) *(suspender, romper)* talks have been broken off (c) *(romper una relación personal)* it wouldn't surprise me if they broke it off soon; they've broken off the engagement

break open **VT SEP** (a) *(derribar, forzar una puerta, etc.)* he broke the desk open (b) **FAM.** *(abrir, descorchar)* let's break open another bottle

break out **VI** (a) *(declararse, comenzar)* fires have broken out all over the city (b) *(salir un sarpullido a)* the baby is breaking out in a rash (c) *(escaparse)* the prisoners broke out late last night

break up 1 **VI** (a) *(romperse, hacerse pedazos)* the ice on the river is breaking up at last; *(romperse, terminar)* their marriage is breaking up; **U.S. FAM.** *(locución)* I just broke up *me moría de risa* (b) *(terminar)* when did the party finally break up?; the schools will be breaking up for summer soon (c) *(separarse)* I've heard that they're breaking up

2 **VT SEP** (a) *(poner fin a, detener)* the warder broke up the fight between the prisoners; *(destruir)* it was his drinking that broke the marriage up (b) *(mullir)* you'll have to break the earth up before you can plant anything

bring about VT SEP *(provocar, causar)* what brought this about?

bring back VT SEP (a) *(traer de vuelta)* Mum told me to bring you back for supper (b) *(devolver la salud)* a couple of days in bed will bring him back to normal; *(reinstaurar)* it will be up to the electors to decide whether to bring back the previous government (c) *(recordar)* that song brings back memories

bring down VT SEP (a) *(derribar)* if that boy doesn't stop jumping up and down like that he's going to bring the house down about our ears; *(locución)* their jokes always bring the house down *sus chistes siempren tienen éxito* (b) *(abatir)* the spy plane was brought down by a missile (c) *(aterrizar)* the badly damaged plane was brought down with no loss of life (d) *(derribar, derrocar)* it was really the students who brought down the government; he brought him down with a rugby tackle (e) *(bajar)* this new drug will bring his temperature down; she would have brought the price down even further if you'd gone on bargaining (f) *(atraer la atención de)* stop making so much noise or you'll bring the headmaster down on us

bring in VT SEP (a) *(hacer entrar)* I've brought Mrs Jones in to see you (b) *(introducir)* new tax legislation will be brought in next year (c) *(hacer intervenir)* the company is bringing consultants in to see if the problems can be solved; this argument is between you two, why bring me in? (d) *(celebrar)* to bring in the New Year (e) *(ganar)* how much money is your eldest son bringing in? (f) *(pronunciar, hablando de un veredicto)* the jury brought in a verdict of not guilty

bring off VT SEP (a) *(salvar o recuperar de un barco, etc.)* the bodies are being brought off the ship today (b) *(conseguir)* did you bring the deal off?

bring on VT SEP (a) *(hacer entrar a)* please bring on our next contestant (b) *(causar, provocar)* damp days always bring on my arthritis; what brought this on? (c) *(hacer florecer)* this mild weather will bring the roses on nicely (d) *(locución)* I brought it on myself *me lo he buscado*

bring out **vt sep** (a) *(sacar, hacer salir)* they brought the man out under armed guard (b) *(ayudar a adquirir confianza)* his granddaughter is about the only one who can bring him out (of himself) (c) *(sacar, hacer aparecer)* the sun has brought out all the bulbs; disasters bring out the best – and worst – in people; they're bringing out the new models very soon; *(provocar, hablando de una alergia)* strawberries bring her out in a rash

bring round **vt sep** (a) *(traer)* I'll bring him round to meet you some time (b) *(persuadir, convencer)* you'll never bring my dad round to that way of thinking (c) *(hacer volver en sí, reanimar)* they brought her round quite quickly after she fainted (d) *(conducir hacia)* I finally managed to bring the conversation round to what I wanted to talk about

bring up **vt sep** (a) *(educar)* we've brought four kids up (b) *(mencionar, sacar a colación)* Madam Chairwoman, I wish to bring up the question of travel expenses (c) *(vomitar)* everything she swallows she brings up ten minutes later

brush aside **vt sep** *(no hacer caso de)* the Minister brushed aside the reporters; she won't listen, she just brushes our objections aside

brush up **vt sep** (a) *(barrer)* I want all those crumbs brushed up off the floor (b) *(pulir)* he'll have to brush up his Spanish

buck up **fam.** **1 vi** (a) *(darse prisa, espabilarse)* buck up or we'll be late (b) *(animarse)* I wish he would buck up a little
2 vt sep (a) *(animar)* the good news bucked me up no end (b) *(locución)* to buck up one's ideas *espabilarse*

bucket down **vi Brit. fam.** *(llover a cántaros)* it's bucketing down

buckle down/to **vi Brit. fam.** *(ponerse manos a la obra)* I suppose I'd better buckle down if I want to finish the housework this morning; if you don't buckle down to your piano practice you'll never pass the exam; he buckled to and finished cleaning the car

buil on **1vs sep** *(añadir, hacer un anexo)* they're building on a conservatory next door
2 vt insep *(apoyarse en, consolidar)* the company is building on its earlier success

build up **1 vi** *(incrementarse, aumentar)* pressure on the government is building up

2 **VT SEP** (a) *(aumentar)* I wouldn't build my hopes up if I were you; we're trying to build up our savings so we can buy a house soon (b) *(fortalecer)* the children need some vitamins to build them up (c) *(crear)* his father built that company up from nothing; you've built up quite a reputation for yourself (d) *normalmente en voz pasiva (construir)* the area has become quite built up (e) *(hacer propaganda de)* the play has been so built up that it's impossible to get tickets for it

bump into VT INSEP (a) *(chocar contra)* I was so engrossed in my thoughts that I bumped into a lamp post (b) *(encontrarse con, toparse con)* he's always bumping into people he knows

bump off VT SEP FAM. *(cargarse a, liquidar)* his job was bumping people off for a fee

bump up VT SEP FAM. *(subir, aumentar)* they've bumped up the price of beer again

bundle off VT SEP *(enviar a toda prisa)* the baby was bundled off to hospital in an ambulance

bundle up 1 **VI** *(abrigarse)* you'd better bundle up, it's freezing out there
2 **VT SEP** *(envolver, abrigar)* she bundled the baby up in a warm blanket

bung up VT SEP FAM. *(atascar, taponar)* who bunged the sink up?; I'm/my nose is all bunged up

burn down 1 **VI** *(quemarse)* the theatre burned down; *(propagarse poco a poco)* the fire is burning down
2 **VT SEP** *(incendiar, quemar)* vandals have burned down a number of derelict buildings in the area

burn out 1 **VI** *(consumirse, apagarse)* the fire is burning out; **FIG.** *(quemarse, perder el entusiasmo)* social workers frequently burn out at an early age
2 **VT SEP** (a) *(estar a la intemperie, p. ej., a causa de un incendio)* they were burned out (b) *(propagarse)* the fire has burnt itself out

burn up 1 **VI** *(entrar en combustión)* the rocket burned up in the atmosphere
2 **VT SEP** *(gastar, consumir)* children burn up a lot of energy playing; this stove burns up a lot of wood

burst into **VT INSEP** (a) *(irrumpir en)* she burst into the room (b) *(romper a, ponerse a)* he burst into tears; then they all burst into song

burst out 1 **VT INSEP** *(romper a, echarse a)* I burst out laughing; *(espetar, gritar)* «where were you last night?» he burst out
2 **VI** *(salir de estampida)* they all burst out of the room

butt in **VI** *(inmiscuirse, entrometerse)* we were just having a cosy chat when she butted in; is this a private argument or can anybody butt in?

buy into **VT INSEP** *(comprar acciones o participaciones de)* he has bought into his neighbour's business

buy off **VT SEP FAM.** *(sobornar, comprar)* the councillor was bought off with an all-expenses-paid holiday in the south of France

buy out **VT SEP** *(comprar acciones de)* all the other shareholders have been bought out

buy up **VT SEP** *(comprar todas las existencias de)* look at all those parcels, she must have bought up the entire store!; *(acaparar)* because of the threatened shortage people have been buying up petrol

buzz off **VI FAM.** *(pirarse, largarse)* tell that kid brother of yours to buzz off; just buzz off and leave me alone

call back 1 **VI** (a) *(volver, volver a pasar)* I'll call back later to see her (b) *(volver a llamar por teléfono)* if you'd like to call back in an hour...
2 **VT SEP** (a) *(volver a llamar por teléfono a)* he said he would call you back (b) *(hacer volver)* I know she's on holiday but she'll have to be called back to deal with this; I think the last pair should be called back for another audition

call for **VT INSEP** (a) *(exigir)* the Opposition is calling for her resignation (b) *(pasar a recoger)* would it be too much of a rush if I called for you at seven? (c) *(necesitar, requerir)* this is the kind of job that calls for good interpersonal skills; that's wonderful news, it calls for a celebration

call in 1 **VI** (a) *(pasarse)* the social worker is going to call in later (b) *(llamar por teléfono)* off-duty nurses called in and offered to help; prison officers are not actually on strike but a great many of them are calling in sick
2 **VT SEP** (a) *(llamar)* they've finally decided to call the doctor in (b) *(retirar de la circulación)* the bank has called in its loans

call off VT SEP (a) *(cancelar, suspender)* the meeting will have to be called off; does this mean we'll have to call our holiday off?; they've called it off (es decir, *cancelar el compromiso o la boda*) (b) *(llamar)* call your dog off!

call out 1 **VI** *(gritar, vociferar)* don't call out in the street like that
2 **VT SEP** (a) *(decir en voz alta)* the master of ceremonies called out the names of the prizewinners (b) *(llamar)* call out the guard!; I don't like calling the doctor out at this time of night (c) *(llamar a la huelga)* the men were called out (on strike) halfway through the morning shift

call up VT SEP (a) *(pedir)* the situation looked dangerous and the lieutenant decided to call up reinforcements (b) *(llamar a filas)* Dad was called up in 1940 (c) *(telefonear, llamar por teléfono)* please don't call me up at midnight (d) *(evocar, traer a la memoria)* the speech called up thoughts of the past

call (up)on VT INSEP (a) *(invitar)* the opposition called on the government to make its position clear (b) *(visitar)* gentlemen used to ask permission to call on young ladies

calm down 1 **VI** *(calmarse)* getting hysterical won't help, just calm down; I want you all to calm down now, children
2 **VT SEP** *(calmar)* leave it to Mum, she'll calm him down

care for VT INSEP (a) *(cuidar de, ocuparse de)* she has spent years caring for her invalid mother (b) *(gustar, apreciar)* you know I don't care for that kind of language; I don't believe he ever cared for you or he wouldn't have treated you the way he did

carry away VT SEP *(emocionarse, entusiasmarse)* he let his enthusiasm carry him away; she gets carried away by the sound of her own voice; take it easy, don't get carried away!

carry forward VT SEP (a) *(aplazar, hablando de una fecha)* can I carry my leave forward and have six weeks next summer? (b) *(poner,* *hablando de cifras)* this amount should have been carried forward to the next page

carry off **VT SEP** (a) *(llevarse)* the thieves carried off all their jewellery (b) *(salir airoso)* it wasn't the easiest of speeches to make but you carried it off very well c) *(llevarse, alzarse con)* she carried off the prizes for Latin and French (d) *(acabar con la vida de)* tuberculosis carried off a great many people in the last century

carry on 1 **VI** (a) *(continuar)* just carry on with what you were doing (b) **FAM.** *(montar un numerito)* he carried on just because his wife wanted an evening out; what a way to carry on! (c) **FAM.** *(tener un lío con, tener una aventura con)* have you been carrying on behind my back?
2 **VT SEP** *(continuar, proseguir)* grandfather wants me to carry on the business after he dies; *(mantener)* we have carried on a correspondence for years

carry out **VT SEP** (a) *(sacar)* they had to carry him out since he couldn't walk (b) *(llevar a cabo)* the coastguard is carrying out a search for the missing crew members (c) *(cumplir)* never make a promise that you cannot carry out

carry through **VT SEP** *(llevar a cabo)* the plan has to be carried through to the last detail

carve out **VT SEP** (a) *(tallar, esculpir)* he has now carved out twenty or so statues (b) **FIG.** *(labrarse un porvenir)* the company plans to carve out its own niche in the market

carve up **VT SEP** (a) *(trinchar)* ask the butcher to carve the meat up for you (b) *(dividir, repartir)* they just carved up the land among themselves with no regard for the native inhabitants (c) **FAM.** *(adelantar bruscamente)* did you see how that fool carved me up?

cash in 1 **VT SEP** *(hacer efectivo)* are you going to cash in your premium bonds?
2 **VI FAM.** *(aprovechar)* she's cashing in on the fact that her father knows a lot of influential people

cast away **VT SEP** *(ser un náufrago)* Robinson Crusoe was cast away on his desert island for a great many years

cast back **VT SEP** *(rememorar)* if you cast your mind back a week, you will recall that...

cast off 1 **VT SEP** (a) *(terminar, cerrar los puntos de)* cast off the remaining stitches (b) *(soltar lastre)* we cast the launch off at dawn 2 **VI** (a) *(rematar)* cast off when only four stitches remain (b) *(soltar amarras)* they will cast off shortl

cast on 1 **VI** *(engarzar una vuelta)* I usually cast on with my thumb

2 **VT SEP** *(cerrar los puntos de)* cast on 80 stitches; have you cast the sleeve on yet?

catch at **VT INSEP** *(tratar de agarrarse a)* she caught at his sleeve and asked for help

catch on **VI** (a) *(cuajar, hacerse popular)* I remember you saying that the Beatles would never catch on (b) fam. *(comprender)* she's so naïve she didn't catch him

catch out **VT SEP** (a) *(pillar, coger desprevenidos)* the police caught him out by asking for a description of the programme he said he was watching (b) *(eliminar, en críquet)* he was caught out very early on

catch up 1 **VI** *(ganar terreno, alcanzar)* the runners behind are catching up; *(recuperar, p. ej., el sueño atrasado)* I wish I could catch up with my work/sleep
2 **VT SEP** (a) *(alcanzar)* you go ahead and I'll catch you up (b) *(bloquear)* they were caught up in a traffic jam for hours

cave in **VI** *(hundirse, ceder)* the walls and roof caved in under the force of the blast

centre on **VT INSEP** *(centrarse en)* the play centres on the idea of survivor guilt

chain up **VT SEP** *(atar, encadenar)* I hope he chains that brute of a dog up at night; in those days people could be chained up in prison for years

chalk up **VT SEP FAM.** (a) *(apuntarse)* the team chalked up another win today (b) *(apuntar en la cuenta)* chalk it up, will you, and I'll pay next week (c) *(locución)* she'll just have to chalk it up to experience *ha sido otra experiencia para ella*

chance on **VT INSEP** *(encontrar por casualidad)* I chanced on this piece of Meissen in a grubby little second-hand shop

change down **VI** *(disminuir la velocidad)* there are traffic lights coming up, so change down

change over **vi** (a) *(cambiar)* is it a good idea to change over entirely to electricity? (b) *(intercambiarse)* let's change over and you wash while I dry; *(cambiar de canal)* as soon as opera or ballet comes on the TV, he changes over

change up **vi** *(cambiar a una marcha más larga)* you have to change up faster than that

chase up **vt sep Brit.** (a) *(reclamar, recordar)* I had to chase him up for the £50 he owed me; I'll chase the matter up for you (b) *(buscar)* why not ask one of the big stores to chase up the pattern for you? (c) *(encontrar)* we finally chased her up in the library

chat up **vt sep fam.** *(ligar)* he's just chatting you up; I wish I could chat up men the way she does

cheat on **vt insep** (a) *(engañar)* why didn't you tell me he was cheating on me? (b) *(hacer trampas)* it's not a good idea to cheat on your expenses

check in **1** **vi** *(registrarse en un hotel, facturar el equipaje en el aeropuerto, etc.)* have you checked in?

2 **vt sep** (a) *(registrar en un hotel, facturar el equipaje, obtener la tarjeta de embarque en el aeropuerto)* they must be here, I checked them in myself (b) *(reservar una habitación para)* she checked me into a four-star hotel

check out **1** **vi** (a) *(dejar un hotel, etc.)* they checked out last night (b) **fam.** *(cuadrar)* it doesn't check out
2 **vt sep** (a) *(registrar la salida de)* the reception clerk will check you out (b) *(investigar)* we've checked her out and she's who she says she is (c) **fam.** *(echar un ojo a)* why don't we check out the restaurant that John told us about? (d) **fam.** *(verificar, comprobar)* check this out

check through **vt sep** (a) *(examinar, registrar)* they checked through everyone's hand luggage (b) *(enviar por avión)* I have to change at Geneva, can my bags be checked right through to London?

cheer on **vt sep** *(animar, vitorear)* he's there every Saturday to cheer his team on

cheer up **1** **vi** *(animarse)* she soon cheered up when she heard she'd got the job

2 **vt sep** (a) *(subir la moral, reconfortar)* a visit to the pub will cheer him up (b) *(dar color, animar)* the new curtains really do cheer the room up

chew on **vt insep** (a) *(mordisquear)* he chewed on his pipe stem for a bit and then said... (b) *(rumiar)* how much longer do you need to chew on it?

chew over **vt sep** *(rumiar)* I've been chewing this problem over in my mind for some time

chew up **vt sep** (a) *(masticar)* chew your food up well before swallowing (b) *(estropear, destrozar)* your machine has chewed up my bank card; it's those heavy lorries that are chewing up the road

chicken out **vi fam.** *(rajarse)* he had a date with my sister but he chickened out at the last minute; don't chicken out on us; *(escaquearse)* he chickened out of his dental appointment

chip in **fam.** 1 **vi** (a) *(intervenir, meter baza)* if I can chip in for a moment... (b) *(contribuir)* we've all chipped in for a present for her
2 **vt sep** *(contribuir)* how much is everyone else chipping in?

chip off 1 **vi** *(desconcharse)* the paint is chipping off
2 **vt sep** *(romper)* be careful with those plates, I don't want any pieces chipped off; *(quitar, arrancar)* we slowly chipped off the old paintwork

choke back **vt sep** *(contener)* looking at these pictures, I find it hard to choke back my tears/anger

choke up **vt sep** (a) *(atascar)* the drain is all choked up with leaves (b) **fam.** *normalmente en voz pasiva (conmover, emocionar profundamente)* she was all choked up

chuck in **vt sep fam.** *(dejar, abandonar)* you're surely not thinking of chucking in your job?; one day I'm going to chuck all this in and buy a farm; he's chucked his latest girlfriend in

chug along **vi fam.** *(ir a paso de tortuga)* Dad always chugs along at about 35, even on the motorway

clam up **vi** *(no decir ni mu, callarse)* don't clam up, talk to me!

clamp down vi *(ser más severo)* the police are clamping down this Christmas so don't drink and drive

clamp down on vt INSEP *(tomar medidas contundentes contra)* the authorities are clamping down on misleading advertising

clean out vt SEP (a) *(limpiar a fondo)* I'll clean out a few cupboards today, I think (b) FAM. *(dejar sin blanca)* the casino cleaned him out (c) FAM. *(dejar pelado)* someone has cleaned the shop out of sugar

clean up 1 vt SEP (a) *(limpiar, lavar)* when are you going to clean this place up? it's a mess; the kids need to be cleaned up before we go to your mother's (b) *(limpiar)* I like those old cowboy films where the sheriff always says «I'm going to clean up this town»
2 vi FAM. *(forrarse)* she really cleaned up at the roulette table

clear away 1 vt SEP *(quitar, retirar)* workmen were clearing away the debris; it's your turn to clear the dishes away
2 vi (a) *(quitarse de en medio)* could you clear away, please? (b) *(disiparse, desaparecer)* the clouds have all cleared away

clear off 1 vt SEP *(quitar, sacar)* clear all those papers off the table
2 vi *(largarse)* clear off!; the boys cleared off when they saw the headmaster coming down the street

clear up 1 vt SEP (a) *(aclarar, resolver)* I'd like to clear up a point or two; we have some problems that need to be cleared up (b) *(ordenar)* I can't come out, I have to clear up my room (c) *(hacer desaparecer)* the doctor said this cream would clear up the acne
2 vi (a) *(despejarse)* it's clearing up (b) *(desaparecer)* don't worry, that rash will soon clear up

climb down vi (a) *(descender)* it took the climbers three hours to climb down (b) *(dar marcha atrás, ceder)* she'll never climb down, however strong the arguments against her

clock in 1 vi (a) *(llegar a una hora o en un tiempo)* the last of the marathon runners clocked in at six hours (b) *(fichar a la llegada al trabajo, etc.)* I have to clock in; you clocked in 10 minutes late
2 vt SEP *(fichar por alguien a la llegada al trabajo, etc.)* do you think just this once you could clock me in?

clock off 1 **VI** *(fichar a la salida del trabajo)* when did you clock off?
2 **VT SEP** *(fichar por alguien a la salida del trabajo)* I'll clock you off if you like

clock up **VT SEP** (a) *(registrar)* he clocked up a faster time than any of his rivals in the race (b) *(conseguir)* the team has clocked up another victory

close down 1 **VI** (a) *(cerrar definitivamente)* the factory is closing down next month; we're closing down soon (b) *(finalizar la emisión)* television used to close down at midnight
2 **VT SEP** *(cerrar definitivamente)* they closed the restaurant down because of health code violations

close in 1 **VI** (a) *(acortarse)* the days are closing in (b) *(acercarse)* winter is closing in
2 **VT SEP** *(cercar, cerrar)* they're thinking of closing the porch in

close in on **VT INSEP** *(ir cercando a)* government troops are said to be closing in on the rebels

close up 1 **VI** *(apretarse)* the photographer asked the people in the front line to close up so he could get them all in
2 **VT SEP** *(cerrar)* they must have gone away for some time, the house is all closed up; the opening in the fence has been closed up to prevent similar tragedies in the future

cloud over **VI** *(nublarse)* it clouded over this afternoon; **FIG.** *(emsombrecerse)* her face clouded over when she saw him

cloud up 1 **VI** *(nublarse)* it's clouding up; *(empañarse, cubrirse de vaho)* the mirror has clouded up
2 **VT SEP** *(empañar, cubrir de vaho)* the bathroom is poorly ventilated, steam always clouds the windows up

club together **VI** *(poner dinero entre todos)* if we club together, we can get one big present instead of lots of small ones

cobble together **VT SEP** *(improvisar)* my speech won't be very good, I'm afraid, I cobbled it together on the train

collect up **VT SEP** *(recoger)* I began to collect up my parcels

comb through **VT INSEP FIG.** *(rebuscar)* I've combed through the entire book and haven't found any reference to him

come across 1 **VI** *(dar una impresión)* how did her story come across?; they come across as (being) rather nice people
2 **VT INSEP** *(encontrar por casualidad)* I came across this when I was tidying up, is it yours?

come across with VT INSEP FAM. *(apoquinar)* if we don't come across with the money, they say they'll kill him

come along VI (a) *(darse prisa)* come along children, please! (b) *(avanzar, progresar)* my speech is coming along rather well (c) *(llegar)* everything was peaceful until you came along (d) *(ir)* can I come along?

come apart VI *(caerse de)* honestly, I don't know how it happened, it just came apart in my hands; **FIG.** *(desmoronarse)* she feels her life is coming apart at the seams

come at VT INSEP *(atacar, ir a por)* the pair of them came at me with a baseball bat; **FIG.** *(asaltar)* questions came at me from all sides

come away VI (a) *(ir)* why not come away with me to Paris for the weekend?; *(apartarse)* come away from the cat, it's got fleas (b) *(desprenderse, soltarse)* the handle has come away from the knife*)*

come back VI (a) *(volver a la memoria)* I've forgotten your name but it will come back to me eventually (b) *(contestar, replicar)* then she came back with one of her usual cutting remarks (c) *(reanudar)* we thought the fight was all over but he's coming back very strongly now (d) *(volverse a poner de moda)* short hair is coming back

come by 1 **VT INSEP** *(conseguir)* how did your brother come by all those bruises?; *(sacar, obtener)* I wonder how he came by all that money
2 **VI** *(pasarse)* I'll come by next week if that suits

come down VI (a) *(bajar)* oil prices have been coming down; her temperature came down overnight; *(bajar el precio, rebajar)* he'll come down a few pounds if you bargain (b) *(caer)* rain was coming down in sheets; *(desplomarse)* the ceiling came down (c) *(llegar hasta)* the curtains should come right down to the floor (d) *(ser un legado)* the necklace came down to her from her great-aunt (e) *(arrancar)* that disgusting poster is coming down right now, or else! (f) *(pronunciarse)* the majority came down in favour of/against abortion

come down on vt insep (a) *(regañar)* one mistake and he'll come down on you like a ton of bricks (b) *(decidirse por)* he'll wait and see what happens and then come down on the winning side

come down to vt insep *(reducirse a)* it all comes down to money; *(tratarse de)* this is what we've come down to – selling the house

come down with vt insep *(pillar)* I always come down with a cold at this time of year

come forward vi *(presentarse)* the police have appealed for witnesses to come forward

come in vi (a) *(llegar)* our new stock will not come in until next week (b) *(entrar sumas de dinero, etc.)* I don't have much coming in at the moment, can you wait a bit? (c) *(ser)* an extra pair of hands always comes in useful (d) *(estar implicado, intervenir)* where does she come in in all this? (es decir, *¿cuál es su papel en todo esto?*) (e) *(hablar, por radio)* are you receiving me? come in, please

come in for vt insep *(ser objeto de)* the government is coming in for a lot of criticism over its latest proposals; he came in for a lot of adverse publicity when he was younger

come in on vt insep *(tomar parte en)* why should we let him come in on the deal?

come into vt insep (a) *(heredar)* she'll come into several hundred thousand pounds when her great-uncle dies (b) *(desempeñar un papel en)* wait a minute, when did I come into this crazy scheme?; *(tener que ver)* ability doesn't come into it, it's who you know that matters (c) *(locución)* to come into blossom *florecer*; to come into effect *entrar en vigor*

come of vt insep (a) *(deducirse, ser el resultado de)* nothing will come of it; this is what comes of being too self-confident (b) *(venir de)* the mare comes of good stock (c) *(locución)* she inherited a fortune when she came of age *heredó una fortuna cuando alcanzó la mayoría de edad*

come off 1 vi (a) *(salirse)* could you fix my bike? the chain has come off; my suede shoes are ruined, the mud won't come off (b) *(salir de un apuro)* considering what he's done, he's come off very lightly; it could have been a serious accident, but they all came off without a scratch; we came off very badly in the debate on capital punishment (c) *(tener lugar)* I shall be very surprised if that wedding ever comes off; the trip did eventually come off but several months later than planned (d) **FAM.** *(funcionar)* yet another attempt to beat the record hasn't come off

2 **VI INSEP** (a) *(despegarse de)* the handle has come off the knife; that kind of mark never comes off silk (b) **FAM.** *(exclamación de impaciencia, incredulidad: ianda ya!)* come off it! you can't expect me to believe that!

come on **VI** (a) *(darse prisa)* come on, or we'll miss the start (b) *(avanzar)* how's the work coming on? (c) *(empezar)* the rain came on about six; I have a sore throat coming on; when does that programme you want to watch come on? (d) *(entrar en escena, aparecer)* the character he plays doesn't come on until halfway through the first act (e) **FAM.** *(hacerse el/la...)* he was coming on a bit too macho

come out **VI** (a) *(aparecer, salir)* the magazine comes out on a Wednesday; when do you expect your latest film to come out?; now that the sun has come out, maybe I'll get my washing dried; *(florecer)* next door's roses always come out early (b) *(darse a conocer)* the election results came out a few hours ago; the truth will come out eventually (c) *(declararse en huelga)* nurses all over the country have come out in protest (d) *(tener una erupción cutánea, un sarpullido)* the baby has come out in a rash (e) *(salir bien, hablando de una fotografía)* they're pleased that their holiday photographs have come out so well (f) *(irse, quitar, hablando de manchas)* I've had this coat cleaned three times and the stain still hasn't come out (g) *(salir del hospital, de la cárcel)* she'll be coming out soon (h) *(resolverse, hablando de una operación aritmética)* of course the equation hasn't come out – you copied the figures down wrongly (i) *(declararse, pronunciarse)* we've come out against the idea of moving; the committee came out in her favour (j) *(librarse de)* she came out of that looking rather silly, don't you think?

come out with **VI INSEP** (a) *(decir de forma inesperada)* I'm always on the edge of my seat wondering what he'll come out with next; she finally came out with what was bothering her

come over 1 vi (a) *(acostumbrarse a)* I doubt if I will ever come over to your way of thinking (b) *(dar la impresión de)* he comes over as (being) a bit pompous, but in fact he's rather shy (c) FAM. *(sentirse)* Granny says she came over all funny in the supermarket
2 vt INSEP *(invadir)* a feeling of fear came over her; *(sobrevenir)* I don't know what's come over her, she's usually so quiet

come round vi (a) *(pasar el mal humor)* give him time, he'll come round eventually; *(aceptar)* I'm sure they'll come round to our point of view in the end (b) *(volver en sí)* imagine that poor woman coming round and seeing all those faces staring at her (c) *(llegar periódicamente)* it's a good thing Christmas only comes round once a year

come through 1 vi (a) *(llegar, obtener, hablando de documentos oficiales, etc.)* he's very annoyed because his visa is taking so long to come through (b) *(sobrevivir, superar)* it must have been a terrifying experience but they have come through all right
2 vt INSEP (a) *(aprobar)* their daughter has come through her law exams with flying colours (b) *(sobrevivir a, salir indemne de)* I am sure you will come through this ordeal; very few people came through the First World War unscarred either physically or mentally

come to 1 vi *(volver en sí)* she came to in a hospital bed
2 vt INSEP (a) *(ascender a)* the bill came to much more than I could afford; *(llegar a, hacer algo en la vida)* that nephew of his will never come to anything; *(llegar a un punto)* has it come to this, that we must leave a house our family has lived in for 400 years? (b) *(ser cuestión de, tratarse de)* when it comes to buying a car, find yourself a reputable dealer (c) *(llegar a)* if it comes to a malpractice suit, the surgeon is in trouble; when does the case come to trial? (es decir, *estar visto para sentencia*); I do wish she would come to the point (d) *(locución)* come to that, where were you last night? *por cierto, ¿dónde estabas ayer por la noche?*

come up vi (a) *(verse, hablando de un caso jurídico)* when does her case come up (for trial)?; *(salir a colación)* he kept quiet when the subject of fee-paying schools came up; *(salir, preguntar)* do you think this question will come up in the exam? (b) *(salir a la venta)* two other houses in our street are coming up for sale soon (c) *(salir, aparecer)* my number never comes up in the draw; the bulbs are starting to come up (d) *(pasar, suceder)* call me if anything comes up that you can't handle

come up against vт iɴsᴇᴘ *(encontrarse con)* you realize that you'll come up against some pretty strong opposition on this?; who does she come up against in the next round?

come up to vт iɴsᴇᴘ (a) *(llegar a, alcanzar)* she's so tall that I only come up to her shoulder; we're coming up to the halfway mark now (b) *(responder a)* his latest play does not come up to expectations

come up with vт iɴsᴇᴘ *(ocurrírsele a alguien)* she's come up with a solution; he keeps coming up with these awful jokes; I'll let you know if I come up with anything that might help

conk out vɪ ꜰᴀᴍ. (a) *(escacharrarse)* the radio has conked out on us (b) *(desmayarse)* he's conked out, better send for a doctor (c) *(quedarse frito)* I conked out as soon as I lay down on the sofa

cool down 1 vɪ (a) *(calmarse)* we'll talk about it once you've cooled down (b) *(refrescar, enfriarse)* it has cooled down quite a bit since yesterday; let the soup cool down a bit; ꜰɪɢ. *(enfriarse)* things have cooled down between them
2 vт sᴇᴘ (a) *(calmar)* I'll try to cool her down but I don't think I'll have much success (b) *(refrescar)* how about a beer to cool you down after all that hard work?

cotton on vɪ ꜰᴀᴍ. *(enterarse, coscarse)* I never did cotton on

cough up 1 vт sᴇᴘ (a) *(escupir, esputar)* if you can cough the phlegm up, you'll soon feel better; people with tuberculosis cough up blood (b) ꜰᴀᴍ. *(apoquinar)* I've got to cough up another £50
2 vɪ ꜰᴀᴍ. *(apoquinar)* he coughed up for the meal

count in vт sᴇᴘ *(contar, incluir)* have you counted the neighbours in?; anybody want to go out for lunch? – count me in! (es decir, *¡cuenta conmigo!*)

count on vт iɴsᴇᴘ *(contar con)* we can always count on you to be late; he counted on me and I let him down

count out vт sᴇᴘ (a) *(contar)* count out the change and see if we have enough (b) *(dejar fuera de combate, en boxeo)* his opponent is on the canvas and being counted out (c) *(excluir, no contar con)* he's teetotal, so count him out of the pub-crawl; a weekend camping out in the snow? no thanks, count me out!

count up **VT SEP** *(sumar)* I've counted these figures up time and time again and get a different answer every time

cover up 1 **VI** *(ocultar, encubrir)* don't try to cover up, I know it was you; the government was accused of covering up
2 **VT SEP** (a) *(cubrir, tapar)* that dress is much too low, cover yourself up a bit (b) *(ocultar)* it's highly unlikely that he meant to cover things up

cover up for **VT INSEP** *(encubrir)* the architects and builders are covering up for each other

crack down **VI** *(volverse más estricto)* in view of the increase in drunk driving the police are going to crack down

crack down on **VT INSEP** *(adoptar medidas más severas contra)* they're going to crack down on drunk drivers

crack up 1 **VI** (a) *(romperse, agrietarse)* the ice on the pond is cracking up (b) **FAM.** *(hundirse, venirse abajo)* if he doesn't take a holiday soon, he'll crack up; do you think their marriage is cracking up?; she cracked up under the pressure (c) **FAM.** *(echarse a reír)* I cracked up when he said that
2 **VT SEP FAM.** *normalmente en voz pasiva* (a) *(hacer reír)* it really cracked me up when I heard about it (b) *(locución)* he's not what he's cracked up to be *no es tan bueno como dicen*; the play is everything it's cracked up to be *la obra es tan buena como dicen*

cream off **VT SEP** *(quedarse con, seleccionar)* the oldest universities cream off the best candidates

cross off **VT SEP** *(borrar, tachar)* cross his name off the list

cross out **VT SEP** *(borrar, tachar)* cross your mistakes out neatly, please

cry off **VI** *(echarse atrás)* I hate it when people cry off at the last minute

cry out **VI** (a) *(lanzar un grito)* the pain made her cry out (b) **FIG.** *(necesitar, pedir a gritos)* that room is just crying out for red velvet curtains

cuddle up **VI** *(arrimarse a)* cuddle up if you're cold; the little girl cuddled up to her grandmother

curl up **vi** (a) *(acurrucarse)* I like to curl up in bed with a good book (b) *(hacerse un ovillo)* hedgehogs curl up into a ball for protection

cut across **vt insep** (a) *(atajar por)* we cut across the playing field (b) *(trascender)* concern for the environment cuts across party lines (c) *(ir en contra de)* it cuts across all my principles

cut back **1** **vi** *(reducir el consumo de, ahorrar)* we're definitely going to have to cut back
2 **vt sep** (a) *(podar)* now is the time to cut your raspberries back (b) *(reducir)* the company is cutting back production until the seamen's strike is over

cut down **vt sep** (a) *(cortar,talar)* they're cutting down the trees that were damaged in the storm (b) *(abatir)* he was cut down by machine-gun fire (c) *(reducir)* we've been asked to cut down the amount of time we devote to sports; if you won't stop smoking then at least cut down

cut in **1** **vi** (a) *(interrumpir)* the interviewer cut in to ask a question (b) *(adelantar bruscamente)* that idiot will cause an accident cutting in in front of people like that
2 **vt sep** *(dejar participar)* can you cut me in on one of your deals?

cut off **vt sep** (a) *(cortar)* they had to cut his clothes off in the emergency room; cut off his head! (b) *(aislar)* the town has been cut off by floods; don't you feel cut off living in the country? (c) *(cortar el suministro eléctrico, la línea telefónica, etc.)* we'd hardly said hello before we were cut off; it's dreadful to think how many people have their electricity cut off because they can't afford to pay the bills (d) *(locución)* her family cut her off without a penny *su familia la ha desheredado*; he was cut off in his prime *murió en la flor de la vida*

cut out **1** **vi** *(calarse, hablando de un motor)* will you have a look at the engine, it keeps cutting out
2 **vt sep** (a) *(cortar)* the hardest part is cutting the dress out (b) *(recortar)* I cut this magazine article out for you (c) *(suprimir)* cut out starchy food for a couple of weeks; **fam.** *(parar)* I've told you already to cut out the silly jokes

cut out for **vt sep fig.** *siempre en voz pasiva (estar hecho para)* I'm not cut out for all these late nights

cut up **vt sep** (a) *(cortar)* cut the meat up quite small (b) **fam.** *normalmente en voz pasiva (afectar, herir)* he was definitely a bit cut up about not being invited

dash off 1 **vi** *(salir corriendo)* she was sorry she missed you but she had to dash off
2 **vt sep** *(escribir a toda prisa)* I dashed off an answer yesterday; *(dibujar rápidamente)* he says he dashes these paintings off in his spare time

deal with **vt insep** (a) *(tener tratos con)* we've been dealing with that company for years (b) *(afrontar, hacer frente a)* she dealt with that problem very well; the case wasn't very professionally dealt with (c) *(tratar de o sobre)* the play deals with euthanasia

die away **vi** *(desvanecerse)* the noise of the car engine died away

die down **vi** *(apaciguarse, disminuir)* he had to wait for the applause to die down

die off **vi** *(morirse, desaparecer)* by the time he was in his twenties, his relatives had all died off; their livestock is dying off as the drought intensifies

die out **vi** *(extinguirse, desaparecer)* entire species are dying out as their habitat is destroyed

dig in 1 **vi** (a) *(atrincherarse)* the first thing the troops had to do when they got to the front was to dig in (b) **fam.** *(empezar a comer, hincar el diente)* dig in, there's plenty for everyone
2 **vt sep** *(mezclar con la tierra)* before planting, dig in a couple of handfuls of fertilizer

dig into **vt insep** (a) **fam.** *(zampar)* dig into that pie as much as you like, I made two (b) *(buscar)* they want us to dig into her past

dig out **vt sep** (a) *(extraer)* dig out the roots (b) *(rescatar)* they hope to have the remaining survivors dug out by nightfall (c) **fam.** *(encontrar)* have you dug those files out yet?; we want more information on the company's early days, so see what you can dig out

dig up **VT SEP** (a) *(arrancar)* this rose bush will have to be dug up and moved (b) **FAM.** *(encontrar, descubrir)* we're hoping to dig up some items to show that there was a Roman encampment here; I've dug something up that might prove he's been lying to us

dip into **VT INSEP** (a) *(remojar rápidamente)* she dipped her toes into the bath water to test it (b) *(echar mano de)* she doesn't want to dip into her savings if she can help it (c) *(echar un vistazo a)* this is the kind of anthology to be dipped into rather than read all at once

dish out **VT SEP** (a) *(servir)* Mum's dishing supper out now (b) **FAM.** *(dar)* you're always dishing out advice!

dish up 1 **VT SEP** *(servir)* somebody dish up the soup
2 **VI** *(servir)* when will you be dishing up?

dispense with **VT INSEP** *(prescindir de, deshacerse de)* let's dispense with formalities, call me Laura

dispose of **VT INSEP** (a) *(deshacerse de)* dispose of your waste paper here (b) *(arreglar)* let's just dispose of the matter now (c) **FAM.** *(matar, liquidar)* we have to dispose of him before he talks (d) **FAM.** *(deshacerse de, quitarse de encima)* so far she has disposed of six opponents who want to take the title away from her

divide out **VT SEP** *(repartir)* they divided the food out

divide up **VT SEP** *(dividir, repartir)* contestants will be divided up into groups of four

do away with **VT INSEP** (a) *(abolir, eliminar)* they should do away with capital punishment (b) *(acabar con, eliminar)* he has threatened to do away with himself

do by **VT INSEP FAM.** *(tratar bien/mal)* the company did very badly by its employees; he'll feel very hard done by if you don't at least send him a birthday card; she did very well by her granddaughter at Christmas (es decir, *su abuela la mimó en Navidad*)

do down **VT SEP BRIT. FAM.** (a) *(timar)* why did you let the salesman do you down? (b) *(hablar mal de)* there's always someone ready to do you down

do for vt insep fam. (a) *(matar)* if he keeps on treating her this way, she'll do for him (b) *(acabar con, agotar)* it was that last hill that did for me (c) *(hacer la limpieza a)* who does for you?

do in vt sep Brit. fam. (a) *(apiolar, liquidar)* somebody on our street was done in last night (b) fig. *(agotar, dejar hecho polvo)* Christmas shopping always does me in

do out vt sep Brit. fam. *(limpiar a fondo)* will you do the kitchen out tomorrow please, Mrs Jones?

do out of vt sep fam. *(estafar)* he always maintained that he had been done out of his inheritance; they did him out of his share of the money

do over vt sep (a) *(reformar)* the whole house needs doing over (b) Brit. fam. *(moler a palos, romper la cara)* the other gang did him over (c) U.S. *(volver a hacer, repetir)* the teacher said I had to do my project over

do up 1 vi *(abrocharse)* the dress does up at the back
2 vt sep (a) *(abrochar)* do your buttons up (b) *(envolver)* it seems a pity to open it when it's done up so nicely (c) fam. *(reformar)* they're doing up all the buildings on the street; *(arreglarse, ponerse guapo)* you've really done yourself up, what's the occasion?

do with vt insep (a) *detrás de «could» (necesitar)* you could do with a haircut; what I could be doing with right now is a hot bath (b) *(estar relacionado con)* he has something to do with computers; *(tener que ver con)* it sounds very fishy to me and you should have nothing to do with it; my business has nothing to do with you; that's got nothing to do with it!; *(tratarse de)* it has to do with your mother, I'm afraid (c) *(acabar de)* I've done with trying to help people; *(acabar una relación con)* he says it's all over, he's done with her (d) *(no necesitar más)* if you've done with the hammer, put it back where it belongs

do without 1 vt insep *(prescindir)* we can do without the sarcasm
2 vi *(arreglárselas sin)* if you don't find anything you like in here then you'll have to do without

double back 1 vi *(volver sobre sus pasos)* they decided to double back since they didn't recognize any landmarks
2 vt sep *(doblar)* double back the bedclothes and let the mattress air

double over/up **VI** *(retorcerse)* the pain struck again and she doubled over; the joke made me double up (with laughter)

double up **VI** *(compartir una cama, una habitación, etc.)* with so many guests coming, some of them are going to have to double up; do you mind doubling up with me?

drag behind **1 VT SP** *(arrastrar)* I ran for the bus, dragging my cases behind me
2 VI *(estar a la cola)* you're dragging behind in maths

drag in **VT SEP** (a) *(meter)* the trunk is too heavy to lift, let's just drag it in (b) *(sacar a colación)* he insisted on dragging in the issue of customer satisfaction

drag on **VI** *(eternizarse)* the play dragged on and on

drag out **VT SEP** *(alargar innecesariamente)* I had to drag my presentation out to fill the time allotted to me

drag up **VT SEP** (a) *(subir arrastrando)* drag it up the stairs (b) **FAM.** *(llevar)* you dragged me up to London for this? (c) *(sacar a relucir)* there's no need to drag up the past (d) **FAM.** *(educar)* those children are being dragged up, not brought up; where were you dragged up?

draw alongside **1 VI** *(ponerse al lado o a la misma altura)* then this big Mercedes drew alongside...
2 VT INSEP *(ponerse al lado o a la altura de)* the Customs launch drew alongside the liner

draw apart **VI** *(separarse físicamente)* they drew apart when I entered the room

draw away **1 VI** (a) *(alejarse)* we waved as the car drew away (b) *(adelantarse)* the first half dozen runners are now beginning to draw away (c) *(apartarse)* I can't help drawing away when he touches me
2 VT SEP *(apartar)* she drew us away from the other guests

draw back **1 VI** *(retroceder)* she drew back from the edge of the cliff
2 VT SEP (a) *(abrir, descorrer)* he drew back the curtains and light flooded into the room (b) *(llevar de regreso)* what drew you back to music?

draw in **1 VI** (a) *(llegar)* the train will be drawing in soon; the car drew in to the drive (b) *(acortarse)* the days have started to draw in again

2 **vt sep** (a) *(aspirar)* fresh air from outside is drawn in by these ventilators (b) *(implicar, mezclar)* they were arguing again and I left because I didn't want to be drawn in

draw on 1 **vi** *(avanzar)* as the day gradually drew on; *(acercarse)* summer is fast drawing on
2 **vt insep** *(echar mano de)* for this essay, I want you to draw on your own childhood memories
3 **vt sep Brit.** *(ponerse)* she drew on a pair of long white gloves

draw out 1 **vi** (a) *(alejarse)* they waved as the train drew out (b) *(alargar)* after Christmas, the days start to draw out
2 **vt sep** (a) *(sacar)* she drew out a gun; *(retirar, sacar)* I've drawn out all my savings (b) *(prolongar)* they drew the meeting out on purpose (c) *(sonsacar)* I managed to draw her out on her plans

draw up 1 **vi** *(parar, hablando de un coche)* he drew up with a squeal of brakes
2 **vt sep** (a) *(acercar)* draw up a chair and join us
(b) *(diseñar)* I think we should draw up a plan of action; *(redactar)* the old lady drew up a new will

dream away vt sep *(pasarse el día soñando)* he'll dream his whole life away at this rate

dream up vt sep *(idear, inventarse)* they've dreamed up some scheme that they say will make us all rich

dredge up vt sep (a) *(dragar)* the barges are dredging up silt (b) *(sacar a relucir)* why did you dredge that old scandal up?

dress up 1 **vi** (a) *(vestirse bien, arreglarse)* it's just an informal get-together, there's no need to dress up (b) *(disfrazarse)* it's a Hallowe'en party and everybody has to dress up
2 **vt sep** (a) *(vestir bien, con elegancia)* she dressed herself up for the wedding (b) *(disfrazar)* you could dress yourself up as Pierrot

drink down vt sep *(tragar, beber de un trago)* drink this down and you'll soon feel better

drink in vt sep (a) *(absorber, beber)* these plants will drink in plenty of water, even in winter (b) **fig.** *(estar pendiente de)* we drank in every word; *(impregnarse de, empaparse de)* we stopped for a moment to drink in the atmosphere

drink up 1 **vi** *(bebérselo todo)* drink up and I'll get the next round
2 **vt sep** *(terminado)* have you drunk up your tea?

drive at **vt insep** *(insinuar)* I'm sorry, but I really don't see what you're driving at; did you think she was driving at something when she said she couldn't afford a holiday this year?

drive back 1 **vi** *(volver en coche)* are you driving back or taking the train?
2 **vt sep** (a) *(llevar en coche)* George will drive you back to your hotel (b) *(repeler)* the soldiers did not have the strength to drive back another attack

drive home **vt sep** (a) *(apretar bien)* once you have driven the screws home... (b) *(hacer comprender)* I tried to drive it home to them that this was not an isolated incident

drive off 1 **vi** *(irse en coche)* he drove off about an hour ago
2 **vt sep** (a) *(llevar en coche)* all three of them were driven off in a police car (b) *(repeler)* the attackers were driven off when reinforcements arrived

drive on 1 **vi** *(seguir adelante)* he decided to drive on rather than stop there for the night
2 **vt sep** *(empujar)* her friends drove her on to sue

drive up **vi** *(llegar, hablando de un coche)* a car has just driven up

drop back **vi** *(quedarse atrás, rezagarse)* he has dropped back and it looks as if he's given up the race

drop behind 1 **vi** *(retrasarse, rezagarse)* you're dropping behind, do try to keep up
2 **vt insep** *(quedarse rezagado)* that last lap exhausted her and now she's dropping behind the leaders

drop in 1 **vi** *(pasarse)* I'll drop in and see mother tomorrow; would you drop in at the supermarket on your way home?
2 **vt sep** *(dejar)* drop this in the night safe for me, will you?

drop off 1 **vi** (a) *(caer)* with all this heavy shopping to carry, I feel as if my arms are going to drop off (b) *(dormirse)* it was 4 a.m. before she dropped off; why don't you go to bed instead of dropping off in the chair? (c) *(disminuir)* church attendance has been dropping off for many years
2 **vt sep** *(dejar)* drop these books off at the library; where do you want to be dropped off?

drop out **vi** (a) *(caerse)* there's a hole in your pocket and the keys must have dropped out (b) **FAM.** *(abandonar o dejar los estudios, un curso, etc.)* he dropped out at the age of 14; so many have dropped out that the course may be cancelled (c) *(escoger una vida al margen de la sociedad)* in the sixties a lot of people dropped out (of society) and went off to places like India

drum into **vt** **SEP** *(repetir hasta la saciedad, meter en la cabeza)* drum it into the children that they mustn't take sweets from strangers

drum up **vt** **SEP** *(encontrar, tratar de conseguir)* how are you drumming up support for the campaign?; we must drum up some more business

dry off 1 **vi** *(secarse)* don't touch the varnish while it's drying off 2 **vt** **SEP** *(secar)* come and dry yourself off in front of the fire

dry out 1 **vi** (a) *(secarse)* leave your wet things in the bathroom to dry out (b) *(desintoxicarse)* I think she's somewhere drying out 2 **vt** **SEP** *(resecar*soap can dry your skin out

dry up **vi** (a) *(secarse, quedarse sin agua)* streams and rivers are drying up because of this long heat wave (b) *(secar los platos)* could you dry up, please? (c) **FAM.** *(cerrar la boca, callarse)* why don't you dry up? (d) **FAM.** *(quedarse en blanco)* why don't you dry up?

dwell (up)on **vt** **INSEP** *(pensar constantemente en)* get on with your life instead of dwelling on what might have been

ease off/up **vi** *(calmarse, frenarse)* he's been told to ease off if he doesn't want a heart attack; *(disminuir la velocidad)* ease up, there's a 30-mile-an-hour limit here

eat away **vt** **SEP** *(erosionar)* the action of the waves is eating the coast-line away

eat in **vi** *(comer en casa)* I'm tired of eating in all the time

eat into **vt** **INSEP** *(mermar)* it's silly to eat into your savings when you could get a bank loan; long-term unemployment eats into people's self-confidence

eat out 1 vi *(ir al restaurante)* let's eat out tonight
2 vt sep *(locución)* the child is eating her heart out for a pony *el niño se muere de ganas de tener un pony*

eat up 1 vt sep (a) *(acabar)* eat up your spinach (b) fig. *(devorar, corroer)* jealousy is eating him up
2 vi *(acabar de comer)* eat up, the taxi's waiting; eat up, there's lots more *(come, come, que hay más)*

edge out 1 vi *(asomarse)* I opened the window and cautiously edged out
2 vt sep (a) *(ir con mucha precaución)* she edged her way out on to the ledge (b) *(apartar)* there's a move to edge him out of the chairmanship

egg on vt sep *(animar, incitar)* it was sickening to hear the crowd egg the boxers on; I wish I hadn't let you egg me on to accept

end up vi *(acabar)* no one ever thought she would end up in prison; *(acabar por)* I ended up telling him in no uncertain terms what I thought

enter into vt insep (a) *(concluir, cerrar)* we entered into this contract with our eyes open (b) *(tener que ver con)* morality rarely enters into foreign policy

enter (up)on vt insep *(embarcarse en)* she has entered on a new career

even out 1 vi *(rondar, hablando de una cantidad)* production figures are evening out at about 5,000 per week
2 vt sep *(repartir o compartir equitativamente)* we need to even out supplies over time

even up vt sep (a) *(igualar)* that last goal evened up the score; if you pay for the meal, that will even things up (b) *(redondear al alza)* just even it up to a pound

explain away vt sep *(justificar)* he tried to explain away his absence from the last meeting; explain this away if you can

eye up vt sep fam. *(desnudar con la mirada, comerse con los ojos)* I passed the time eyeing up all the men; he eyed up every one of the women at the party

face up to **vt insep** *(hacer frente a)* it might help if she faced up to her fears of rejection; *(aceptar, hablando de un hecho)* we'll have to face up to the fact that we're not getting any younger

fade away **vi** *(desvanecerse)* the sound of the procession faded away; her smile faded away when she realized he hadn't been joking

fade in 1 **vi** *(aparecer gradualmente)* the music faded in
2 **vt sep** *(hacer aparecer gradualmente)* fade in the crowd scenes

fade out 1 **vi** *(desaparecer gradualmente)* the music fades out for the last few seconds
2 **vt sep** *(hacer desaparecer gradualmente)* fade out the crowd scenes

fall about **vi** **Brit, fam.** *(partirse de risa)* her scripts always make me fall about

fall away **vi** (a) *(descender)* be careful, the ground falls away here (b) *(bajar, disminuir)* attendance at committee meetings has been falling away recently

fall back **vi** *(retroceder)* the demonstrators fell back when they saw the water cannon

fall back on **vt insep** *(recurrir a, echar mano de)* I suppose we can always fall back on temporary staff

fall behind **vi** (a) *(quedarse atrás)* he began well but now seems to be falling behind (b) *(retrasarse)* you mustn't fall behind with the payments

fall down **vi** (a) *(caer al suelo)* he fell down and bumped his head (b) *(caerse)* why don't they demolish that old building instead of letting it fall down? (c) *(no sostenerse, fallar)* that's where their argument falls down

fall down on **vt insep** *(fracasar)* if you fall down on this, she won't give you another chance

fall for **vt insep** (a) *(enamorarse de)* he's fallen for the girl next door;

(encantar algo) I've really fallen for that Victorian chair in the antique shop (b) *(tragarse)* you didn't fall for that old story, did you?

fall in with vt insep (a) *(aceptar)* I fell in with the plans for a picnic because the children were so keen (b) *(juntarse con)* the teenager next door has fallen in with a bad crowd

fall off vi (a) *(caerse)* I was terrified of falling off and clung to the chimney for dear life (b) *(disminuir)* enrolment is falling off

fall on vt insep (a) *(recaer sobre)* if anything goes wrong you can be sure that the blame will not fall on him (b) *(abalanzarse sobre)* they fell on the meal as if they hadn't eaten for days

fall out vi (a) *(caerse)* the window is open so be careful you don't fall out (b) *(reñir, pelearse)* my sister and I have fallen out

fall over 1 vi *(caerse, volcarse)* the vase is top-heavy, that's why it keeps falling over
2 vt insep (a) *(tropezar con)* move your suitcase before someone falls over it (b) fam. *(desvivirse por)* he was falling over himself to buy the woman a drink

fall through vi *(fracasar)* their plans for a skiing holiday have fallen through

farm out vt sep *(subcontratar)* if deadlines are to be met then some of the work will have to be farmed out; *(confiar el cuidado de)* those two next door are always farming their kids out

feed in vt sep *(introducir, en el ordenador)* feed the data in then let the computer perform the calculation

feed up vt sep *(cebar, hacer comer más de lo normal)* Mum always wants to feed us up when we come home for the weekend

feel up vt sep fam. *(meter mano a, sobar)* he's always feeling her up in public, it's so embarrassing

feel up to vt insep *(verse capaz de)* he suggested a long walk but she didn't feel up to it; I don't feel up to cooking a big meal tonight, let's go out; do you feel up to a visit from my mother?

fetch up vi *(ir a parar)* we eventually fetched up in a tiny little village in the middle of nowhere; the road was very icy and they fetched up in a ditch

fiddle about/around VI FAM. (a) *(juguetear)* he fiddled about for ages and still couldn't get the car to go (b) *(perder el tiempo)* why don't you stop fiddling about and get down to some work?

fight back 1 VI (a) *(defenderse)* everybody encounters a bully at some time – you must learn to fight back (b) *(recuperarse)* he was critically ill but managed to fight back
2 VT SEP *(reprimir, contener)* I fought back my anger and tried to answer calmly

fight down VT SEP *(contener)* you must fight down these fears

fight off VT SEP *(repeler, librarse de)* government troops have fought off a number of attacks; his bodyguards had to fight off over-eager fans

fight on VI *(seguir luchando)* she regards this as merely a setback and is determined to fight on

fight out VT SEP *(decidirlo luchando, discutiendo)* you'll have to fight this one out; I left them to fight it out

figure on VT INSEP *(contar con, esperar)* I didn't figure on your mother coming too; when are you figuring on leaving?

figure out VT SEP (a) *(lograr entender)* she can't figure you out at all; the dog figured out how to open the door (b) *(calcular)* we figured out that they must be paying three times as much rent as we are

fill in 1 VI *(sustituir)* this isn't her normal job, she's just filling in; who'll be filling in for you while you're on holiday? (es decir, *¿quién va a sustituirte...?*)
2 VT SEP (a) *(tapar, rellenar)* workmen are filling those potholes in at last (b) *(rellenar, hablando de un formulario)* there are several forms to fill in when you apply for a mortgage (c) *(informar, poner al corriente)* will someone please fill us in on what's been happening? (d) *(hacer tiempo)* are you busy or just filling in time?

fill out 1 VI *(coger peso, engordar)* he's beginning to fill out at last after his long illness
2 VT SEP *(rellenar, hablando de un formulario)* will you fill out this form, please?

fill up 1 VI *(llenar hasta los topes)* the room was filling up

2 vt sep (a) *(llenar el depósito)* fill it up, please; *(llenar, hablando de un recipiente)* let me fill your glass up (b) *(rellenar, hablando de un formulario)* there are one or two forms to be filled up first

filter out 1 vi *(salir poco a poco)* mourners filtered out of the church; *(trascender, llegar a saberse)* the news was beginning to filter out that several arrests had been made
2 vt sep *(filtrar hasta eliminar)* filter out the impurities

find out 1 vt sep *(descubrir)* I could have found that out for myself
2 vi *(descubrir, enterarse)* has your wife found out yet?

finish off 1 vt sep (a) *(acabar)* let me just finish this chapter off; finish off your lunch; you can finish off the cream if you like (b) *(matar, acabar con)* the men were finished off with a bullet through the skull (c) **fig.** *(agotar, acabar con)* all that heavy digging has finished him off
2 vi *(acabar)* what did you have to finish off with?

finish up 1 vt sep *(acabar)* finish up your lunch; don't finish up the pie
2 vi *(acabar)* we finished up in the pub down the road; he'll finish up in court; *(acabar por)* any more of this uncertainty and I'll finish up a nervous wreck

fire away vi fam. *(empezar, especialmente a hablar o a hacer preguntas)* fire away, I'm all ears *(es decir, ¡adelante! soy todo oídos)*

fish out vt sep (a) *(sacar del agua)* they fished him out of the river (b) **fig.** *(sacar)* just let me fish the keys out

fit in **1 vt sep** (a) *(meter, hacer sitio en)* could you fit this pair of shoes in the case? (b) *(coger, atender)* the hairdresser says she can fit me in tomorrow
2 vi (a) *(caber)* there's not enough room, the books won't fit in (b) *(concordar)* that doesn't fit in with what I was told (c) *(adaptarse, encajar)* how does that fit in with your plans?; *(integrarse)* I hate parties like this, I never feel that I fit in

fix on **1 vt sep** *(sujetar)* he fixed the handle on for me
2 vt insep *(fijar, decidirse por)* have you fixed on a date yet?

fix up **1 vt sep** (a) *(instalar)* the marquee will be fixed up on their front lawn (b) *(conseguir)* I've fixed up an interview for you (c) *(proporcionar)* our in-laws will fix us up with a bed (d) *(reformar)* they're busy fixing up the house; *(arreglarse)* if

you're going out, don't you think you should fix yourself up
a bit first?
2 **VI** *(prever, planear)* I'm sorry but I've already fixed up to go
out

fizzle out **VI** *(decaer)* people's enthusiasm is starting to fizzle out;
(quedar en agua de borrajas) all those big plans we had have
just fizzled out

flag down **VT SEP** *(parar)* it's impossible to flag a taxi down when it's
raining; *(hacer señales para que se detenga)* I was cycling
along when a policeman flagged me down

flake out **VI FAM.** *(quedarse roque)* six late nights in succession, no
wonder you flaked out; I just want to flake out on the couch

flare up **VI** (a) *(llamear)* the fire flared up, turning night into day (b)
FIG. *(estallar)* the argument flared up when she said something
about favouritism; *(irritarse)* he flares up at the least little
thing

flip over 1 **VT SEP** *(revolver)* do you want your egg flipped over?;
(pasar) she was flipping over the pages of a magazine
2 **VI** *(darse la vuelta)* the plane just seemed to flip over

float about/around **VI FAM.** (a) *(circular, correr)* rumours have been
floating around about your resignation (b) *(estar por ahí)* my
keys must be floating about somewhere but I just can't find
them; I spent a lazy weekend just floating around

flood in **VI** *(entrar a raudales)* when she opened the door water flooded
in; light flooded in through the windows; *(entrar en masa)* the
concert doesn't start for another hour but people are already
flooding in

flood out 1 **VT SEP** *normalmente en voz pasiva (estar obligado a marchar a
causa de las inundaciones)* thousands of people in Bangladesh
have been flooded out
2 **VI** *(salir en masa)* people flooded out of the cinema; *(salir)*
light flooded out of the open casement

fly in 1 **VI** *(llegar en avión)* the royal visitors will fly in tomorrow
2 **VT SEP** *(enviar por avión)* the army will fly troops in if necessary

fly off 1 **VI** (a) *(salir volando)* they flew off in a helicopter (b) *(levantarse)* his toupee flew off in the wind
2 **VT SEP** (a) *(evacuar en avión, etc.)* the rescue team came to fly

the oil rig workers off (b) *(transportar en avión)* the army flew
the troops off to another country

fly out 1 **vi** *(salir en avión)* the President flew out this morning;
which airport are you flying out of?

2 **vt sep** *(transportar en avión)* troops are being flown out as
quickly as possible; the company is flying her out to be with
her husband

fly past 1 **vt insep** *(sobrevolar)* the squadron will fly past the airfield at
precisely two o'clock

2 **vi** *(pasar volando)* the weekend has just flown past

fold away 1 **vi** *(plegarse)* does this table fold away?

2 **vt sep** *(doblar, plegar)* fold your clothes away neatly; she
folded the tablecloth away

fold in **vt sep** *(incorporar, añadir)* fold in the sugar

follow on **vi** (a) *(seguir)* you go ahead, we'll follow on (b) *(continuar)*
how did the story follow on? (c) *(resultar, ser consecuencia de)*
it follows on from this that...

follow out **vt sep** **U.S.** *(llevar a cabo)* he followed out his plans

follow through 1 **vt sep** *(llevar hasta el final)* she firmly intends to follow the idea through

2 **vi** *(acompañar con el propio cuerpo el golpeo de una pelota,
etc.)* the problem is that you're not following through after
you hit the ball

follow up 1 **vt sep** (a) *(hacer un seguimiento de)* the police are following up a number of leads; I want you to follow the matter up
(b) *(apoyar, completar)* he followed up his complaint to the
shop with an angry letter to the manufacturer

2 **vi** *(proseguir la acción, continuar)* he followed up with a right
to the jaw

fool around **vi** (a) *(perder el tiempo, gandulear)* stop fooling around
and get up! (b) *(hacer el tonto, jugar)* don't fool around with
that glue or you'll get it all over you; stop fooling around
with that computer! (c) **fam.** *(tener una aventura)* she thinks
her husband is fooling around behind her back

fork out **fam.** 1 **vt sep** *(pagar, soltar la pasta)* I have to fork out the cash
for everything just because I have a better-paid job than him

2 **vi** *(apoquinar, soltar la pasta)* we're all going to have to fork out

freak out vi FAM. (a) *(ponerse hecho una furia)* Mum will freak out when she sees that you've dyed your hair blue (b) *(bailar como un loco)* look at him freaking out on the dancefloor!

frighten away/off vt SEP *(asustar, ahuyentar)* we keep a couple of Doberman to frighten off potential burglars; don't look so grim or you'll frighten people away

frown on vt INSEP *(desaprobar)* they all frowned on my suggestion; her parents frowned on her marriage to a man so much younger

gain on vt INSEP *(ganar terreno)* they're gaining on us

gear up 1 **vi** *(prepararse)* the shops are already gearing up for Christmas
2 **vt SEP** (a) *(preparar)* shops are getting geared up for the January sales (b) *(aumentar)* we must gear up production to meet the demand

get about vi (a) *(moverse)* he doesn't get about much these days (b) *(difundirse)* a rumour has got about that you're leaving

get across 1 **vi** (a) *(cruzar)* there are no traffic lights there so I found it difficult to get across (b) *(ser comprendido)* our message is not getting across
2 **vt SEP** (a) *(hacer cruzar)* the flooding will prevent them from getting much-needed supplies across the river (b) *(hacer comprender)* did you get your point across to her?

get ahead vi *(abrirse camino, llegar lejos)* he got ahead in life; if you want to get ahead, you have to work extremely hard

get along vi (a) *(irse)* I must be getting along (b) *(ir bien, mal)* how are you getting along in the new house? (c) *(llevarse bien)* I wish I got along better with my neighbours

get around 1 **vi** (a) *(moverse)* elderly people often find it hard to get around; *(tener una vida social intensa)* that young man really gets around! (b) *(circular, hablando de una noticia)* I wonder how that story got around

2 **VT INSEP** *(evitar)* there's no getting around it, you'll have to tell him what happened; can we get around this difficulty?

get at VT INSEP (a) *(llegar a, alcanzar)* I can't get at that shelf, it's too high (b) *(descubrir)* he intends to get at the truth (c) *(querer decir)* do you mind telling me what you're getting at? (d) **FAM.** *(criticar, meterse con)* his father is always getting at him (e) **FAM.** *(comprar, sobornar)* the trial could not continue because a number of witnesses had been got at and refused to testify

get away 1 VI (a) *(irse, marcharse)* I usually get away by six; will they manage to get away this year? (b) *(escaparse, huir)* the terrorists got away in a stolen car
2 **VT SEP** *(apartar)* get that child away from the road!; *(coger, arrancar de las manos)* the policeman managed to get the gun away

get away with VT INSEP (a) *(huir con)* the thieves got away with the old lady's life savings (b) *(irse con)* he got away with a small fine (c) *(locución)* that child gets away with murder! *ieste crío siempre se sale con la suya!*

get back 1 VI (a) *(apartarse)* get back from the edge of the cliff! (b) *(regresar)* when did you get back?; I must be getting back soon
2 **VT SEP** (a) *(recuperar)* I'll get it back from him tomorrow (b) *(devolver)* get the file back to me as soon as you can

get back at VT INSEP *(vengarse de)* I'll get back at you for that

get back to VT INSEP (a) *(reincorporarse a)* I must get back to work soon (b) *(volver a telefonear a, volver a hablar con)* can we get back to you on that point later?

get behind 1 VI *(retrasarse)* I've got so behind that I'm working late every night this week
2 **VT INSEP** *(esconderse detrás)* get behind that tree

get by 1 VI (a) *(pasar)* the car could not get by because of the roadworks (b) *(arreglárselas)* he thinks he'll get by without studying; it must be difficult getting by on so little money; do you think I'll get by in Greece without speaking the language?
2 **VT INSEP** (a) *(pasar al lado de)* can I get by you? (b) *(escapar de)* his latest book did not get by the censor

get down 1 **vi** (a) *(bajar)* get down at once! (b) *(agacharse)* get down or she'll see us c) *(levantarse de la mesa)* may I get down?
2 **vt sep** (a) *(bajar)* will you get my case down for me? (b) *(hacer bajar, reducir)* the doctors have got his temperature down at last (c) *(tomar notas, anotar)* I didn't manage to get that down, she was speaking too quickly (d) *(deprimir)* this kind of weather gets everybody down (e) *(tragar)* her throat is so swollen she can't get anything down; get this soup down and you'll soon feel better

get down to **vt insep** *(ponerse a hacer)* when are you going to get down to your homework?

get in 1 **vt sep** (a) *(llamar)* I was so worried about the baby that I got the doctor in (b) *(entrar, meter)* just let me get the washing in before the rain starts; farmers are only now getting their crops in (c) *(lograr hacer)* she got some last-minute revision in the night before the exam (d) *(meter baza)* she was talking so much I couldn't get a word in (e) *(garantizar la entrada en)* these excellent exam results will get you in anywhere (f) *(hacer ganar las elecciones a)* it was the government's mistakes that got the opposition in (g) *(plantar, sembrar)* you should get your bulbs in earlier than this
2 **vt insep** *(meterse en)* the smoke from the camp fire got in their eyes; *(subir a)* get in the car!
3 **vi** (a) *(entrar)* if they didn't have a key, how did they get in? (b) *(volver a casa, etc.)* we got in about 4 a.m. (c) *(llegar)* when does the train get in? (d) *(ser admitido)* he applied to Oxford but he didn't get in (e) *(ser elegido)* she got in with a very small majority

get in on **vt insep** *(tomar parte en)* they'd all like to get in on the deal

get into 1 **vt insep** (a) *(ponerse)* she got into her clothes; *(caber en)* she hasn't been able to get into any of her clothes since the baby was born (b) *(entrar en)* only a small percentage of candidates get into university; the thieves got into the house through an open window (c) *(pasar, ocurrir algo a)* I don't know what's got into her these days (d) *(meterse en)* he wants to get into politics (e) *(locución)* there's no need to get into a panic *no vale la pena asustarse*; you'll get into trouble *te vas a meter en problemas*; they've got badly into debt *se endeudaron mucho* (f) *(acostumbrarse a)* she'll soon get into our ways (g) *(interesarse por)* he got into Eastern religions;

(engancharse) everyone says this is an excellent book, but I just can't get into it

2 vt sep (a) *(meter en)* did you manage to get everything into the suitcase?; you got me into this mess, now get me out of it **(b)** *(meter a alguien en un sitio)* he got his friend into the club **(c)** *(arrastrar a)* you're the one who got us into this **(d)** *(poner de mal humor, etc.)* she knows just what to do to get her father into a good mood; don't get her into one of her rages

get in with vt insep (a) *(congraciarse con alguien)* if you want to get in with him, tell him how much you enjoyed his singing **(b)** *(frecuentar)* she's worried about her daughter getting in with a bad crowd

get off 1 vi (a) *(bajar de un vehículo)* he got off at the traffic lights **(b)** *(irse, marcharse)* I have to be getting off to work **(c)** *(salir del trabajo, acabar)* I'd like to get off early tomorrow **(d)** *(librarse)* he shouldn't have got off; you got off lightly! *(es decir, salir bien librado)* **(e)** *(soltar)* hey! get off! that's my book! **(f)** *(dormir)* I couldn't get off at all last night

2 vt sep (a) *(enviar)* it's time to get the children off to bed; I must get this letter off in time to catch the last post **(b)** *(sacar de)* get your hands off that child; get those football boots off the chair **(c)** *(hacer pagar)* he has a reputation for always getting his clients off **(d)** *(tomar unas horas libres)* maybe I could get the afternoon off **(e)** *(obtener de)* I got it off the woman next door **(f)** *(dispensar de)* the burns were not very serious but they got him off work **(g)** *(dormirse)* it always takes ages to get her off

get off with vt insep Brit. (a) fam. *(enrollarse con)* she used to get off with a different guy every night **(b)** *(marcharse)* he got off with just a fine

get on 1 vi (a) *(subir a un autobús, un tren, etc.)* where did you get on? **(b)** *(ir* how did you get on at the dentist's?; *(arreglárselas)* how is the old man going to get on without his dog? **(c)** *(avanzar, progresar)* if he wants to get on, the best thing he can do is work hard; time is getting on *(es decir, se hace tarde)* **(d)** *(hacerse mayor)* my grandmother is getting on **(e)** *(llevarse bien)* we don't get on

2 vt sep *(poner)* I can't get the lid on; get your coat on and we'll be off; *(subir a)* you won't be able to get that on the bus, it's far too big; I got her on (the train) with seconds to spare

get on for **vt insep** *(rondar)* she must be getting on for 90 but she's very active; *(ser cerca de)* it's getting on for four o'clock; there were getting on for 500 guests at the wedding

get onto **vt insep** (a) *(encontrar, encontrar el nombre de)* how did you get onto me? (b) *(ponerse en contacto con)* I'll get onto the bank about it c) *(hablar de)* I'd like to get onto the question of expenses

get on with **vt insep** (a) *(continuar, proseguir)* please get on with what you're supposed to be doing; I would like to get on with my reading; that will do to be going on with (es decir, *irá bien de momento*) (b) *(progresar, avanzar)* how are you getting on with the painting? (c) *(llevarse bien con)* I don't get on with my parents

get out 1 **vi** (a) *(irse)* I told her to get out (b) *(salir)* when does he get out? (c) *(salir de casa, etc.)* she doesn't get out much; he ought to get out more (d) *(filtrarse)* how did the news get out? 2 **vt sep** (a) *(sacar)* I got my purse out to pay the delivery man; get your books out and turn to page 54 (b) *(liberar)* our prime concern must be to get the hostages out (c) *(decir)* he couldn't get a word out when they told him his wife had had triplets; *(sacar, publicar)* we have to get this report out by Monday (d) *(eliminar, en críquet)* John got their best batsman out for ten

get out of 1 **vt insep** (a) *(salir de)* let's get out of here; he got out of the country before the police came looking for him; the children get out of school at about three o'clock (b) *(librarse de)* he always gets out of the washing up (c) *(perder, hablando de una costumbre)* I've got out of the habit of studying 2 **vt sep** (a) *(sacar de)* get the big pot out of the cupboard; *(sonsacar)* the detective finally got the truth out of the suspect (b) *(disfrutar, hablando de una satisfacción)* I don't see what pleasure he gets out of all this studying; *(sacar provecho de)* she really gets the most out of life, doesn't she?

get over 1 **vi** (a) *(cruzar)* the Channel Tunnel makes it easier to get over to France (b) *(transmitir, hablando de una idea, una opinión, etc.)* her ideas don't get over to her audience very well 2 **vt insep** (a) *(recuperarse de)* he hasn't got over the shock of

his wife's death yet; I'm getting over it gradually (b) *(superar)* they've managed to get over their marital problems; you must get over these silly fears
3 **VT SEP** (a) *(hacer cruzar)* it's not easy getting fifty children over a busy road (b) *(transmitir una opinion, etc.)* you got your point over very well

get over with VT SEP *(acabar con)* once I got my appointment with the dentist over with, I thoroughly enjoyed my day off; can we get this over with quickly?

get round 1 VI (a) *(llegar a casa)* he won't get round until later, we may as well have dinner now (b) *(difundirse)* the news is getting round quickly
2 **VT INSEP** (a) *(evitar)* there's no getting round it, you'll have to own up; how did they get round the export regulations? (b) *(ganarse)* I can always get round my father
3 **VT SEP** *(convencer)* you've got me round to your way of thinking

get round to VT INSEP *(encontrar tiempo para)* I'll get round to it eventually, I promise

get through 1 VI (a) *(pasar)* the cars could not get through because the pass was blocked with snow; will the message get through? (b) *(comunicarse telefónicamente)* the lines must be down, I can't get through (c) **U.S.** *(acabar)* the evening class does not usually get through until nine o'clock (d) *(aprobar un examen)* only three of the class didn't get through
2 **VT INSEP** (a) *(franquear)* you will not be able to get through the roadblock (b) *(aprobar)* I got through my exams second time around (c) *(acabar, terminar)* will you get through your homework in time to come to the match? (d) *(utilizar, ponerse)* he gets through a dozen shirts a week (e) *(ocupar el tiempo)* since she retired, she's been finding it difficult to get through the days
3 **VT SEP** (a) *(hacer llegar)* they got the food supplies through just in time (b) *(hacer comprender)* I finally got it through to him that I wasn't interested (c) *(hacer aprobar un examen)* it was your essay that got you through

get to VT INSEP (a) *(llegar a)* how do we get to their house from here? (b) *(poder, conseguir)* did you actually get to speak to the Prime Minister? (c) *(comenzar a, empezar a)* you know, I've

got to wondering if maybe he's right after all (d) **FAM.**
(molestar, fastidiar) she really got to me with her sarcastic
remarks; don't let it get to you! (es decir, *ino dejes que eso te
afecte!*)

get together 1 **VI** *(reunirse)* when can we get together to discuss the
project?; *(verse, quedar)* he's getting together with the bank
manager tomorrow
2 **VT SEP** *(recoger)* get your things together

get up 1 **VI** (a) *(levantarse de la cama)* it's time to get up (b) *(levantarse, ponerse de pie)* he got up to address the audience (c)
(avecinarse) there's a storm getting up
2 **VT SEP** (a) *(despertar)* will you get me up early tomorrow? (b)
(subir) how are we going to get this up to the top floor? (c)
(aumentar) we'll get up speed when we reach the motorway
(d) *(organizar)* we've got up a petition to protest about the
closure (e) *(vestir)* the children are always nicely got up

get up to **VT INSEP** (a) *(llegar a, ir por)* I've got up to the fifth chapter (b)
(hacer tonterías) those children are always getting up to mis-
chief; I don't want you getting up to anything while I'm out

give away **VT SEP** (a) *(dar)* I gave it away to someone who needed it
more (b) *(llevar al altar)* her uncle is to give her away (c)
(traicionar, denunciar) who gave us away?; *(locución)* to give
the game away *irse de la lengua*

give in 1 **VT SEP** *(entregar)* give your homework in; I gave the wallet
in to the police
2 **VI** *(ceder)* try not to give in to temptation; *(darse por vencido)* I give in, tell me what the answer is

give off **VT SEP** *(producir, desprender)* this fire gives off a lot of heat;
something is giving off a bad smell

give onto **VT INSEP** *(dar a)* the windows give onto the main road so it's
a noisy flat

give out 1 **VT SEP** (a) *(distribuir)* they were giving out leaflets about
abortion (b) *(anunciar)* the Chancellor gave out the trade figures today (c) *(producir, generar)* the radiators are not giving
out much heat
2 **VI** (a) *(averiarse)* the old car has finally given out
(b) *(agotarse, faltar)* supplies have given out; *(estar al límite,
agotarse)* my patience is giving out

give over vt sep (a) *(confiar)* he gave the children over to his mother; *(poner a disposición de, dejar)* the vicar gave the hall over to the scouts (b) *(consagrar, dedicar)* they gave the entire evening over to a discussion of the film

give up 1 vt sep (a) *(perder la esperanza, etc.)* the climbers gave up hope of being found before nightfall; *(dejar estar, dejar correr)* give it up as a bad job (b) *(renunciar, dejar de)* she is giving up chocolate as part of her diet; I've given up trying (c) *(dejar, ceder)* I gave up my seat on the bus to a pregnant woman (d) *(entregarse)* the scaped prisoner gave himself up after two days (e) *(dar por)* to give someone up for dead/lost (f) *(consagrar, dedicar)* I gave the entire week up to studying (g) *(no esperar más)* we had almost given you up
2 vi *(rendirse)* don't shoot, we give up; *(rendirse, darse por vencido)* OK, tell me the answer then, I give up

give up on vt insep *(no esperar más, dejar de esperar)* we gave up on you after waiting for an hour; *(desahuciar)* how can a mother give up on her daughter and say she's no good?

gloss over vt sep (a) *(pasar por alto, ignorar)* she very kindly glossed over my mistakes; I tend to gloss those things over (b) *(ocultar algo de)* he glosses over his past

go about 1 vi *(circular)* there's a story going about that they've separated; there seems to be a virus going about; you can't go about saying things like that (es decir, *no puedes ir contando ese tipo de cosas*)
2 vt insep (a) *(hacer)* what's the best way to go about buying a house? (b) *(ocuparse de)* just go about your business as usual

go about with vt insep *(salir con)* my son has been going about with her for a year now

go after vt insep (a) *(atrapar)* go after them! (b) *(intentar conseguir)* she's going after the world record; she really goes after what she wants

go ahead vi (a) *(ir delante)* you go ahead, we'll follow later (b) *(seguir adelante)* if you have something to say to me, just go ahead!; they have decided to go ahead with the wedding; he just went ahead and did it (c) *(avanzar)* the project is going ahead quite satisfactorily

go along VI (a) *(pasar por)* she met him as she was going along the road (b) *(hacer sobre la marcha)* please check your punctuation as you go along

go along with VT INSEP *(aceptar)* that's what they decided and I went along with it; *(estar de acuerdo con)* I cannot go along with you on that; *(respetar)* he went along with his father's wishes

go at VT INSEP *(abalanzarse sobre)* he went at the wall with a hammer; the children ignored the sandwiches and went at the cakes instead

go back VI (a) *(volver)* let's go back some day (b) *(devolver)* when do these library books have to go back?; my new shoes will have to go back - they don't fit properly (c) *(retrasar)* don't forget that the clocks go back tomorrow (d) *(remontarse a)* the church has records going back to the 16th century

go back on VT INSEP *(faltar a)* I cannot go back on my promise to her; he never goes back on his decisions

go by 1 VI *(pasar)* as the parade was going by...; many years have gone by since we met; don't let this opportunity go by 2 VT INSEP (a) *(guiarse por)* don't go by my opinion – I hate that kind of film; if you go by that clock, you'll miss the train (b) *(seguir)* he never goes by the rules; go by your brother's example (c) *(ser conocido por)* she has been going by her maiden name since the divorce

go down VI (a) *(ponerse el sol, etc.)* the sun is going down (b) *(hundirse)* the ship went down with all hands (c) *(bajar)* house prices may go down; *(descender)* flood waters are going down (d) *(degradarse, venir a menos)* my old neighbourhood has really gone down; his family has gone down in the world (es decir, *su familia ha conocido tiempos mejores*); *(tener en menos estima)* she went down in my estimation when I found out hat really happened (e) *(perder contra)* Mexico went down to Germany; I won't go down without a fight (es decir, *no voy a rendirme sin luchar*) (f) *(ser recibido)* my suggestion did not go down very well; how did your proposal go down with the director?; British actors often go down well in the States (g) *(bajar)* some water will help the pill go down; *(beberse, pasar)* this wine goes down very nicely, don't you think? (h) *(dejar huella)* she will go down in history as a woman of great courage (i) *(colgarse, hablando de un orde-*

nador) the computer's gone down (j) *(caer enfermo)* he went down with flu on the first day of the holidays, the poor thing

go for **VT INSEP** (a) *(ir a buscar)* he went for a doctor (b) *(atacar)* what was I supposed to do when she went for me with a knife?; we heard them going for each other in the street (c) *(intentar conseguir)* with this next jump, he's going for the gold medal; she's going for his job; **FAM.** go for it! (es decir, *iadelante!, ia por ello!)* (d) **FAM.** *(gustar)* I don't really go for that idea; he really goes for her in a big way (es decir, *está loco por ella)*; *(preferir)* she's always gone for the tall, dark and handsome type (e) *(ir por, concernir)* what I said goes for both of you (f) *(servir para)* his twenty years of service went for nothing

go in **VI** (a) *(entrar)* it's cold, let's go in (b) *(ponerse el sol, etc.)* the sun's gone in

go in for **VT INSEP** (a) *(dedicarse a)* they have decided to go in for catering (b) **FAM.** *(sentirse atraído por)* he doesn't go in for team sports; my parents don't go in for opera (c) *(participar, tomar parte en)* are you going in for the four hundred metres?

go into **VT INSEP** (a) *(entrar en, ingresar en)* our special training programme is now going into its third year; she has to go into hospital (b) *(dedicarse a)* she wants her daughter to go into teaching (c) *(empezar a, ponerse a)* the car went into a skid; he nearly went into hysterics (es decir, *estuvo a punto de ponerse histérico)*; *(abordar)* we won't go into that for the moment (d) *(lanzarse a)* my grandmother then went into a long and detailed description of her childhood

go off 1 **VI** (a) *(irse)* she has gone off with the man next door; he's gone off on some business of his own (b) *(echarse a perder, hablando de la comida)* the milk has gone off (c) *(apagarse)* the lights went off all over the city last night (d) *(sonar)* the alarm went off at the usual time; *(dispararse)* he said that the gun just went off in his hand (e) *(ser acogido)* how did the play go off?; my presentation went off well/badly
2 **VT INSEP** *(perder el interés por)* I've gone off him since I found out how unpleasant he is; she says she has gone off Spain

go on 1 **vi** (a) *(continuar)* go on, what did he say then?; just go on with what you were doing; do we have enough coffee to be going on with or should I buy some more? (b) *(combinar)* your coat won't go on unless you wear a different sweater; *(ir, colocarse, etc.)* the lid goes on this way (c) *(encenderse)* the street lights go on when it gets dark (d) **fam.** *(hablar sin parar)* once he starts, he goes on and on (e) *(pasar, suceder)* what's going on? (f) *(pasar, hablando del tiempo)* as time went on, I realized that I'd made the right decision 2 **vt insep** (a) *(empezar, comenzar)* most people go on a diet at least once (b) *(guiarse por, basarse en)* I have nothing concrete to go on, I just don't trust him (c) *(rondar, hablando de una edad)* she's going on forty-five (d) **fam.** *(estar colado por, gustar)* my sister is really gone on the boy next door; I don't go much on abstract art

go on at **vt insep fam.** *(dar la lata a, molestar)* my parents keep going on at me to get a job

go out **vi** (a) *(salir)* they were just about to go out; *(salir de casa)* she doesn't go out much these days; we're going out for dinner (b) *(salir con)* she's been going out with him for years (c) *(ser eliminado)* I bet his team goes out in the first round (d) *(apagarse)* put some wood on the fire before it goes out; the lights went out (e) *(ser enviado)* has that letter gone out? (f) *(locución)* I went out like a light *me dormí al instante* (g) *(pasar de moda)* jeans will never go out (h) *(descender, hablando de la marea)* the tide has gone out

go over 1 **vi** (a) *(ir a un lugar preciso)* I went over and tapped him on the shoulder (b) *(pasarse, cambiarse)* they've gone over to the Conservative Party; he's thinking about going over to cigars (c) *(ser aceptado)* my suggestion didn't go over at all well 2 **vt insep** (a) *(revisar)* we should go over the accounts (b) *(revisar, repasar)* let's go over your speech a second time (c) *(hablar de)* we must have gone over this point a dozen times already

go round 1 **vi** (a) *(visitar, ir)* you ought to go round and see him; she's gone round to her mother's (b) *(bastar)* there won't be enough to go round *(es decir, no habrá suficiente para todo el mundo)* (c) *(coger un desvío)* there was a road accident so we had to go round the long way (d) *(dar vueltas)* everything is going round

2 vt insep (a) *(tomar, hablando de un camino)* I went round the long way to be sure of not getting lost (b) *(visitar)* we must have gone round every museum in town; she went round the neighbourhood looking for her cat (c) *(bastar, ser suficiente)* is the roast big enough to go round everyone?

go through 1 vi *(ser aceptado, concluir)* the deal has gone through; *(consumarse)* when does the divorce go through?
2 vt insep (a) *(sufrir)* she has gone through a lot in recent years (b) *(examinar, estudiar)* the detective went through the witness's statement very carefully (c) *(buscar en)* I've gone through all the papers and I still can't find it (d) *(repetir, para memorizar)* how often do you have to go through your lines before you know them by heart? (e) *(gastar, por el uso)* children go through a lot of shoes; *(consumir)* we've gone through six pints of milk in two days (f) *(ser aprobado)* the bill went through Parliament last week

go through with vt insep *(llevara a término)* he decided at the last moment that he couldn't go through with the wedding; management went through with its threat to close the factory

go together vi (a) *(combinar)* do these colours go together? (b) *(salir juntos)* we've been going together for a long time

go towards vt insep *(estar destinado a)* the proceeds from the fête are going towards a new village hall

go under 1 vi (a) *(hundirse)* it's too late, he's gone under (b) **fig.** *(hundirse, venirse abajo)* his business is going under and there isn't much he can do about it
2 vt insep *(ser conocido como)* since the divorce she's been going under her old name of Williams

go up vi (a) *(subir)* just go up, he's expecting you (b) *(subir, aumentar)* the patient's temperature had been going up for some time; house prices are going up again (c) *(levantarse)* the curtain will go up at eight o'clock (d) *(ser destruido)* the building went up in flames; *(locución)* his hopes went up in smoke *sus esperanzas se esfumaron*

go with vt insep (a) *(ir con, llevar aparejado)* mathematical skills usually go with an ability to play chess (b) *(combinar, no pegar con)* change your tie, it doesn't go with that shirt

go without 1 vi *(pasar sin)* those are too dear – if you don't like any of the others you'll just have to go without
2 vt insep *(prescindir de)* I went without breakfast so I wouldn't be late

grow apart vi *(distanciarse)* they have grown apart over the years

grow in vi *(crecer de nuevo)* your hair will grow in soon

grow out of vt insep (a) *(hacerse demasiado grande, no caber en)* he has grown out of those shoes we bought just a few months ago (b) *(ser más maduro que)* I've grown out of my friends; *(abandonar la costumbre de)* when are you going to grow out of biting your nails?

grow up vi (a) *(crecer, hacerse mayor)* children grow up so fast nowadays (b) *(comportarse como un adulto)* I wish you would grow up! (c) *(surgir)* a theory has grown up that...

guard against vt insep *(prevenir)* take vitamin C to guard against colds

hammer home vt sep (a) *(clavar bien con un martillo)* be sure to hammer all the nails home (b) *(insistir en, machacar)* we hammered home the importance of wearing seat belts

hammer out vt sep (a) *(desabollar)* I'll have to hammer these dents out (b) *(llegar a)* they have finally managed to hammer out an agreement on the withdrawal of troops

hand back vt sep *(devolver)* I'll hand it back to you as soon as I've finished

hand down vt sep (a) *(pasar, alcanzar desde un lugar elevado)* hand that plate down to me (b) *(dejar en herencia)* she handed the necklace down to her granddaughter (c) *(dictar una sentencia)* will be handed down soon

hand in vt sep *(entregar)* I want you to hand in your essays tomorrow

hand out vt sep (a) *(repartir)* I've offered to hand leaflets out (b) *(dar)* you can always rely on him to hand out advice

hand over 1 vt sep (a) *(pasar, dar)* hand over your wallet (b) *(entregar)* she handed the papers over to the lawyer for safekeeping (c) *(ceder)* he will be handing over the reins of power very soon; we now hand you over to our foreign affairs correspondent (es decir, *ahora conectamos con nuestro corresponsal...*)

2 **vi** *(ceder la palabra)* I now hand over to the weatherman; *(pasar el poder)* when will he be handing over to the new chairman?

hang about/around **FAM.** 1 **vi** (a) *(esperar)* I had to hang about for ages before he finally arrived (b) *(entretenerse)* don't hang about or we'll never finish

2 **vt INSEP** *(frecuentar, pasearse por)* I don't want you hanging about amusement arcades

hang back **vi** *(quedarse atrás)* if you have a contribution to make to the discussion, please don't hang back; *(dudar)* I hung back from saying anything as it wasn't really my place to do so

hang down **vi** *(caer)* her hair hung down in ringlets

hang in **vi** **FAM.** *(aguantar)* hang in there, we'll get you out soon; he'll just have to hang in until a better job comes along

hang on 1 **vi** (a) *(agarrarse)* hang on tight (b) **FAM.** *(esperar)* can you hang on for a couple of minutes?

2 **vt INSEP** (a) *(escuchar atentamente)* the audience was hanging on the speaker's every word (es decir, *el público no se perdía ni una palabra del orador*) (b) *(depender de)* the fate of the project hangs on the availability of supplies

hang on to **vt INSEP** (a) *(agarrarse a)* he hung on to the cliff face (b) *(conservar)* I'd hang on to those documents if I were you

hang out **vi** (a) *(colgar)* your shirt tails are hanging out (b) **FAM.** *(andar)* I'm looking for Bill – any idea where he hangs out? (c) **FAM.** *(insistir)* I'm hanging out for a rise

hang together **vi** *(tenerse en pie, ser consistente)* the plot of the film doesn't hang together

hang up 1 **vi** *(colgar el teléfono)* don't hang up until you've heard what she has to say; hang up immediately

2 **vt SEP** *(colgar)* hang your coat up

happen along **vi** **FAM.** *(llegar por casualidad)* then, thank goodness, a policeman happened along

hark back to vt insep *(volver a, hablando de un tema)* he keeps harking back to the war

have around vt sep *(tener a mano)* it's always a good idea to have some candles around

have back vt sep (a) *(recuperar)* can I have it back? (b) *(devolver la invitación)* we're having them back next Saturday

have in vt sep (a) *(llamar)* we'll have to have the plumber in to fix that leak (b) *(invitar a casa)* the old ladies across the street like having people in for tea (c) *(locución)* to have it in for someone *(tenerla tomada con alguien)*

have off vt sep (a) *(quitar)* the doctor had the plaster off in no time at all (b) *(mandar quitar)* she's having the plaster off next week (c) Brit. fam. *(echar un polvo)* he's been having it off with a different woman every weekend for years

have on vt sep (a) *(llevar puesto, hablando de una prenda)* he looks totally different when he doesn't have his business suit on (b) Brit. fam. *(tomar el pelo)* didn't you realize I was having you on? (c) *(tener algo que hacer)* she has a lot on this week; I have something else on, I'm afraid (d) *(tener pruebas contra)* he told the police they had nothing on him – he'd been in hospital at the time (e) *(poner, instalar)* once we have the roof rack on, we'll be ready to go

have out vt sep (a) *(operarse, sacarse)* he's in hospital having his appendix out (b) *(aclarar)* let's have this out once and for all (es decir, *aclaremos las cosas de una vez por todas*)

have up vt sep (a) *(montar, instalar)* they worked all night to have the exhibits up in time for the opening (b) *(invitar al vecino de abajo o a alguien que procede del sur)* he had them up (to his flat) for tea; we're having them up from London for the weekend

head for vt insep (a) *(ir a, dirigirse a)* where is he headed for?; let's head for home (b) *(ir camino de)* the country is heading for civil war; she's heading for a disappointment if she thinks he's going to propose

head off vt sep (a) *(desviar la atención de, mantener distraído a)* head Mum off for a couple of minutes while I finish wrapping her present (b) *(evitar)* to head off accusations of favouritism...

head up VT SEP *(presidir, estar a la cabeza de)* how many committees does she head up?

hear of VT INSEP (a) *(oír hablar de)* I've never heard of her; *(estar al corriente de)* the whole town had heard of his success
(b) *normalmente en forma negativa (aceptar, dejar)* I won't hear of you going to a hotel when we've got a spare room

hear out VT SEP *(escuchar hasta el final)* please hear me out; the committee heard her out before reaching a decision

heat up 1 VI (a) *(calentarse, caldearse)* the room will soon heat up (b) FIG. *(acalorarse, subir de tono)* the discussion heated up and turned into an argument
2 VT SEP *(calentar)* heat up some milk; *(calentar, hacer entrar en calor)* a bowl of soup will heat you up

hide out VI *(esconderse)* he's hiding out in some hotel to get away from his fans

hit back 1 VI *(replicar, responder)* he hit back with accusations that they were accepting bribes
2 VT SEP *(devolver)* hit the ball back; *(devolver el golpe a)* he hit her so she hit him back

hit off VT SEP (a) *(imitar)* he hits the Prime Minister off very well (b) FAM. *(locución)* we hit it off immediately *enseguida hicimos buenas migas*

hit on VT INSEP *(encontrar)* I've hit on a possible solution

hit out VI (a) *(repartir golpes)* all of a sudden he started hitting out (b) *(atacar)* all the speakers at the conference hit out at the proposals

hive off 1 VI *(diversificarse)* they're hiving off into the retail side of things
2 VT SEP *(deshacerse de)* my boss is furious that the company wants to hive off the research team

hold against VT SEP *(reprochar, recriminar)* why do you hold my past against me?; she's very naive but you can't hold that against her

hold back 1 VI *(permanecer en silencio, contenerse)* I held back while the two of them discussed old times; he held back from making any comment

2 **vt sep** (a) *(retener, contener)* security guards held the fans back; he held back his rage (b) *(impedir progresar)* your poor performance in maths is holding you back (c) *(ocultar)* she's holding something back, I know she is; don't hold anything back

hold down **vt sep** (a) *(sujetar, controlar)* it took two of us to hold him down (b) *(limitar, impedir la subida de)* the government must take action to hold down interest rates (c) *(tener, hablando de un empleo)* she is holding down a fairly high-powered job; *(mantener, hablando de un empleo)* can he hold this job down?

hold forth **vi** *(explayarse sobre)* she held forth a great length on the benefits of aromatherapy (es decir, *ella hizo un largo discurso sobre los beneficios de la aromaterapia*)

hold in **vt sep** (a) *(meter tripa)* for heaven's sake, hold your stomach in (b) *(retener, contener)* she shouldn't hold her emotions in

hold off 1 **vi** (a) *(no decidirse a llover, hablando de lluvia)* the rain seems to be holding off (b) *(abstenerse)* hold off from smoking for a few weeks
2 **vt sep** *(mantener a distancia)* the troops held off the enemy; *(resistir)* the remaining men managed to hold off the attack until reinforcements arrived

hold on **vi** (a) *(guardar, quedarse con)* hold on to this contract for me (b) *(agarrarse)* hold on tightly!; *(aguantar, sujetar bien)* hold on to your hat! (c) *(aguantar, resistir)* I can't hold on much longer (d) *(esperar)* hold on, how do I know I can trust you?

hold out 1 **vi** (a) *(durar)* our supplies will not hold out for long (b) *(aguantar)* can you hold out until the doctor gets here?
2 **vt sep** (a) *(tender)* she held out her hand (b) *(dar, hablando de esperanzas, una posibilidad)* the doctor doesn't hold out much hope for a complete recovery

hold out on **vt insep** *(ocultar a)* you've been holding out on me – I didn't know you played the saxophone

hold to 1 **vt insep** *(aferrarse)* he held to his decision
2 **vt sep** *(hacer cumplir)* we held him to his promise

hold up 1 **vi** (a) *(aguantar en pie)* the centuries-old house continues to hold up (b) *(aguantar, estar tranquilo)* she held up magnificently under the strain

2 **vt sep** (a) *(levantar)* she held her face up to the sun (b) *(mantener, sostener)* the tent is held up with just a couple of pegs (c) *(retrasar)* bad weather is holding the project up (d) *(atracar)* armed men held up another bank yesterday

hold with **vt insep** **Brit.** *(aprobar, estar de acuerdo con)* I don't hold with private education

hole up **vi** **fam.** *(esconderse)* the bank robbers decided to hole up for a while

home in on **vt insep** (a) *(dirigirse a)* the missiles can home in on the heat of aircraft engines (b) *(señalar)* she homed in on my one mistake

hook up 1 **vi** (a) *(abrocharse)* the dress hooks up at the back (b) *(conectar)* we will be hooking up with European networks to bring you this very special programme
2 **vt sep** *(abrochar, hablando de una prenda de vestir)* hook me up

hot up **fam.** 1 **vi** *(acalorarse)* the argument hotted up when one of them swore at the other; things are hotting up again on the industrial relations front
2 **vt sep** *(aumentar, forzar)* they are hotting up the pace

hunt down **vt sep** (a) *(perseguir)* they are being hunted down by state and federal police (b) *(capturar)* he was finally hunted down

hunt out(up) **vt sep** *(lograr encontrar, dar con)* I've hunted out those old family photographs you wanted to see

hurry along 1 **vi** *(darse prisa)* you're hurrying along as if we were late; hurry along please, the museum is now closed
2 **vt sep** *(acelerar)* I'm trying to hurry the project along but it's not easy; you can't hurry these things along

hurry up 1 **vi** *(darse prisa)* do hurry up or we'll be late
2 **vt sep** *(meter prisa)* I'll go and hurry them up; *(acelerar)* could you hurry things up a bit, please, the deadline is fast approaching

ice over vi *(helarse)* this river is too fast-flowing to ever ice over

ice up vi *(helarse)* the crash was attributed in part to the plane's wings having iced up; I can't get the key in – the lock must have iced up

improve on vt insep *(mejorar)* we have to improve on last year's performance; she'll have to improve on that score with her next jump

iron out vt sep (a) *(planchar)* I'll iron out these creases in your shirt for you (b) fig. *(limar)* have you ironed out your differences?; *(resolver)* there are one or two little problems that must be ironed out

jack in vi sep Brit. fam. (a) *(dejar)* I'm going to jack this job in as soon as I can (b) *(cerrar el pico)* jack it in!

jack up vt sep (a) *(alzar con el gato)* he had to jack up the car to change the wheel (b) fam. *(aumentar, subir)* they've jacked up the price of petrol again

jam in(to) 1 vt sep (a) *(empujar)* the crowd were jamming him in (b) *(meter)* can you jam anything else in?; he had jammed as many quotations as he could find into the essay 2 vi *(apretujarse)* hundreds of people jammed in to hear her speech

jam on vt sep *(pisar bruscamente)* I had to jam on my brakes or I would have hit him; *(encasquetarse)* she jammed her hat on and marched out

jam up vt sep *(provocar atascos)* Sunday motorists in search of a good spot for a picnic have jammed up the roads

jar on vt insep *(iriritar)* that constant banging is jarring on my nerves

jazz up vt sep fam. *(crear ambiente, animar)* it's very dull in here tonight – couldn't we jazz things up a bit?; *(alegrar, animar)* jazz up a plain dress with some costume jewellery

jockey for VT SEP *(luchar por, sobre todo hablando de un empleo o un puesto de trabajo)* everyone is jockeying for the position of chairperson

jog along VI *(avanzar, seguir su ritmo)* the work is jogging along

join in 1 VI *(participar)* I want everyone to join in
2 VT INSEP *(tomar parte en, participar)* I joined in the fun

join on 1 VI *(engancharse)* where does this bit join on?
2 VT SEP *(enganchar)* they've joined on another carriage

join up 1 VI (a) *(alistarse)* he joined up as soon as war was declared
(b) *(reunirse)* the two groups will join up here
2 VT SEP *(juntar, unir)* join the ends up

jot down VT SEP *(apuntar, anotar)* he jotted down a few notes for his speech; just jot it down

jump at VT INSEP *(no dejar escapar)* I jumped at the chance of a holiday in Spain; when he offered her the position she jumped at it

jump down 1 VI *(saltar)* there aren't any steps, you'll have to jump down; he jumped down from the window
2 VT INSEP FAM. *(locución)* to jump down someone's throat *echar los perros a alguien*

jump on 1 VI *(tomar, coger)* there was a bus sitting at the traffic lights so he decided to jump on
2 VT INSEP FAM. (a) *(abalanzarse sobre)* the hooligans jumped on the old man at the corner of the street (b) *(echar la bronca a)* he jumps on me for the least little thing

keel over VI (a) *(zozobrar)* the lifeboat keeled over (b) *(desmayarse)* he keels over at the sight of blood; *(caerse)* the hat stand just keeled over

keep at 1 VT INSEP (a) *(continuar trabajando en)* if he wants to get into university, he'll have to keep at his maths (b) *(atosigar)* she kept at me until I agreed
2 VT SEP *(hacer trabajar)* the boss kept us hard at it all morning

keep away 1 **vi** *(mantenerse alejado)* keep away from the cooker!; I knew you had visitors so I kept away (es decir, *sabía que tenías visita y por eso no he venido*); *(no sucumbir, resistirse)* she can't keep away from chocolates

2 **vt sep** *(mantener alejado)* keep him away from me

keep back 1 **vi** *(no acercarse)* a policeman was telling people to keep back

2 **vt sep** (a) *(mantener alejado)* the security guards at the concert had trouble keeping the fans back from the stage (b) *(contener)* I couldn't keep back my tears; *(no decir, ocultar)* she's keeping something back from us (c) *(hacer repetir, hablando de un alumno)* he has been kept back a year (d) *(entretener)* am I keeping you back?

keep down 1 **vi** *(mantenerse agachado)* keep down or he'll see us

2 **vt sep** (a) *(no levantar, bajar)* the policemen surrounding the house were told to keep their heads down; please keep your voice down, some people are trying to concentrate (b) *(mantener, alimentos)* I think it must be a virus, I haven't been able to keep anything down for days (**es decir,** *creo que es un virus, llevo días vomitando todo lo que como*) (c) *(contener)* the government is not doing anything to keep inflation down; he's trying to keep his weight down (**es decir,** *intenta mantener la línea*); *(evitar que algo prolifere)* it's a full-time job keeping the weeds down in this garden

keep from 1 **vt sep** (a) *(esconder, ocultar)* they kept the news from the old lady for as long as possible; what are you keeping from me? (b) *(impedir)* the climber hung on to his partner's hand to keep him from falling over the edge; I'm trying to keep you from harm (**es decir,** *intento protegerte*) (c) *(distraer de)* I mustn't keep you from your work

2 **vt insep** *(evitar hacer)* he was such a boring speaker that I couldn't keep from nodding off

keep in with **vt insep** *(llevarse bien con)* if you want to keep in with him, just agree with everything he says

keep off 1 **vi** *(no acercarse)* that's my property, keep off!

2 **vt insep** (a) *(no pisar)* keep off the grass (b) *(evitar)* they tactfully kept off the subject of divorce; the doctor has ordered him to keep off alcohol

3 **vt sep** (a) *(alejar, proteger de)* this cream will keep the mosquitoes off; Mum said to keep our hands off the cakes (es decir, *no tocar*) (b) *(quitarse, hablando de una prenda de vestir)* don't keep your coat off for long or you'll get cold

keep on 1 **vi** (a) *(continuar)* if they keep on like this much longer, I'm going to call the police (b) **FAM.** *(hablar sin parar)* he keeps on about his kids
2 **vt sep** (a) *(mantener, hablando de un empleado)* we can't afford to keep the cleaning woman on (b) *(dejarse puesto, hablando de una prenda de vestir)* make sure the baby keeps her gloves on

keep on at **vt insep** *(amonestar, echar la bronca a)* the headmaster keeps on at his pupils about their behaviour

keep out 1 **vi** (a) *(no entrar)* danger – keep out!
(b) *(mantenerse al margen de)* try to keep out of trouble; *(no mezclarse en, no intervenir en)* I'm keeping out of this argument
2 **vt sep** (a) *(impedir la entrada a)* lock the door to keep people out; *(proteger de)* these boots are supposed to keep the rain out (b) *(locución)* keep out of the reach of children *mantener fuera del alcance de los niños* (c) *(no mezclar, mantener al margen)* I'll do my best to keep you out of this

keep to 1 **vt insep** (a) *(cumplir)* we must keep to the agenda and introduce new subjects for discussion; people should keep to their promises (b) *(mantenerse en)* keep to the right
2 **vt sep** (a) *(ceñirse a)* we are endeavouring to keep delays to a minimum (b) *(locución)* to keep something to oneself *guardarse algo para sí*

keep up 1 **vi** (a) *(continuar)* if this snow keeps up much longer the roads will be blocked (b) *(seguir el ritmo)* she dictated so quickly that her secretary couldn't keep up (c) *(seguir en contacto)* have you kept up with them since they moved away?
2 **vt sep** (a) *(sostener, sujetar)* he needs a belt to keep his trousers up; keep your spirits up! (es decir, *¡mantén el ánimo!*) (b) *(mantener, continuar)* we kept up a fairly regular exchange of letters until quite recently; keep it up, you're doing fine (c) *(seguir)* it seems impossible for him to keep this pace up (d) *(cuidar)* the garden hasn't been kept up very well (e)

(tener en vela) our dinner guests kept us up until three o'clock this morning

kick about/around 1 **vi** **FAM.** *(estar por ahí)* don't leave the paper kicking about; find yourself something to do instead of kicking around
2 **vt sep** (a) *(dar patadas a)* they're not doing any harm kicking a ball around (b) **FAM.** *(pisotear, tratar a patadas)* you've kicked me around long enough (c) **FAM.** *(debatir)* we kicked the proposal around for a while but finally decided against it

kick in **vt sep** *(derribar a patadas)* we lost our key and had to kick the door in; **FAM.** *(locución)* I'll kick his teeth in! *¡voy a partirle la boca!*

kick off 1 **vi** (a) *(hacer el saque inicial)* when do they kick off? (b) **FAM.** *(empezar)* our speaker will now answer questions – who's going to kick off?; let's kick off with a situation report
2 **vt sep** (a) *(quitar de una patada)* it's always such a relief to kick your shoes off (b) **FAM.** *(expulsar de, echar de)* they're going to kick him off the team for misconduct

kick out 1 **vi** *(dar coces)* the mules kicked out whenever anyone approached; *(dar patadas)* she would kick out at anyone who came near
2 **vt sep FAM.** *(poner de patitas en la calle a)* his wife has kicked him out and he's got nowhere to go

kick up **vt sep FAM.** *(crear problemas)* he'll kick up an awful fuss when he finds out (es decir, *cuando lo sepa montará un número*)

knock about/around 1 **vi** = kick about/around
2 **vt sep FAM.** (a) *(pegar)* he knocks her about regularly (b) *(sufrir desperfectos)* the car was knocked about a good bit but the driver is unharmed (c) *(traquetear)* we were really knocked about in the back of the truck (d) **FAM.** *(debatir, discutir)* we knocked the idea about for a while

knock back **vt sep** (a) **FAM.** *(chuparse, hablando de una bebida)* he's knocking the whisky back a bit, isn't he? (b) **FAM.** *(costar)* how much did that knock you back? (c) **BRIT.** *(dar calabazas a)* she knocked him back; *(rechazar)* they knocked the invitation back

knock down **VT SEP** (a) *(demoler)* the council wants to knock those houses down (b) *(atropellar)* the car that knocked her down was moving much too fast; *(derribar)* the champion knocked his opponent down in the first round (c) *(hacer bajar el precio a)* we're trying to knock them down to something we can afford; *(bajar el precio de)* she knocked it down a fair bit (d) **BRIT.** *(adjudicar)* both paintings were knocked down to dealers

knock off 1 **VI FAM.** *(acabar de trabajar)* I'll try to knock off early
2 **VT SEP** (a) *(tirar, volcar)* there's water everywhere, the cat must have knocked the vase off

 (b) *(rebajar)* could you knock a pound or two off?

(c) **FAM.** *(hacer de cualquier manera, chapucear)* she knocks those sketches off by the dozen

(d) **FAM.** *(birlar, mangar)* those watches that he's trying to sell have probably been knocked off

(e) **FAM.** *(cargarse)* she's terrified he'll be knocked off for informing on the gang leader

(f) **FAM.** *(locución)* knock it off! *¡déjalo ya!*

knock out **VT SEP** (a) *(dejar K.O.)* the challenger knocked the champion out with a single punch; *(anestesiar, dormir)* will they knock you out or just give you a local anaesthetic? (b) *(eliminar)* that's her knocked out of Wimbledon already! (c) **FAM.** *(agotar, dejar hecho polvo)* those children have knocked me out (d) **FAM.** *(dejar alucinado)* his performance absolutely knocked me out (e) *(destruir)* the government jets knocked out two rebel encampments; the storm has knocked out power supplies to a great many homes (f) *(vaciar, limpiar)* knocking his pipe out, he said...

knock over **VT SEP** *(derribar, atropellar)* he knocked several people over as he ran away; a bus knocked her over

knock together 1 **VI** *(entrechocarse)* my knees were knocking together at the thought of the interview
2 **VT SEP FAM.** *(hacer deprisa y corriendo)* I've promised to knock a tree house together for the kids

knock up 1 **VI BRIT.** *(pelotear, en tenis)* the players are allowed two minutes to knock up

2 vt sep (a) Brit. *(despertar, llamando a la puerta)* will you knock me up at six o'clock? **(b) fam.** *(hacer deprisa y corriendo)* if you don't mind leftovers, I'll knock a quick meal up for you **(c) fam.** *(dejar preñada a)* he's knocked her up

know of vt insep (a) *(saber)* has Bill arrived? – not that I know of **(b)** *(haber oído hablar de)* I don't know him personally, but I know of him; *(saber de)* nothing is known of her whereabouts

knuckle under vt insep *(ceder)* I won't knuckle under to threats

lash down 1 vt sep *(sujetar, atar firmemente)* the lorry driver lashed the tarpaulin down
2 vi *(llover a cántaros)* it's lashing down

lash into vt insep Brit. (a) *(atacar)* the two men lashed into each other **(b)** *(arremeter contra)* I lashed into her for making such silly mistakes

lash out 1 vi (a) *(dar patadas o puñetazos)* he lashed out at the police officer who was trying to arrest him; **fig.** *(arremeter contra)* she lashes out at anyone who opposes her **(b) Brit. fam.** *(pulirse el dinero)* I think I'll lash out and treat myself to a new coat
2 vt sep Brit. fam. *(pulirse)* they lashed out a couple of thousand pounds on that holiday to the States

last out 1 vi (a) *(resistir)* how long will he last out?; I don't think I can last out at this job **(b)** *(alcanzar, llegar)* will our water last out?
2 vt sep *(pasar)* she is not expected to last out the night; we have enough supplies to last out the winter

laugh off vt sep *(burlarse de, reírse de)* he laughed off everyone's warnings

launch into vt insep *(embarcarse en, lanzarse a)* he launched into a glowing description of the car he had just bought

launch out vi *(diversificarse)* the company is going to launch out and add textiles to its product range; *(locución)* to launch out on one's own *trabajar por cuenta propia*

lay about **VT INSEP FAM.** *(repartir golpes a diestro y siniestro a)* the old lady laid about him with her stick

lay down **VT SEP** (a) *(dejar)* he laid his glass down on the table; *(deponer)* the rebels have announced that they will lay down their arms (b) *(renunciar a)* she laid down her life for her beliefs (c) *(establecer, estipular)* it is laid down in the regulations; *(locución)* to lay down the law *dar órdenes*

lay in **VT SEP** *(proveerse de)* we have laid in enough canned goods to feed an army; you had better lay some wood in

lay off 1 **VI FAM.** *(dejar)* I've had as much criticism as I can take, so lay off
2 **VT INSEP FAM.** *(dejar en paz a)* my sister doesn't want to go out with you so lay off her
3 **VT SEP** *(despedir)* the company will be laying 350 employees off within the next few weeks

lay on **VT SEP** *(proveer de)* water and electricity are both laid on at the cottage; extra buses will be laid on if necessary; *(ofrecer)* I'll lay on a meal for everyone

lay out **VT SEP** (a) *(extender, tender)* lay the pattern out on the floor (b) *(preparar)* she always lays her clothes out the night before (c) *(amortajar)* the old lady was laid out for her relatives to view her (d) *(acondicionar)* I don't like the way the office has been laid out (e) *(dejar K.O. a)* he laid me out with one blow (f) *(gastarse)* your parents have laid out a considerable sum on your education

lay up **VT SEP BRIT.** (a) *(guardar cama)* this flu has laid her up (b) *(desarmar, hablando de un barco)* the severely damaged vessel will be laid up for repair; *(estar en el garaje)* my car is laid up

lead on 1 **VI** *(ir delante)* lead on, you know the way better than I do
2 **VT SEP** (a) *(ilusionar, dar esperanzas a)* he led her on with promises of marriage; you led me on to believe that the job was mine (b) *(llevar a)* this leads me on to my second point; *(incitar)* it was those so-called friends of his that led him on to do it

lead up **VI** (a) *(llevar a, conducir a)* a narrow path led up to the house (b) *(preceder)* in the years leading up to the Declaration of Independence...; *(desencadenar)* these events led up to the war (c) *(preparar para)* her opening remarks were plainly leading up to a full-scale attack on her critics; what are you leading up to? (es decir, *¿adónde quiere llegar?*)

lean on VT INSEP (a) *(contar con)* his mother leans on him for advice (b) *(presionar)* the company is leaning on her to take early retirement

leave behind VT SEP (a) *(dejar)* drivers are advised to leave their cars behind and use public transport; I think we should leave the children behind (b) *(olvidar)* I came out in such a rush that I left my keys behind (c) *(dejar atrás)* when it comes to maths, she leaves most of the others far behind

leave off 1 VT SEP *(quitar)* it was such a beautiful day I left my coat off; who keeps leaving the lid off the coffee jar?; she wants to leave most of her relations off the guest list
2 VI *(pararse)* we'll carry on from where we left off; BRIT. FAM. *(parar)* leave off, will you!

leave out VT SEP (a) *(olvidarse, omitir)* you've left out an entire line (b) *(excluir)* I felt completely left out at the party; the old lady decided to leave her son-in-law out of her will (c) *(no mezclar, dejar fuera)* leave me out of this (d) *(dejar fuera)* I'll leave out the instructions for the washing machine; do you want to leave the car out?

let down VT SEP (a) *(bajar)* they let a rope down to the men stranded on the beach; *(soltar)* she let her hair down (b) *(decepcionar)* you must stop letting people down like this (c) *(alargar, bajar)* she always has to let down the hems of her daughter's clothes (d) *(desinflar, deshinchar)* the boys let his tyres down as a joke

let in 1 VT SEP (a) *(dejar entrar)* don't let him in; these shoes are letting water in (es decir, *estos zapatos le calan*) (b) *(revelar)* they let me in on the secret
2 VI *(calar)* are your boots letting in?

let in for VT SEP *(causar)* your absence let us all in for a lot of extra work; *(meterse en)* he didn't realize what he was letting himself in for

let off VT SEP (a) *(hacer explotar)* animal rights activists have let off a number of bombs (b) *(producir, emitir)* the fire was letting off a lot of smoke (c) *(liberar, dejar en libertad)* he was let off because of lack of evidence; the judge let him off with a fine (d) *(dejar salir)* the teacher lets us off early on Fridays (e) *(dejar, hablando de un vehículo)* I asked the taxi driver to let me off at the corner

let on VI FAM. (a) *(contar)* he never let on that he was married; I'm pregnant but don't you let on
(b) *(fingir, hacer creer)* he likes to let on that he went to university

let out VT SEP (a) *(dejar salir)* they're letting him out on parole soon; *(acompañar a la puerta)* my secretary will let you out; don't get up, I'll let myself out *(es decir, no se levante, conozco el camino)* (b) *(revelar)* he let the truth out; who let it out that we had a party? (c) *(dejar escapar, emitir)* she let out a yelp of pain (d) BRIT. *(alquilar)* they let out rooms to students (e) *(ensanchar, hablando de una prenda de vestir)* I'm either going to have to go on a diet or let all my clothes out

let up VI *(parar, hablando de algo que dura mucho)* I wish this rain would let up; don't you ever let up?

lie back VI (a) *(estirarse)* you lie back and rest (b) *(no hacer nada)* he just lay back and let the rest of us do the work

lie in VI *(levantarse tarde)* most people lie in on Sundays; I wish I could have lain in this morning

lie up VI (a) *(guardar cama)* the doctor says she's to lie up for a couple of days (b) *(esconderse)* the police are convinced that the wanted men are lying up somewhere (c) *(no ser utilizado)* that boat has been lying up for years

light up 1 VI (a) *(iluminarse)* his face suddenly lit up; the room seemed to light up when she came in (b) *(encender un cigarrillo, etc.)* he lit up and sighed with contentment
2 VT SEP (a) *(alumbrar, iluminar)* the fireworks lit up the sky (b) *(encender)* they both lit up their pipes

line up 1 VI *(hacer cola)* people are already beginning to line up outside the cinema
2 VT SEP (a) *(poner en fila)* the headmaster lined everybody up in the playground (b) *(fijar)* I've lined a date up for you; he's got something else lined up for tomorrow

listen in vi *(escuchar)* it's fascinating listening in on other people's conversations; do you mind if I listen in?

live down vt sep *(perdonar)* they'll never let him live that down; *(hacer olvidar)* he won't let her live it down that she made one stupid mistake; you'll never live this down! (es decir, *¡seguirás oyéndolo!*)

live in/out vi *(estar interno/estar externo)* they have at least three maids living in; I would rather live out than stay in a hall of residence

live off vt insep (a) *(vivir de)* she lived off what she earned as a cleaner; *(alimentarse solo de)* that child would live off ice cream if he could (b) *(vivir a costa de)* he lives off his parents

live on 1 vi *(seguir vivo, perdurar)* the memory of their sacrifice will live on
2 vt insep (a) *(vivir de, alimentarse de)* she lives on fruit and vegetables (b) *(vivir de)* this salary is not enough to live on (es decir, *este sueldo no da para vivir*)

live up to vt insep (a) *(estar a la altura de)* the holiday didn't live up to our expectations (b) *(mostrarse digno de)* there's no point in trying to live up to my sister's reputation

load down vt sep *(cargar de)* he was loaded down with packages; I'm loaded down with work

load up 1 vi *(cargar)* there are a number of ships waiting to load up
2 vt sep *(cargar)* we loaded the car up with everything we needed

lock away vt sep *(poner bajo llave)* lock those papers away for the night; *(encerrar, encarcelar)* the police said they could lock him away for ten years

lock in vt sep *(encarcelar)* she's locked in a cell with three other women; *(encerrar)* you almost locked me in

lock out vt sep (a) *(dejar en la calle)* they've gone to bed and locked me out (b) *(realizar un cierre patronal)* the company has threatened to lock its employees out unless they return to work immediately

lock up 1 vi *(cerrar con llave)* you go to bed, I'll lock up

2 vt sep (a) *(cerrar con llave)* could you lock the house up? (b) *(guardar bajo llave)* lock up your valuables; *(encerrar)* the dogs are locked up every night; *(cerrar, meter en la cárcel)* he was locked up for fraud

long for vt insep *(tener muchas ganas de, esperar con impaciencia)* I'm longing for the holidays

look after vt insep *(hacerse cargo de)* we've been looking after our grandchildren for the weekend; the car has been well looked after

look at vt insep (a) *(mirar)* look at that gorgeous man! (b) *(examinar, mirar)* I'll need to get someone in to look at that damp patch (c) *(ver, considerar)* he doesn't look at it that way at all; *(tomar en consideración)* they won't even look at the idea

look back vi (a) *(mirar hacia atrás, volverse)* he stopped and looked back (b) *(volver la vista atrás, hacia el pasado)* looking back over the last five years, do you have any regrets?

look down on vt insep *(despreciar, mirar por encima del hombro)* he looks down on anyone who hasn't gone to university

look for vt insep (a) *(buscar)* I'm really looking for something a bit bigger (b) *(esperar)* it's not the result we were looking for

look forward to vt insep *(esperar con impaciencia)* you must be looking forward to their visit; I look forward to hearing from you soon (es decir, *a la espera de tu respuesta* o *de tus noticias*)

look in vi *(pasarse, hacer una visita rápida)* I'll look in again tomorrow; they looked in for a minute

look into vt insep *(estudiar, examinar)* the company has promised that it will look into my complaint

look on 1 vi *(mirar)* a crowd looked on as firemen fought the blaze **2 vt insep** *(considerar)* they look on her as a daughter; I used to look on him with envy

look onto vt insep *(dar a)* our house looks onto open fields

look out 1 vi (a) *(mirar fuera)* she opened the window and looked out (b) *(tener cuidado)* look out, you're very close to the edge **2 vt sep** *(buscar, encontrar)* look out a scarf for me; she has promised to look those letters out

look out for **VT INSEP** (a) *(buscar)* you could always ask the garage to look out for a good second-hand car (b) *(ocuparse de)* he promised his parents he would always look out for his younger brother (c) *(tener cuidado con)* look out for the bones in this fish

look over **VT SEP** (a) *(examinar, estudiar)* look over the papers carefully before you sign them; *(observar, juzgar)* I'm sure I've been invited for the weekend just so his mother can look me over (b) *(visitar)* we're looking over a flat this evening

look to **VT INSEP** *(contar con)* you must stop looking to other people to solve your problems

look up **1 VI** (a) *(levantar la vista)* she looked up when I entered the room; he didn't even look up from his book (b) *(mejorar)* his business must be looking up if he's bought a new car
2 VT SEP (a) *(visitar, pasar a ver)* you must look us up again (b) *(buscar en un libro, etc.)* look it up in the encyclopedia

look up to **VT INSEP** (a) *(levantar la cabeza para mirar)* he's so tall I have to look up to him (b) *(admirar)* everyone looks up to her for her courage

loosen up **1 VT SEP** (a) *(relajar, desentumecer)* a nice massage will loosen you up (b) *(suavizar, flexibilizar)* they've promised to loosen up the rules
2 VI (a) *(relajarse)* he began to loosen up once the meal was served (b) *(mostrarse menos severo)* will they loosen up on immigration? (c) *(calentar)* the athletes take a couple of minutes to loosen up

lose out **VI** *(salir perdiendo)* you're the one who'll lose out; he lost out on a deal

louse up **VT SEP FAM.** *(fastidiar)* you're always lousing things up for me; he really loused that race up

make for **VT INSEP** (a) *(dirigirse hacia)* he was making for the exit when they stopped him (b) *(contribuir a, facilitar)* handling a complaint in that way does not make for good customer relations

Diccionario de *phrasal verbs*

make of 1 **vt sep** (a) *(comprender algo de)* can you make anything of these instructions? (b) *(dar importancia a)* you're making too much of this – I've known him since we were children; strangely, the press isn't making much of this scandal
2 **vt insep** *(pensar de)* well, what do you make of that?

make off **vi** *(irse, escabullirse)* the boys made off at a run when they saw the policeman

make off with **vt insep** *(llevarse)* who's made off with the scissors again?; don't leave your bag lying around, someone might make off with it

make out 1 **vt sep** (a) *(rellenar, hacer)* make the cheque out to me (b) *(distinguir, ver)* can you make out who it is? (c) *(descifrar)* he can't make out his own handwriting (d) *(comprender, entender)* I can't make her out at all (e) *(pretender)* don't make yourself out to be something you're not; the insurance company is making out that I was negligent
2 **vi fam.** *(arreglárselas)* how is she making out in her new job?

make over **vt sep** *(ceder)* she has made her entire estate over to her granddaughter

make up 1 **vt sep** (a) *(maquillar)* she was heavily made up (b) *(inventar)* she is making the whole thing up, it's not true (c) *(preparar, hacer)* the chemist made up the prescription; would you make these up into three separate packages? (d) *(aumentar)* for your birthday, I'll make your savings up to the price of a new bike (e) *(locución)* to make it up with someone *hacer las paces con alguien*
2 **vt insep** (a) *(recuperar)* overtime will be necessary to make up the time we lost because of the weather (b) *(componerse)* the community is made up primarily of old people (c) *(completar)* we need two more players to make up the team
3 **vi** *(reconciliarse)* haven't you two made up yet?

make up for **vt insep** *(compensar)* the pay doesn't make up for the poor conditions; *(hacerse perdonar por)* how can I make up for forgetting your birthday?; *(recuperar)* he's certainly making up for lost time now

make up to 1 **vt sep** *(locución)* I promise I'll make it up to you some-

day *algún día te recompensaré por esto*
2 **VT INSEP** *(hacer la pelota)* they got the money by making up to the old man

map out VT SEP (a) *(trazar)* have you mapped out the route yet? (b) *(organizar, prever)* I've mapped out a programme

mark up VT SEP (a) *(apuntar)* the menu is marked up on the blackboard (b) *(aumentar el precio de)* most restaurants mark up wine by about three hundred percent

marry off VT SEP *(casar, hablando de un matrimonio de conveniencia)* she married off her daughter to an aristocrat

measure up 1 VT SEP (a) *(valorar)* after measuring up the timber... (b) *(juzgar)* she measured her mother's new boyfriend up with one glance
2 **VI** *(estar a la altura)* I don't think you're going to measure up to the job

meet up VI *(volver a verse, reencontrarse)* let's meet up again soon

meet with VI INSEP (a) *(tropezar con, encontrarse con)* the proposal has met with fierce opposition; rescue attempts have so far met with failure; the suggestion met with acclaim (b) *(tener una cita con, reunirse con)* the senator is meeting with his advisors next week

melt away VI (a) *(deshacerse completamente)* the ice has melted away (b) *(dispersarse)* the onlookers melted away after the initial excitement

melt down VT SEP *(fundir)* the gold jewellery will have been melted down by now and will be impossible to identify

mess about/around FAM. 1 VT SEP (a) *(burlarse de, tomar el pelo a)* first we're going, then we're not going – I wish you would stop messing me about! (b) *(cambiar el orden de algo provocando confusión)* they've messed the programmes around again
2 **VI BRIT.** (a) *(hacer el tonto)* stop messing about! (b) *(holgazanear)* would you stop messing about and get on with your work (c) *(ocuparse de)* he's been messing about in the garden all day (d) *(toquetear, enredar)* don't mess around with something that doesn't belong to you

mess up VT SEP (a) *(desordenar, ensuciar)* don't mess the kitchen up

(b) FAM. *(estropear)* you've really messed your marriage up; by changing his mind at the last minute he's messed things up for all of us

miss out 1 VT SEP *(omitir, olvidar)* have I missed anyone out?
2 VI *(fallar)* you missed out there; *(estar en desventaja)* he missed out because he couldn't afford to go to college

miss out on VT INSEP *(perderse)* you missed out on a great concert

mix up VT SEP (a) *(mezclar)* mix up all the ingredients in a large bowl (b) *(liar)* don't talk to me when I'm trying to count or you'll mix me up (c) *(confundir)* he mixes her up with her mother (d) *normalmente en voz pasiva (implicar, meter)* everyone in that family is mixed up in something dishonest

move along 1 VT SEP *(dispersar)* the police had to move the crowd along
2 VI (a) *(correrse, echarse a un lado)* move along and let the lady sit down (b) *(partir, irse)* I really ought to be moving along (c) *(pasar a)* moving along to my next question...

move in 1 VT SEP (a) *(enviar)* the government has decided to move troops in to quell the riots in the city (b) *(colocar)* when are they going to move the bookcase in?
2 VI (a) *(avanzar, aproximarse)* troops are now moving in on the beleaguered capital (b) *(mudar de casa)* people are moving in next door

move on 1 VT SEP *(dispersar)* the police moved us on
2 VI (a) *(seguir su camino, circular)* a policeman told me to move on (b) *(pasar a)* can we move on to the next item on the agenda?

move out 1 VT SEP *(sacar)* you'll have to move the car out of the garage; *(hacer mudarse de casa)* they're being moved out of their homes to make way for a new road; *(retirar)* the new government has promised to move its soldiers out
2 VI (a) *(mudarse de casa)* the people next door have decided to move out (b) *(retirarse)* troops are already moving out

move up 1 VT SEP (a) *(subir)* he's been moved up a class (b) *(promocionar)* they've moved him up to be assistant manager (c) *(hacer avanzar)* another division has been moved up
2 VI (a) *(correrse, echarse a un lado)* move up and let me sit

down (b) *(avanzar)* troops are moving up to the combat zone

muddle along/on **vi** *(arreglárselas)* they were muddling along quite happily before management brought in a team of consultants to look at efficiency

muddle up **vt sep** *(mezclar, confundir)* he's managed to muddle the dates up; *(liar)* you're muddling me up

muscle in **vi fam.** *(imponerse, introducirse por la fuerza)* a lot of big companies are muscling in; I'm not going to let anyone muscle in (es decir, *no dejaré que nadie se meta en mis asuntos*); *(locución)* to muscle in on someone's territory *meterse en el terreno de alguien*

narrow down **1** **vi** *(reducirse)* the question narrows down to this... **2** **vt sep** *(reducir)* we've narrowed the candidates down to four

nod off **vi fam.** *(dormirse, quedarse traspuesto)* to my embarrassment, I nodded off in the middle of the board meeting

notch up **vt sep fam.** *(apuntarse)* she has notched up yet another win

open onto **vt insep** *(dar a)* the back door opens onto a paved courtyard

open out **1** **vi** (a) *(abrirse, florecer)* the roses are beginning to open out (b) *(extenderse)* miles of wheatfields opened out before us **2** **vt sep** *(abrir, desplegar)* it's difficult to open out your newspaper on a crowded train

open up **1** **vi** (a) *(abrir)* police, open up!; the shopkeeper was just opening up when I passed (b) *(abrirse)* another couple of warm days and the roses will have opened up; new markets are opening up all the time; there are some new shops opening up on the high street (c) *(abrirse, sincerarse)* he never opens up to anybody **2** **vt sep** (a) *(abrir)* when did you open the shop up this morning? (b) *(abrir, inaugurar)* opening up a restaurant in this part of town is a risky venture (c) *(empezar a explotar)* the rainforest is being opened up for development

opt out VI *(optar por no participar, retirarse)* I'm opting out of the committee because I have too many other commitments

own up VI *(confesar)* I know it was you I saw so you might as well own up; he rarely owns up to his mistakes

pack away 1 VT SEP (a) *(guardar)* maybe we packed our winter clothes away a little too soon (b) FAM. *(atiborrarse, papear)* I've never seen anyone who can pack it away like you (c) FAM. *(mandar, enviar)* I packed the kids away to bed
2 VI *(plegarse, guardarse)* this tent packs away easily

pack in 1 VT SEP (a) *(meter, introducir)* you can't possibly pack anything more in (b) BRIT. *(atraer masivamente)* her latest film is packing them in (c) FAM. *(parar)* go next door and tell them to pack that noise in (d) FAM. *(dejar, abandonar)* he's decided to pack his job in; are you going to pack him in or not?
2 VI BRIT. FAM. *(averiarse)* the lawnmower's packed in again

pack off VT SEP FAM. *(enviar, mandar)* I'll call you back once I've packed the kids off to school

pack out VT SEP FAM. *(llenar hasta los topes)* the fans packed the hall out; the pub was packed out so we went somewhere else

pack up VI (a) *(hacer las maletas)* pack up, we're not staying here another night (b) BRIT. *(descansar, dejar de trabajar)* are you packing up already? (c) BRIT. FAM. *(averiarse)* the lawnmower has just packed up so I can't cut the grass

palm off VT SEP FAM. *(encasquetar)* be careful he doesn't try to palm any rotten fruit off on you; they're palming the children off on us for the weekend; *(librarse)* the last time I complained, the company palmed me off with a standard letter

pass away 1 VT SEP *(pasar)* we read to pass the time away
2 VI *(fallecer)* the old lady passed away in her sleep

pass by 1 **vi** (a) *(pasar)* luckily a taxi was passing by just at that moment (b) *(pasar, venir)* she passed by to say hello (c) *(pasar, hablando del tiempo)* time is passing by, are you going to meet the deadline?
2 **vt insep** *(pasar delante de)* we pass by that house every morning
3 **vt sep** *(locución)* life is passing me by *la vida se me escurre de las manos*; life has passed her by *la vida se le ha escurrido de las manos*

pass off 1 **vi** *(transcurrir)* the ceremony passed off without a hitch
2 **vt sep** *(hacer pasar por)* he passed her off as a duchess

pass on 1 **vi** (a) *(fallecer)* when did your father pass on? (b) *(pasar)* why don't we pass on to the next item on the agenda and come back to this later?
2 **vt sep** *(contar)* don't pass this on, but...; *(pasar, dar)* I passed the file on to him yesterday

pass out 1 **vi** *(desmayarse)* I always pass out at the sight of blood
2 **vt sep** *(distribuir)* he passed out copies of the memo to the people at the meeting

pass over 1 **vt sep** *(olvidar, ignorar)* they've passed me over for promotion again
2 **vi** *(fallecer)* the clairvoyant began to talk about «our loved ones who have passed over»

pass up **vt sep** (a) *(pasar)* pass me up the light bulb (b) *(dejar escapar)* imagine passing up a job like that!; she has had to pass up the offer

patch up **vt sep** (a) *(reparar provisionalmente)* I've managed to patch up the car so that it gets us into town at least; *(hacer una cura de urgencia a)* the army doctor just patched him up and sent him back to the front
(b) *(locución)* to patch things up with someone *hacer las paces con alguien*

pay back **vt sep** (a) *(devolver)* have you paid back that money yet? (b) *(pagar con la misma moneda)* I'll pay you back for this! (es decir, *¡me las pagarás!*)

pay off **vt sep** (a) *(despedir)* the company is going to pay half its labour force off at the end of the month (b) *(devolver)* in ten

years' time, we'll have paid the mortgage off (c) **FAM.**
(sobornar) the policeman admitted to having been paid off

pick off **VT SEP** (a) *(rascar)* I spilled some paint on the carpet and had
to pick it off when it dried in; *(recoger)* pick those papers off
the floor (b) *(abatir)* the sniper picked them off one by one

pay out **VT SEP** (a) *(gastar)* he's had to pay out a lot on car repairs late-
ly (b) *(pagar)* the wages were paid out this morning (c) *(soltar
poco a poco)* pay out some more rope

pay up 1 **VT SEP** (a) *(pagar, hablando de una deuda)* has she paid up
what she owes you? (b) *(liquidar, pagar)* my suscription is
paid up
2 **VI** *(pagar)* I've asked him to pay up but I'm still waiting

pick on **VT INSEP** (a) *(elegir)* why pick on me to answer? (b) **FAM.**
(meterse con) stop picking on him, he's doing his best

pick out **VT SEP** (a) *(elegir)* I've picked out one or two patterns you
might like; he picked out the best peaches (b) *(identificar)* she
picked the man out from the identity parade; *(localizar)* I
picked you out immediately – you were the only one wearing a red coat (c) *(resaltar)* the panels on the door are picked
out in a deeper shade of the colour used on the walls (d)
(tocar de oído) he can pick out a few tunes on the piano but
that's all

pick up 1 **VT SEP** (a) *(coger)* he picked up a book and started to read (b)
(recoger, ir a buscar) will you pick up my prescription at the
chemist's?; when did he say he would be picking us up?;
(recoger) the bus stopped to pick up passengers (c) *(encontrar,
dar con)* they picked up that wonderful old table at an auction; I picked it up cheap (es decir, *la compré barata*) (d) **FAM.**
(ligar) he picks up a different woman every night (e) *(coger,
pescar, hablando de una enfermedad)* she's constantly picking
up colds (f) *(adquirir)* that child has picked up some very bad
habits; *(aprender)* he managed to pick up the rules of bridge
quite quickly (g) *(detener, hablando de la policía)* he's been
picked up for shoplifting (h) *(retomar)* to pick up my story...
(i) *(descubrir)* the police have picked up a trail that might
lead them to the suspect (j) *(sintonizar)* you can pick up a lot
of foreign stations with a short-wave radio (k) *(corregir)*
please pick me up if I make any mistakes (l) **FAM.** *(animar)* a
weekend away will pick her up; what would really pick me

up would be a holiday in the sun
2 **vi** (a) *(mejorar)* the weather is picking up; *(restablecerse, recuperarse)* he's been quite ill but he's picked up in the last day or two (b) *(continuar, retomar)* let's pick up where we left off

pile up 1 **vi** *(acumularse)* the work tends to pile up at this time of year
2 **vt sep** *(amontonar)* pile the leaves up there; *(acumular)* they're piling up the evidence against him

pin down vt sep (a) *(atrapar, inmovilizar)* they were pinned down by wreckage; he has his opponent pinned down on the canvas (b) *(obligar a decidirse)* I've tried to pin her down to a time (c) *(definir)* it's just one of those feelings that are very difficult to pin down; *(identificar)* I was sure I had seen him before but I couldn't pin him down

pipe down vi fam. (a) *(hacer menos ruido, callarse)* I wish you two would pipe down while I'm trying to watch television (b) *(cerrar el pico)* just pipe down about it, OK?; *(cerrar el pico, callarse)* he finally piped down when he realized she knew more about it than he did

play about/around vi *(jugar)* it's about time he stopped playing around and settled down; you shouldn't play around with people's feelings

play along 1 **vi** *(colaborar)* if that's what you've decided then I'm quite happy to play along
2 **vt sep** *(jugar con, manipular)* he's just playing her along until he gets what he wants

play back vt sep *(reproducir, hablando de una grabación)* play that last bit back

play down vt sep *(restar importancia a)* she played down the extent of her injuries; the government is trying to play down its involvement

play off vi *(jugar para desempatar)* the two teams will play off next week

play off against vt sep *(enfrentar... entre)* she's playing David off against James; you take pleasure in playing people off against each other, don't you?

play on 1 **vi** *(seguir tocando)* the orchestra played on despite the bomb scare
2 **vt insep** *(jugar con)* the government is playing on people's fears

play out **vt sep** (a) *(representar)* that was quite a scene they played out for our benefit (b) *normalmente en voz pasiva (estar agotado, estar exhausto)* he's played out as a world-class boxer (c) *(acompañar con música la salida de)* the organist played the congregation out

play up **Brit. fam.** 1 **vi** (a) *(hacer de las suyas)* the car is playing up again (b) *(hacer la pelota, dar coba)* he plays up to anyone who can further his career
2 **vt sep** *(molestar, dar guerra a)* the baby has been playing me up all day

plough back (**U.S.** = plow back) **vt sep** *(reinvertir)* all the profits are ploughed back into the company

plug in **vt sep** *(enchufar)* plug the iron in

plug up **vt sep** *(taponar, tapar, obstruir)* that gap will have to be plugged up

plump for **vt insep fam.** *(optar por)* I see you plumped for a car instead of a holiday

point out **vt sep** (a) *(mostrar, señalar)* can you point him out? (b) *(señalar, indicar)* he pointed out that two people were missing

point up **vt sep** *(destacar, poner de relieve)* why point up the difficulties?; the accident points up the need for proper health and safety measures

poke about/around 1 **vi** (a) *(rebuscar, husmear)* poke about and see what you can find; the dog was poking about in the bushes (b) *(husmear, meter las narices)* that social worker is always poking about
2 **vt insep** *(rebuscar en)* I love poking about antique shops

poke out 1 **vi** *(sobresalir)* the label on your coat is poking out
2 **vt sep** (a) *(asomar)* she opened the window and poked her head out (b) *(sacar)* careful or you'll poke my eye out! (es decir, *¡ten cuidado, casi me sacas un ojo!*)

polish off **vt sep fam.** (a) *(zamparse, cepillarse)* the two of them polished that whole bowl of pasta off between them! (b) *(acabar/terminar con)* he polished his opponent off in three straight sets

polish up VT SEP (a) *(pulir, sacar brillo a)* the silver needs to be polished up (b) *(mejorar, perfeccionar)* I'm going to evening classes to polish up my Spanish

pop off VI FAM. (a) *(largarse)* they're popping off home to pick up their kids (b) *(estirar la pata, palmarla)* more people pop off in the winter than at any other time of year

pop in VI FAM. *(pasar, hacer una visita rápida)* he popped in to say hello

pop out VI FAM. *(salir un momento)* I only popped out for five minutes; *(ir en un salto)* I'll pop out to the tobacconist's

pop up VI FAM. *(aparecer)* a head popped up through the trap door; this question has popped up again (**es decir**, *se ha vuelto a plantear*)

pore over VT INSEP *(sumergirse en)* he spends all his time poring over old manuscripts

pour out 1 VI *(salirse)* smoke was pouring out of the windows; *(salir a raudales)* once she had composed herself, the words just poured out
2 VT SEP (a) *(servir)* will I pour out the tea?; *(echar)* pour some sugar out into a bowl (b) *(desahogar)* I hope you didn't mind me pouring out my troubles like that

print out VT SEP *(imprimir)* the text is edited on screen and then printed out to be sent back to the author

prop up VT SEP *(apuntalar)* they've had to prop the castle walls up; *(sostener)* the regime is being propped up by the military; *(apoyar)* he propped himself up against the gate; FAM. he's always propping up the bar (**es decir**, *se pasa el día entero en el bar*)

pull away 1 VT SEP *(retirar)* she pulled her hand away; *(arrancar)* she pulled the book away from him; *(alejar, apartar)* he pulled me away from the window
2 VI (a) *(arrancar, ponerse en marcha)* the train slowly pulled away (b) *(apartarse)* the dog pulled away when I tried to pat it (c) *(sacar ventaja en una carrera)* she's beginning to pull away

pull down VT SEP (a) *(bajar)* pull the blind down (b) *(demoler, derribar)* how many more buildings are they going to pull down? (c)

U.S. FAM. *(ganar, hablando de dinero)* considering his qualifications, he doesn't pull down much of a salary

pull in 1 **VT SEP** (a) *(atraer)* the play is really pulling people in (b) *(detener)* the police pulled him in for questioning
2 **VI** (a) *(aparcar)* pull in here; we'll pull in to the next garage we see (b) *(llegar, hablando de un tren o un autocar)* the coach pulled in two hours late

pull off VT SEP (a) *(quitar)* help me pull the dirty sheets off the bed; he pulled off his clothes (b) *(conseguir)* I never thought we would pull it off; he has pulled off a remarkable achievement

pull out 1 **VT SEP** (a) *(sacar tirando hacia fuera)* my car's stuck in the mud, you'll have to pull me out; *(extraer, sacar)* he's having a tooth pulled out tomorrow (b) *(retirar)* the president has promised that all troops will be pulled out by the end of the year
2 **VI** (a) *(salir)* look in your mirror before you pull out (b) *(retirarse)* troops have begun to pull out

pull over 1 **VT SEP** (a) *(llevar arrastrando)* he pulled the chair over to the window (b) *(tirar)* be careful or you'll pull the filing cabinet over on top of you
2 **VI** *(detenerse)* the policeman asked us to pull over; *(hacerse a un lado)* she's pulling over to let the other cars past

pull through 1 **VT SEP** *(hacer salir adelante)* he says it was his faith that pulled him through
2 **VI** *(recuperarse)* I think we can confidently say that she will pull through

pull together 1 **VT SEP** (a) *(preparar)* I've pulled together a few suggestions (b) *(locución)* pull yourself together! *¡cálmate!* 2 **VI** *(unir los esfuerzos, cooperar)* we must pull together on this

pull up 1 **VT SEP** (a) *(acercar)* he pulled up a chair and joined us; *(subir, levantar)* pull the blind up (b) *(parar, hablando de un coche)* he was pulled up by the police (c) *(reprender)* she pulled him up about his bad language
2 **VI** (a) *(pararse)* why are you pulling up?; the horse pulled up lame (b) *(remontar, mejorar su posición en una carrera)* he is beginning to pull up, but I think he's left it too late

push about VT SEP *(maltratar)* he didn't hit her but he was pushing her about

push ahead vi (a) *(avanzar, progresar)* research on this is pushing ahead in various countries (b) *(seguir adelante)* I think we should push ahead nonetheless

push along 1 vt sep *(empujar)* I saw her pushing a pram along 2 vi fam. *(largarse, abrirse)* I suppose I should be pushing along soon

push around vt sep fam. *(pisotear)* I'm not going to let him push us around like this

push for vt insep *(pedir, presionar para obtener)* the company is pushing for more government funding

push off 1 vt sep (a) *(tirar, hacer caer)* they pushed me off the ladder (b) *(retirar, sacar)* push the lid off 2 vi fam. *(salir pitando)* everyone's pushing off at five o'clock; *(largarse)* I wish you would push off and let me finish what I'm doing

push on 1 vi *(continuar)* we decided to push on 2 vt sep (a) *(empujar)* you need to push it on quite firmly (b) *(animar)* both runners are being pushed on by the crowd

push through 1 vt insep *(abrirse camino a empujones)* we'll have to push through the crowd 2 vt sep *(imponer, hacer aprobar)* the government is pushing this bill through

push up vt sep (a) *(levantar)* you have to push up the handle (b) *(aumentar)* excessive wage increases are pushing up inflation

put about vt sep *(difundir)* who put that rumour about?; it's being put about that she's pregnant *(es decir, corre el rumor de que está embarazada)*

put across vt sep *(imponer, hablando de ideas)* he didn't put that across very well; a politician who certainly knows how to put herself across *(es decir, imponerse)*

put away vt sep (a) *(guardar, poner en su sitio)* put your wallet away, I'm paying for this; *(aparcar)* could someone put the car away for the night? (b) *(ahorrar)* she puts something away every month for her holidays (c) fam. *(zamparse, tragar)* you should see how much junk food he can put away!; *(beber alcohol, empinar el codo)* he's down at the pub every night putting it away (d) **FAM.** *(encerrar)* that maniac should be put away somewhere

put back VT SEP (a) *(poner en su sitio)* put that back where you found it (b) *(aplazar)* the meeting's been put back till next month (c) *(atrasar, hablando de la hora, un reloj, etc.)* isn't this the week we put the clocks back?

put down VT SEP (a) *(dejar)* put that down before you drop it (b) *(dejar, hablando de una persona)* if you put me down at the next corner, I can walk the rest of the way (c) *(reprimir)* the revolt was put down by armed police (d) *(criticar, menospreciar)* he's always putting her down; why do you keep putting yourself down? (e) *(sacrificar, hablando de un animal)* the cat's in a great deal of pain, I think we should have her put down (f) *(depositar, dejar)* how much do you have to put down as a deposit? (g) *(escribir)* have you put all the details down? (h) *(hacer aterrizar)* the pilot had to put the plane down in a field

put down to VT SEP *(atribuir)* she puts it down to laziness

put forward VT SEP (a) *(presentar, proponer)* somebody put forward the idea that...; they've put him forward for a knighthood b) *(adelantar, hablando de una fecha o un reloj)* the meeting has been put forward to noon today; did you put your watch forward?

put in 1 **VT SEP** (a) *(meter)* have you put everything in? (b) *(instalar)* we're having cable TV put in (c) *(trabajar, hacer)* I put in a lot of overtime last month; don't you think you should put in a bit of piano practice? (d) *(inscribir)* we're putting him in for the 500 and 1000 metres
2 **VI** *(presentar una solicitud o una candidatura)* has he put in for that job we saw advertised?

put off VT SEP (a) *(dejar)* could you put me off at the corner?; *(hacer bajar)* the bus conductor put the boys off because of their behaviour (b) *(aplazar, posponer)* let's put lunch off to another time (c) *(anular una cita con)* you can't keep putting him off like this – just tell him you don't want to go out with him (d) *(apagar)* put the TV off (e) *(quitar las ganas de)* their stories have put me off foreign travel; that programme on slaughterhouses put him off eating meat for a while (f) *(molestar, incordiar)* you would think that all those people standing round watching would put her off

put on vt sep (a) *(ponerse, hablando de una prenda de vestir)* put your coat on; she put on her glasses (b) *(fingir)* she puts on a posh accent sometimes; the boss can put on a show of being fierce (es decir, *hacer ver que*); fam. don't worry!, he's just putting it on (es decir, *itranquila!, está marcándose un farol*) (c) *(representar)* they're not putting Hamlet on again, are they?; *(emitir)* why can't they put on something decent on TV for a change? (d) *(ganar, hablando de peso)* he's put on a few inches round the waist (e) *(añadir)* the tax increase will put another 10p on a gallon of petrol (f) *(encender)* put the radio on

put onto vt sep *(recomendar)* I can put you onto a good lawyer; *(poner sobre la pista, llevar a sospechar)* what put the police onto him as the culprit?

put out vt sep (a) *(sacar)* have you put the dustbin out? (b) *(poner, sacar)* remember to put the side plates out as well (c) *(tender)* she put her hand out (d) *(publicarr)* we'll be putting out a new edition very soon (e) *(apagar)* put the light out (f) *(dormir, hablando de un enfermo)* the drug will put you out very quickly (g) *(irritar)* everyone was put out by the two-hour delay (h) *(molestar)* would one more guest put you out?; I don't want to put anyone out (i) *(dislocar)* don't lift that table or you'll put your back out again

put through vt sep (a) *(someter)* a bill has been put through Parliament (b) *(poner en comunicación telefónica)* will you put me through to the book department, please? (c) *(causar)* you've put your mother through a great deal of worry with your behaviour

put up vt sep (a) *(levantar)* put up your hand if you know the answer (b) *(construi)* a new block of flats is being put up just behind their house (c) *(colgar en la pared)* I want to put up a few more pictures in this room (d) *(aumentar)* car manufacturers are putting their prices up again (e) *(hospedar)* could you put us up while we're in town? (f) *(poner)* a lot of people have put their houses up for sale (g) *(presentar)* we are not putting up any candidates (h) *(oponer)* they put up a lot of resistance; she put up a good fight but had to concede defeat in the end (es decir, *se ha defendido bien, pero...*)

put up with vt insep *(aguantar, soportar)* why do you put up with that kind of behaviour?; it's a lot to have to put up with

quieten down 1 **vi** (a) *(calmarse)* if you lot don't quieten down I'm going to get very cross; business always quietens down after Christmas (b) *(moderarse)* he's quietened down a lot since he got married

2 **vt sep** *(calmar)* it took me ages to quieten the class down; the nurse tried to quieten the child down but he kept crying for his mother

rain off (U.S. = rain out) **vt sep** *siempre en voz pasiva (suspender a causa de la lluvia)* the match was rained off

rattle through vt insep (a) *(circular chirriando)* the two old cars rattled through the streets (b) *(terminar rápidamente)* she tends to rattle through her work; the speaker rattled through his talk

read out vt sep *(leer en voz alta)* he read out the names of the injured

read up on vt insep *(empaparse de)* the play might have meant more to you if you'd read up a bit on the events it depicted

rein in 1 **vt sep** (a) *(llevar al paso)* the girl reined her pony in and turned back towards the stables (b) *(frenar)* he tried very hard to rein in his anger; *(restringir, disminuir)* the council wants to rein in its spending on sports facilities

2 **vi** *(reducir la velocidad)* they reined in so they could talk

rest up vi *(descansar)* the doctor has told him to rest up

ring back BRIT. 1 **vt sep** *(volver a llamar por teléfono)* he's not in but I'll ask him to ring you back

2 **vi** *(volver a llamar por teléfono)* could you ring back in half an hour?

ring in vi BRIT. *(telefonear)* you ought to have rung in to say you were ill and couldn't come to work

ring off vi BRIT. *(colgar)* I must ring off now, there's someone at the door

ring out **vi** *(resonar)* her voice rang out; *(sonar)* the church bells were ringing out

ring up **Brit.**1 **vt sep** *(telefonear)* why not ring her up and ask? 2 **vi** *(telefonear)* I'll ring up and find out

rip off **vt sep** (a) *(arrancar)* as soon as they got their hands on the presents, the children ripped the paper off (b) **fam.** *(estafar)* let's choose another restaurant – I was ripped off the last time I was at this one (c) **fam.** *(atracar)* they ripped off a bank; *(birlar)* he ripped off our idea

rip up **vt sep** *(romper en pedazos)* just rip his letter up and forget the whole business

root for **vt insep** *(apoyar)* which side are you rooting for?; the candidate I root for invariably loses

rough out **vt sep** **Brit.** *(esbozar)* could you rough out a publicity campaign?

rough up **vt sep** (a) *(despeinar)* don't rough up my hair (b) **fam.** *(dar una paliza a)* he was roughed up by some thugs; *(maltratar)* they roughed her up a bit but she's all right

round down **vt sep** *(redondear a la baja)* the price will be rounded down

round off **vt sep** (a) *(redondear)* round off the edges (b) *(acabar, terminar)* we rounded the meal off with coffee and liqueurs; she rounded off her presentation with a joke

round on **vt insep** *(volverse contra, atacar)* he rounded on his tormentors

round up **vt sep** (a) *(reunir)* about this time of year the cattle are rounded up; round everyone up for the meeting, will you? (b) *(redondear al alza)* just round the bill up to £50

rub down **vt sep** *(cepillar)* the groom will rub your horse down; *(secar frotando)* he rubbed himself down with the towel

rub in **vt sep** (a) *(aplicar frotando)* rub the cream in well (b) **fam.** *(restregar)* I know I was wrong, don't keep rubbing it in!

rub off 1 **vt sep** *(quitar frotando)* rub those dirty marks off the wall; *(borrar)* the teacher rubbed the equations off the blackboard

2 VI (a) *(irse frotando)* the stain won't rub off (b) **FIG.** *(influir)* I hope his bad behaviour doesn't rub off on you

rub out VT SEP (a) *(quitar frotando)* try rubbing the stain out with a damp cloth (b) *(borrar)* don't rub out your calculations (c) **U.S. FAM.** *(liquidar, eliminar)* one of the key witnesses to the shooting was rubbed out by a gang member

run about/around 1 VT INSEP *(ir de arriba abajo por)* I spent all day running about the shops looking for a birthday present **2 VI** *(correr por todas partes)* the children were running about on the beach; I've been running about all day looking for you! *(es decir, ¡me he pasado el día buscándote por todas partes!)*

run across VT INSEP *(encontrar por casualidad, toparse con)* if you should run across John give him my regards; I've run across a word I don't know

run away with VT INSEP (a) *(irse con, huir con)* his daughter has run away with a married man; *(largarse con)* one of his employees has run away with the week's takings (b) *(dejarse llevar por un sentimiento, la imaginación, etc.)* she tends to let her imagination run away with her *(es decir, ella suele dejarse llevar por su imaginación)* (c) *(locución)* don't go running away with the idea that it will be easy *no te pienses que será fácil* (d) *(hacerse con)* they ran away with nearly all the medals

run back 1 VI (a) *(volver corriendo)* I ran back to the car (b) *(volver con su pareja, etc.)* he'll come running back once he realizes what he's missing
2 VT SEP *(llevar en coche)* don't worry about the last bus, I'll run you back

run down 1 VI (a) *(bajar corriendo)* run down and see who's at the door (b) *(debilitar, decaer)* the government is accused of letting the industry run down; *(pararse, hablando de un reloj, etc.)* don't wind up the clock until it has completely run down; *(descargarse)* you've let the battery run down
2 VT SEP (a) *(atropellar)* she was run down by a bus (b) *(hablar mal de)* you shouldn't run everyone down like that (c) *(descargar)* remember to switch off the lights or they'll run the battery down; *(bajar la producción de)* the factory is being deliberately run down (d) *(encontrar tras una larga búsqueda, dar con)* the police finally ran him down in Brighton

run in 1 **vi** *(entrar corriendo)* she came running in to tell us
2 **vt sep** (a) **Brit.** *(rodar)* it will be another couple of weeks
before we've run the new machine in (b) **fam.** *(detener,*
arrestar) the police ran him in for drunk driving

run into vt insep (a) *(chocar contra)* he ran into an old lady as he raced
for his train (b) *(encontrar por casualidad)* guess who I ran
into last week! (c) *(ascender a)* the cost will run into millions

run off 1 **vi** *(irse corriendo)* he ran off when he saw me coming; *(irse,*
huir) he's run off with the woman next door
2 **vt sep** (a) *(sacar)* will you run off six copies of this? (b)
(escribir rápidamente) she runs these magazine articles off in
her spare time (c) *(perder corriendo)* he's a bit overweight and
wants to run off a few pounds

run out 1 **vi** (a) *(agotarse, faltar)* money is running out; your time is
running out (es decir, *ya no tenéis mucho tiempo*) (b) *(expirar,*
caducar) my passport is going to run out soon
2 **vt sep** *(eliminar, en críquet)* he was run out for ten

run out of vt insep *(acabarse)* I have run out of patience with you;
(quedarse sin) we're running out of butter; they ran out of
petrol (es decir, *se quedaron sin gasolina*)

run over 1 **vi** (a) *(ir rápidamente)* I won't be a minute, I'm just running
over to the shops (b) *(sobrepasar el tiempo en antena)* the live
broadcast of the football match run over into the next programme (c) *(desbordarse)* the sink is runnin over
2 **vt insep** *(examinar rápidamente)* the doctor will want to run
over your case history; *(recapitular)* let's run over the
arrangements one last time
3 **vt sep** (a) *(llevar en coche)* I'm running Mum over to her sister's, do you want to come? (b) *(atropellar)* he ran an old lady
over

run through 1 **vt insep** (a) *(consumir)* we ran through several cases of
wine over the Christmas holidays (b) *(repasar)* would you like
me to run through your speech with you?

2 **vt sep** *(atravesar con una espada)* the coachman ran the
highwayman through

run up 1 **vi** (a) *(subir corriendo)* run up and fetch my purse for me
(b) *(ir corriendo a ayudar)* people ran up to see if they could
help

2 **VT SEP** (a) *(coser rápidamente)* the dressmaker said she could run the suit up for me in a couple of days (b) *(acumular)* you've run up a lot of bills this month (c) *(izar, hablando de una bandera)* they run the flag up on special occasions

rush at **VI** *(lanzarse sobre)* he rushed at the burglar

rush through **VT SEP** (a) *(enviar urgentemente)* the necessary equipment has been rushed through to the rescue workers (b) *(hacer rápidamente)* could you rush my order through? (c) *(hacer pasar a toda prisa)* they rushed us through Customs; *(meter prisa para acabar de)* you rushed me through lunch and now you're rushing me through dinner – what's the hurry?

rustle up **VT SEP FAM.** *(improvisar)* could you rustle up a meal for me?

save up **1** **VI** *(ahorrar)* if you want a new motorbike you'll have to start saving up, won't you?
2 **VT SEP** (a) *(ahorrar)* you should save up part of your pocket money for Christmas presents (b) *(guardar)* I always save up the money-off coupons in all the magazines

score off **1** **VT SEP** *(tachar)* score his name off the guest list
2 **VT INSEP** *(marcarse un tanto sobre)* the speaker scored off the government when he reminded them of their campaign promises

score out **VT SEP BRIT.** *(tachar)* score any mistakes out neatly

scrape along **VI** *(arreglárselas)* she's scraping along until her next pay cheque

scrape by **VI** *(arreglárselas)* he's just been scraping by since he lost his job (es decir, *le cuesta llegar a final de mes...*)

scrape through **1** **VT INSEP** *(ganar por los pelos)* the government will probably just scrape through the next election
2 **VI** *(aprobar por los pelos)* I don't mind scraping by, as long as I pass the exam

scrape together/up **VT SEP** *(reunir con mucha dificultad)* I'll scrape the money together somehow

scream out 1 **VI** *(lanzar un grito)* the pain made him scream out
2 **VT SEP** *(gritar)* the sergeant major screamed out his orders

screw up **VT SEP** (a) *(atornillar)* screw it up tightly (b) *(arrugar)* she screwed the letter up and threw it in the bin (c) **BRIT.** *(entornar)* she screwed up her eyes (d) **FAM.** *(estropear, arruinar)* this rush job has screwed up my plans for the weekend; you screwed the whole thing up – next time let me do the talking (e) **FAM.** *(volver loco)* he claims it was his parents that screwed him up; she's all screwed up over that affair with the married man

see about **VT INSEP** (a) *(encargarse de)* you'll have to see about those cracks in the ceiling (b) *(pensar, ver)* I'll see about it; **FAM.** so they're going to win, are they? well, we'll see about that

see across **VT SEP** *(hacer cruzar)* she saw me across the road

see in 1 **VI** *(ver el interior)* they always keep the curtains drawn so people can't see in
2 **VT SEP** *(hacer entrar)* see the guests in, could you, please?

see off **VT SEP** *(despedirse de,en la estación, el aeropuerto, etc.)* who's coming to see you off?

see out 1 **VI** *(mirar afuera)* another passenger changed seats with the little boy so he could see out
2 **VT SEP** (a) *(acompañar a la puerta)* my husband will see you out, doctor (b) *(aguantar, pasar)* we've got enough food to see the week out

see over/round **VT INSEP** *(visitar)* would you like to see round our new house?

see through 1 **VT INSEP** *(no dejarse engañar por)* why do you persist with these stories when everyone can see through them?
2 **VT SEP** *(ayudar a pasar por)* friends and neighbours are seeing them through this bad time; *(ser suficiente para)* a couple of hundred gallons of oil should see us through the winter

see to **VT INSEP** *(ocuparse de)* let your husband see to the baby – you relax for a bit; *(reparar, arreglar)* you should get the brakes seen to

see up **VT SEP** *(acompañar a un lugar superior)* do you know where his room is or do you want me to see you up?

seize up **vi** (a) *(atascarse, bloquearse)* if you don't put some oil in soon the engine will seize up (b) *(agarrotarse)* my knee always seizes up in the cold weather

seize (up)on **vt insep** *(aprovecharse de)* it seemed like an excellent idea and we seized on it immediately (es decir, *la adoptamos enseguida*)

sell off **vt sep** *(rebajar, liquidar)* the shoe shop is closing down soon and has started to sell off its stock

sell out **1 vt sep** (a) *normalmente en voz pasiva (quedarse sin existencias)* how can a supermarket be sold out of butter?; the tickets are sold out (es decir, *se han agotado las entradas*) (b) *(traicionar)* the rebel leaders were accused of selling out their supporters **2 vi** (a) *(quedarse sin existencias)* all of the shops I tried had sold out (b) *(agotar las existencias)* they are selling out since they want to retire (c) *(renegar de sus principios)* we will negotiate but we will never sell out

sell up **1 vt sep** *normalmente en voz pasiva (liquidar el negocio)* something has to be done to prevent farmers being sold up and losing their livelihood
2 vi *(venderlo todo)* since she can no longer run the business on her own, she has decided to sell up

send away **vt sep** *(enviar)* he's too young to be sent away to school (es decir, *es demasiado joven para enviarlo a un internado*)

send away for **vt insep** *(pedir por correo)* send away for your free gift now; you should send away for an application form

send down **vt sep** (a) *(hacer bajar)* the tenants upstairs sent their daughter down with the rent money (b) *(disminuir)* the rumours have sent share prices down (c) **Brit. fam.** *(enchironar)* the judge sent her down for two years (d) **Brit.** *(expulsar)* all of the students involved in the incident were sent down for a term

send for **vt insep** *(llamar)* I think we should send for the doctor

send in **vt sep** (a) *(hacer entrar, hacer pasar)* send Mr Martin in as soon as he arrives, please (b) *(enviar)* a lot of viewers have sent in comments on the programme we aired last week

send off **vt sep** (a) *(enviar por correo)* have you sent that letter off yet?

(b) *(expulsar, hablando de un jugador)* he was sent off for spitting at the referee

send on **vt sep** (a) *(hacer llegar)* would you send on any letters that come for me?; *(enviar por adelantado)* we've decided to send our luggage on so we don't have as much to carry (b) *(hacer entrar al terreno de juego)* the coach decided to send him on

send out **vt sep** (a) *(enviar por correo)* those invitations should have been sent out a week ago (b) *(expulsar, echar)* the teacher sent him out of the classroom for talking; *(enviar fuera)* send the children out to play (c) *(emitir)* the satellite has stopped sending out signals

send out for 1 **vt insep** *(pedir que traigan)* do you want to send out for a sandwich?
2 **vt sep** *(enviar a por)* send him out for coffee for everyone

send up **vt sep** (a) *(lanzar al espacio, etc.)* the crew sent up a distress rocket (b) *(hacer subir)* news of the takeover bid sent the company's share prices up (c) **Brit.** *(parodiar)* politicians are very easy to send up; *(burlarse de)* don't you know when you're being sent up? (d) **U.S. fam.** *(enviar a chirona)* he was sent up for armed robbery

serve out **vt sep** (a) *(repartir, servir)* you can start serving out the soup while I finish preparing the main course (b) *(acabar)* my father had only just served out his apprenticeship when the war started; *(cumplir)* he served out a prison sentence

set about **vt insep** (a) *(ponerse a, hablando de una tarea)* she set about the washing up (b) *(empezar a)* be sure to take expert advice before you set about rewiring the house (c) *(atacar, física o verbalmente)* the old lady set about the boys with her stick; Mum set about me for leaving my room in such a mess

set against **vt sep** (a) *(poner en contra de)* something must have set him against the idea; it was her friends who set her against me (b) *(deducir)* some expenses can be set against taxes (c) *(comparar con)* we must set the government's promises against its performance in the past

set apart **vt sep** *(distinguir)* what sets her apart from all the other children in my class is her confidence

set aside **vt sep** (a) *(dejar de lado)* could you set aside what you're working on and do this instead?; let's set that particular aspect of the issue aside for a moment; I've decided to set aside some money every week (b) *(anular)* the Supreme Court has set aside the decision

set back **vt sep** (a) *(estar apartado de)* the cottage is set back quite a bit from the road (b) *(retrasar)* the strike has set the company back at least a month in its deliveries (c) **fam.** *(costar)* that new car must have set him back a bit; will it set me back more than a thousand?

set down **vt sep** (a) *(dejar en el suelo)* you can set those cases down in the hall (b) **Brit.** *(dejar bajar)* the bus stopped to set down one or two passengers (c) *(fijar, hablando de leyes, normas, etc.)* permissible levels of pollution are set down in the regulations (d) *(anotar)* the policeman set down the details in his notebook

set forth **vt sep** *(exponer)* would you like to set forth your suggestions to the committee?; this document sets forth a detailed description of the service provided

set in **vi** *(declararse)* the doctors are worried that gangrene might set in; *(llegar)* winter seems to be setting in early this year

set off 1 **vt sep** (a) *(hacer explotar)* terrorists have set off yet another bomb in a crowded street (b) *(desencadenar, provocar)* what set the argument off? (c) *(hacer reír, llorar, etc.)* that last joke of his set us all off; if you say any more you'll only set her off again; he is so allergic to pollen that even a vase of flowers sets him off (d) *(realzar)* those velvet curtains really set the room off (e) *(deducir)* can I set these expenses off against my tax liability?
2 **vi** *(partir, ponerse en camino)* we'll have to set off at dawn

set on 1 **vt sep** *(azuzar)* if you don't get off my land immediately, I'll set the dogs on you; *(vigilar de cerca)* they set the police on his trail
2 **vt insep** *(atacar)* travellers were often set on by highwaymen

set out 1 **vt sep** (a) *(exponer, presentar)* a mouthwatering display of desserts was set out on a side table (b) *(indicar, presentar)* this document sets out the steps that must be taken
2 **vi** (a) *(partir, ponerse en camino)* they set out late last night

(b) *(empezar)* I didn't realize when I set out just how long the job was going to take me **(c)** *(locución)* to set out to do something *querer hacer algo*

set to 1 **VI** *(empezar a trabajar, ponerse manos a la obra)* isn't it about time that we set to and cleaned out the garage?
2 **VT INSEP** *(empezar)* when are the builders going to set to work?

set up 1 **VI** *(establecerse)* they've decided to set up in business for themselves; she's setting up as a hairdresser
2 **VT SEP** **(a)** *(instalar)* marquees will be set up on the front lawn **(b)** *(organizar, concertar)* I'd like to set up an appointment with a careers adviser; *(constituir)* a task force will be set up to investigate the matter **(c)** *(instalar)* he's set her up in a flat of her own **(d)** **FAM.** *(pegársela a)* there's no point in claiming you were set up – no one will believe you

settle down 1 **VI** **(a)** *(acomodarse)* I had just settled down with a book when the phone rang **(b)** *(calmarse)* settle down, please, children **(c)** *(concentrarse en)* he must settle down to his homework **(d)** *(sentar la cabeza)* when are you going to settle down and get married?
2 **VT SEP** **(a)** *(acomodar)* just let me settle the baby down for the night **(b)** *(calmar)* I couldn't settle my class down at all today

settle for **VT INSEP** *(contentarse con, aceptar)* we haven't got any drink at all, I'm afraid – will you settle for a cup of coffee?; is that a fixed price for the house or would the seller settle for less?

settle in 1 **VI** *(instalarse)* once we're settled in, we'll invite you round; *(acostumbrarse, adaptarse)* he'll soon settle in at the job
2 **VT SEP** *(ayudar a situarse)* I'm just going to settle the new secretary in and then I'm having a holiday

settle on **VT INSEP** *(decidirse por)* have you settled on a date for the wedding yet?

settle up **VI** **(a)** *(pagar)* can I leave you to settle up? **(b)** *(saldar cuentas)* he said he would settle up with us later

shake off **VT SEP** **(a)** *(sacudir de)* shake the snow off your coat before you come in **(b)** *(quitarse de encima, hablando de una enfermedad, una costumbre, etc.)* I can't seem to shake this cold off; *(librarse de)* she shook the detective off by going into the ladies and leaving by a back door

shake up vt sep (a) *(agitar)* shake it up a bit, all the solids are at the bottom; don't shake the champagne bottle up (b) *(ahuecar, hablando de una almohada, etc.)* let me shake your pillows up for you (c) *(sacudir, conmocionar)* the news of the accident shook her up; I was badly shaken up by my narrow escape (d) fam. *(remodelar)* this committee needs shaking up a bit; *(animarse)* he needs shaking up

shell out vt sep fam. *(apoquinar)* I'm not going to shell out any more on that motorbike of his; how much do we each have to shell out for petrol?

shoot down vt sep (a) *(abatir, especialmente de un disparo)* he was shot down over France; the guerrillas claim to have shot down three planes in the last week (b) fam. *(rebatir, echar por tierra)* she shot his argument down; if he doesn't like your proposal he'll shoot it down

shoot out 1 vi *(salir con fuerza)* the water shot out of the hose
2 vt sep *(tender enérgicamente)* she shot out her hand and grabbed him before he could fall

shoot up 1 vi (a) *(dispararse)* house prices have shot up in the last year; *(levantarse)* hands were shooting up all over the room to ask questions (b) *(pincharse, inyectarse droga)* a government poster showing kids shooting up
2 vt sep *(bombardear)* the runways are so badly shot up that they are unusable

shop around vi *(comparar precios)* it pays to shop around

shout down vt sep *(rechazar con violencia)* union members shouted down management's proposal; *(impedir hablar)* don't shout her down – listen to what she has to say

show off 1 vi *(alardear)* he was flexing his muscles and generally showing off
2 vt sep (a) *(enseñar)* I think I'll go for a drive round town and show off the new car (b) *(resaltar, realzar)* wearing white always shows off a tan

show up 1 vi (a) *(notarse, verse)* the dirt really shows up on a pale carpet (b) fam. *(aparecer, presentarse)* he showed up wearing a new suit; she's always showing up late

2 **vt sep** (a) *(poner de manifiesto)* the loss of export markets shows up the company's failure to modernize (b) *(poner en evidencia)* I don't want you showing me up in front of people, so don't tell any of your crude jokes (c) *(acompañar arriba)* the porter will show you up to your room

shrug off **vt sep** *(restar importancia a)* he shrugs off all criticism

shut away **vt sep** *(encerrar)* he's been shut away in prison for the last year; ever since her husband's death, she has shut herself away

shut down **vt sep y vi** = close down

shut in **vt sep** *(encerrar)* shut the dog in

shut off 1 **vt sep** (a) *(cortar)* the electricity had to be shut off (b) *(aislar)* don't they feel shut off living in the depths of the countryside?

2 **vi** *(pararse)* the kettle shuts off automatically when the water is boiling

shut out **vt sep** (a) *(dejar fuera)* the door's locked, they've shut us out; I've forgotten my key and now I'm shut out (b) *(impedir entrar)* he drew the curtains to shut out the light; *(tapar)* we're going to plant some trees to shut out the view of the railway line (c) **fig.** *(excluir)* people want to help – why do you insist on shutting them out?

shut up 1 **vt sep** (a) *(encerrar)* the cat got accidentally shut up in the airing cupboard (b) *(cerrar)* they're away shutting up their cottage for the winter (c) **fam.** *(hacer callar)* shut those kids up, I'm trying to concentrate

2 **vi fam.** *(cerrar el pico)* don't tell me to shut up!; please can you shut up for five minutes?

shy away **vi** *(retroceder asustado)* she shied away when he tried to put his arm around her

shy away from **vt insep** *(evitar)* he has shied away from driving ever since the accident

sift out **vt sep** (a) *(quitar con el colador)* sift out any impurities (b) *(eliminar)* we have sifted out the most obviously unsuitable candidates

sign away vt sep *(renunciar a)* read the small print to be sure you're not signing away any of your rights

sign for vt insep *(firmar, hablando de un recibo)* there's a registered letter for
you – will you sign for it, please?

sign in 1 vi *(firmar el registro de entrada al llegar)* it's a rule of the club that all visitors must sign in
2 vt sep *(firmar el registro para avalar la admisión de)* I'm a member, so I can sign you in

sign off vi (a) *(acabar un programa)* they usually sign off for the day at midnight; he always signs off with that catchphrase (b) *(frase que se utiliza al final de una carta: te dejo)* I think I'll sign off now and go to bed

sign on vi Brit. *(inscribirse en el paro, sellar el paro)* how long do you have to be out of work before you can sign on?; I have to sign on every second Monday

sign up 1 vt sep *(contratar, fichar)* the committee wants to sign up more volunteers to help with the fundraising campaign
2 vi (a) *(firmar un contrato)* he signed up as a crew member (b) *(alistarse en el ejército)* my uncle tried to sign up when he was only 15 (c) *(incribirse en, hablando de un curso)* she has signed up for a class in car maintenance

simmer down vi *(calmarse)* I'll tell you what he said once I've simmered down

single out vt sep *(distinguir)* why single her out for praise? after all, we all contributed to the success of the project (es decir, *¿por qué la han felicitado a ella?*)

sink in vi (a) *(penetrar, hablando de un líquido)* pour the syrup over the cake and allow it to sink in (b) *(hacer efecto, calar)* his remark didn't sink in until she was halfway down the stairs

sit about/around vi *(estar sin hacer nada, esperar sin hacer nada)* we had to sit about in the airport lounge for two hours

sit back vi (a) *(ponerse cómodo)* I just want to sit back, put my feet up and watch some TV (b) *(quedarse de brazos cruzados)* we can't just sit back and do nothing if we think something's wrong

sit down 1 **vi** *(sentarse)* you'd better sit down, I've got some bad news 2 **vt sep** *(hacer sentar)* the doctor sat her down and explained the operation

sit in vi (a) *(asistir como oyente)* do you mind if I sit in on the class? (b) *(hacer una sentada)* students used to sit in regularly in the sixties

sit in for vt insep *(sustituir)* the chairwoman is ill and has asked me to sit in for her at the meeting

sit on vt insep (a) *(ser miembro de)* how many people sit on the committee? (b) *(guardar silencio sobre)* reporters were asked to sit on the news until the hostages were safely out of the country (c) *(guardar en secreto, no revelar)* the company decided to sit on the consultant's recommendations (d) **fam.** *(cerrar el pico a)* I'm sorry I had to sit on you like that but you were about to be indiscreet

sit out vt sep (a) *(no bailar)* I'd rather sit this one out (b) *(aguantar hasta el final)* we sat the concert out to the bitter end but it didn't get any better

sit up 1 **vi** (a) *(estar sentado)* she was sitting up in bed when I arrived; sit up straight! (es decir, *¡ponte recta!, ¡incorpórate!*) (b) *(sentarse)* sit up, I've brought you breakfast in bed (c) *(quedarse levantado, quedarse despierto)* we sat up until midnight waiting for them to arrive 2 **vt sep** *(incoporar)* the nurse sat the old man up

size up vt sep *(observar)* she looked round the room, sizing everyone up

skim off vt sep *(quitar con una espumadera)* let the soup cool and then skim off any fat on the surface; **fig.** *(quedarse con)* he always skims off the best applicants for his department

skim over/through vt insep *(echar un vistazo a)* the lawyer skimmed over his client's statement

slap on vt sep fam. (a) *(aplicar de cualquier manera)* just slap some paint on and that will hide the marks (b) *(añadir)* the government has slapped ten pence on the cost of a gallon of petrol

sleep around vi fam. *(ser promiscuo)* before she met her husband she had quite a reputation for sleeping around

sleep in vi (a) *(levantarse tarde, no despestarse a la hora)* this is the third morning this week I've slept in and been late for work (b) *(hospedarse en el lugar de trabajo)* she has two maids sleeping in

sleep off vt sep *(dormir para recuperarse de)* he's upstairs sleeping off his hangover

sleep on 1 vi *(seguir durmiendo)* let her sleep on for as long as she likes
2 vt insep *(posponer para el día siguiente, hablando de una decisión, etc.)* you don't have to make your mind up now – sleep on it and then call me; I'll sleep on it (es decir, *la noche es buena consejera*)

sleep together vi *(acostarse juntos)* when did you start to sleep together?

sleep with vt insep *(acostarse con)* she's been sleeping with him for a year

slip away vi *(desaparecer, irse discretamente)* she slipped away from the party; *(pasar deprisa)* the time just slips away when I'm with him (es decir, *las horas me pasan volando cuando estoy con él*)

slip by 1 vi *(pasar deprisa)* the time has slipped by
2 vt insep *(pasar por alto a)* how did that mistake manage to slip by you?

slip in 1 vi *(entrar, colarse discretamente)* I just slipped in for five minutes
2 vt sep *(introducir)* she slipped in a remark about his affair

slip off 1 vi *(marcharse)* we didn't see you go – when did you slip off?
2 vt sep *(quitarse)* she slipped off her coat

slip on vt sep *(ponerse, hablando de una prenda de vestir)* she slipped a dressing gown on and ran to answer the door

slip out vi (a) *(salir discretamente)* we slipped out halfway through the concert (b) *(escapársele a alguien)* I didn't mean to give the secret away, it just slipped out

slip up vi fam. *(meter la pata)* slip up one more time and you're fired

slow down/up 1 **vi** *(aminorar la velocidad)* slow down, there's a speed limit here; slow down, I can't understand what you're saying 2 **vt sep** *(aflojar el paso)* can't you walk any faster? you're slowing everyone down

smooth down **vt sep** (a) *(alisar)* smooth down your hair – it's sticking up all over the place (b) *(calmar, tranquilizar)* he's really very upset – give me a few minutes to smooth him down

smooth out **vt sep** (a) *(alisar, hablando de arrugas, pliegues, etc.)* she smoothed out the creases from the tablecloth (b) *(resolver)* we have a little problem we hope you can help us smooth out

smooth over **vt sep** *(tranquilizar)* the chairman smoothed over the dispute with a light remark; *(arreglar, solucionar)* I smoothed things over

snap out **vt sep** *(decir en un tono seco)* the sergeant snapped out an order

snap out of **vt insep** *(quitarse de encima, referido a un estado de ánimo)* you must snap out of this depression

snap up **vt sep fam.** *(quitarse de las manos)* the towels are so cheap people are snapping them up

snarl up **vt sep Brit.** *(atascarse)* because of the accident, traffic is all snarled up on the motorway

snow under **vt sep fam.** *normalmente en voz pasiva (estar desbordado)* we have been snowed under with orders

soldier on **vi** *(seguir adelante)* I know you're all very tired but if you could soldier on till the project is finished, I'd be very grateful

sort out **vt sep** (a) *(ordenar)* I've sorted out all those tools that you had just thrown in the drawer (b) *(seleccionar)* I've sorted out some books for you to take away with you (c) *(resolver)* maybe he needs some counselling to sort out his problems (d) *(fijar)* we need to sort out a date for the next meeting (e) **fam.** *(saldar cuentas verbal o físicamente con)* it's about time someone sorted him out

sound off **vi** *(refunfuñar)* she is always sounding off about rude shop assistants

sound out **VT SEP** *(pedir la opinión de)* I want to recommend you for the job but I thought I should sound you out first and see if you'd be interested

spell out **VT SEP** (a) *(deletrear)* it's rather an unusual name so I'll spell it out for you (b) *(explicar con claridad)* the chairman spelled out what a strike would mean for the company's future; do I have to spell it out for you?

spin out **VT SEP** *(hacer durar, estirar)* I have to spin my spending money out until the end of the holiday

splash down **VI** *(amerizar)* the capsule splashed down at 13.00 hours just off Haiti

splash out 1 **VI FAM.** *(gastarse un dineral)* let's splash out for once and stay in the best hotels
2 **VT INSEP** *(gastarse)* she splashed out a lot of money on a camera

split up 1 **VT SEP** (a) *(partir)* he split the wood up into small pieces (b) *(compartir, repartir)* we're going to split the money up among our children (c) *(separar)* the teacher split the boys up
2 **VI** *(separarse, hablando de una pareja)* I hear they're splitting up

spring up **VI** (a) *(levantar bruscamente)* several hands sprang up (b) *(crecer)* hasn't Lisa sprung up this year! (c) *(surgir, aparecer bruscamente)* weeds are springing up all over the garden after the rain; the company sprang up almost overnight

square up **VI** (a) *(hacer cuentas con)* can we square up later?; I'll square up with you when I get paid if that's all right (b) *(ponerse en guardia)* the two men were so angry with each other that they began to square up (c) *(hacer frente a)* it was wonderful the way you squared up to that bully

stamp out **VT SEP** *(acabar con)* the military government has vowed to stamp out unrest

stand by 1 **VI** (a) *(quedarse sin hacer nada)* people just stood by and watched the policeman being beaten up (b) *(mantenerse al margen)* viewers were told to stand by for further developments; *(estar preparado)* the police were standing by to disperse the crowd

2 **vt insep** *(mantener)* the government has promised to stand by its election promises

stand down vi *(dimitir, retirarse)* he will stand down as chairman of the football club at the end of the year

stand for vt insep (a) *(presentarse a, hablando de unas elecciones)* I have decided to stand for the chairmanship of the committee; she is standing for election (b) *(querer decir, significar)* what does the F stand for in JFK? (c) *(tolerar)* I won't stand for that kind of behaviour

stand in vi *(sustituir a)* Mr Wilson has very kindly agreed to stand in at short notice for our scheduled speaker

stand out vi (a) *(destacar)* he is so tall that he stands out in a crowd; what makes her stand out is her platinum blonde hair (b) *(resistir)* we are standing out against management's attempts to break our strike

stand up 1 vi (a) *(levantarse)* everyone stood up when the president entered the room (b) *(sostenerse, ser válido, hablando de un argumento)* the prosecution hasn't got enough evidence for the charge to stand up
2 **vt sep fam.** *(dar plantón a)* that's the second time this month I've been stood up!

stand up for vt insep *(defender, luchar por)* my parents stood up for me when I was in trouble; stand up for what you believe in

stand up to vt insep *(hacer frente a)* I admired the way she stood up to that aggressive drunk

start off 1 vi (a) *(salir)* the runners will be starting off in the coolness of the early morning (b) *(comenzar)* to put your audience at ease, start off with a joke or two; *(debutar, estrenarse)* he started off as a cashier
2 **vt sep** (a) *(empezar)* start your presentation off with a brief history of the problem (b) *(disparar, hablando de un dispositivo)* what started the alarm off?; *(hacer reír, llorar, etc.)* there's the baby crying again – what started her off this time?

start up 1 vi (a) *(arrancar, ponerse en marcha)* she heard a car starting up next door (b) *(montar un negocio)* there's a new dry cleaner's starting up on the corner

2 **vt sep** (a) *(arrancar, poner en marcha)* start the engines up (b) *(montar)* they're starting up another restaurant

stay off 1 **vi** (a) *(quedarse en casa)* he's decided to stay off and see if he can cure this cold (b) *(no empezar a llover)* do you think the rain will stay off until the washing's dry?
2 **vt insep** *(no ir a)* can I stay off school today?

stay out **vi** (a) *(no volver a casa)* I can't stay out late like I used to, not when I have work the next day (b) *(continuar la huelga)* the women have decided to stay out until their demands are met

step in **vi** *(intervenir)* the government should step in and order the strikers back to work

step up **vt sep** *(acelerar, aumentar)* research into this disease must be stepped up; the company is stepping up production of the vaccine

stick around **vi fam** *(quedarse)* stick around, we may need you

stick out 1 **vi** (a) *(asomar, sobresalir)* the label on your dress is sticking out; his ears stick out (es decir, *tener las orejas salidas*) (b) *(destacar, sobresalir)* she sticks out because of the way she dresses
2 **vt sep** *(asomar por, sacar por)* stick your head out the window and see if they're coming

stick to **vt insep** (a) *(seguir en)* the cloth is sticking to the table (b) *(seguir, hablando de una decisión, unos planes, etc.)* she's sticking to her plans despite her parents' opposition; it's a very tough exercise regime – do you think you'll stick to it?; *(contentarse con)* if red wine gives you a headache, stick to white

stop by 1 **vi insep** *(pasarse por)* stop by the post office on your way home
2 **vi** *(pasarse)* we'll stop by and see you next week

stop off **vi** *(parar, hacer un alto)* they're stopping off at Bali for a couple of days on their way back

stop over **vi** *(hacer escala)* we stopped over at Singapore on the flight to Sydney

straighten out 1 **vt sep** (a) *(alisar, estirar, hablando de un tejido)* she straightened out the crumpled bedclothes (b) *(resolver, esclarecer)* we need to straighten a few things out in this relationship

2 **vi** *(hacerse recto, hablando de una carretera, un camino, etc.)* after twisting and turning for a couple of hundred yards, the path finally straightened out

straighten up 1 **vt sep** (a) *(poner recto, poner derecho)* can you straighten up that picture for me? (b) *(ordenar)* straighten your room up a bit, it's very untidy
2 **vi** *(ponerse derecho)* she straightened up and rubbed her back

strike back **vi** (a) *(contestar, responder)* the government struck back at its critics with a strong defence of its actions (b) *(marcar un tanto tras haber encajado otro antes)* two minutes later, the home team struck back

strike off **vt sep** *(tachar)* your name has been struck off (the list)

strike out 1 **vt sep** *(tachar)* strike out whichever answer does not apply
2 **vi** (a) *(golpear, pegar)* he struck out at his opponent (b) *(ir hacia)* we're all tired, let's strike out for home (c) *(locución)* I'm striking out on my own *me establezco por cuenta propia*

strike up 1 **vt sep** (a) *(empezar a tocar)* the orchestra struck up a waltz (b) *(empezar, iniciar)* he immediately struck up a conversation with me; they struck up a friendship at school (es decir, *se hicieron amigos en la escuela*)
2 **vi** *(empezar a tocar, hablando de una orquesta, etc.)* the band struck up

string along **vt sep fam.** *(hacer caminar)* that garage is just stringing you along – the car can't possibly be repaired; he just strung her along till he'd taken all her money and then he vanished

string up **vt sep fam.** *(colgar, ahorcar)* they should string child abusers up from the nearest lamp post

strip down **vt sep** *(desmontar)* the garage can't find the fault without stripping down the engine completely

strip off 1 **vt sep** *(hacer caer)* the wind stripped all the leaves off the trees; *(quitar)* he stripped off all his clothes and jumped into the water; we'll have to strip off about six layers of paint from this door
2 **vi** *(desnudarse)* strip off and let the doctor examine you

sum up 1 **vt sep** (a) *(resumir)* the chairman summed up the committee's discussions (b) *(evaluar)* he summed us up immediately; he began his address by summing up the situation
2 **vi** *(recapitular)* when summing up, the judge warned the jury against jumping to conclusions

summon up **vt sep** *(armarse de)* I summoned up all my courage and asked to speak to the manager

swallow up **vt sep** *(tragarse)* the sea swallowed them up; they were soon swallowed up by the mist (es decir, *la bruma los envolvió*)

swear in **vt sep** *(tomar juramento a)* as soon as the witness had been sworn in, the lawyer began questioning her; the new president was sworn in today

sweat out **vt sep** (a) *(sudar)* have a sauna and sweat your cold out (b) *(locución)* oh, just leave him to sweat it out, he'll find out soon enough *oh, pues deja que se las arregle él solo...*

switch back **vi** *(volver a)* we tried electricity but we've decided to switch back to gas

switch off/on **Brit.** 1 **vt sep** *(apagar/encender, hablando de un aparato eléctrico, un interruptor, etc.)* switch the radio off/on
2 **vi** *(apagarse/encenderse)* where does the power switch off/on?

switch over 1 **vi** *(cambiar, hablando de una cadena de de televisión, de una emisora de radio)* shall I switch over? the news is on the other side

switch round **vt sep** *(cambiar de sitio)* someone switched the drinks round and the Duchess got the poison by mistake

tail away/off **vi** *(disminuir, debilitarse)* the noise of the lorry tailed away in the distance; *(desvanecerse)* her voice tailed off as she realized that no one was listening

tail back **vi Brit.** *(formar un embotellamiento)* the traffic tailed back all the way to the intersection

take aback VT SEP *(sorprender, desconcertar)* his ignorance really took me aback; *(coger por sorpresa)* the enemy was completely taken aback by the speed of our attack

take after VT INSEP *(parecerse a)* don't blame me, it's her father she takes after

take apart VT SEP (a) *(desmontar)* the radio hasn't worked since he took it apart (b) FAM. *(criticar)* the critics have really taken her new film apart

take around VT SEP *(hacer visitar)* would you like someone to take you around?

take away 1 VI *(quitar)* the fact that he lost in the first round doesn't take away from his overall skill (es decir, *no le quita talento*) 2 VT SEP (a) *(restar)* what do you get if you take 28 away from 70? (b) *(llevarse)* they took her father away in an ambulance last night (c) *(llevar)* how about some curry to take away?

take back VT SEP (a) *(devolver)* take these library books back, will you? (b) *recoger, buscar)* when is Tony coming to take back those records you borrowed? (c) *(retirar, hablando de un comentario)* now that I know her better, I take back all that I said about her (d) *(admitir devoluciones)* will the shop take it back if it doesn't fit?; she's a fool to take him back (e) *(traer recuerdos de)* these old songs take me back to when I was a teenager

take down VT SEP (a) *(quitar, descolgar)* it's time we took the curtains down for a wash; take all your posters down (b) *(desmontar, quitar)* when are the workmen going to take down the scaffolding?; the shops still haven't taken down their Christmas decorations (c) *(anotar, apuntar)* the reporter took down very little of what was said at the meeting

take in VT SEP (a) *(llevar a)* take your coat in to the cleaner's tomorrow (b) *(recoger, acoger)* they take in all the stray cats in the neighbourhood; *(admitir)* she has to take in lodgers to make ends meet (c) *(volver a ponerse, hablando de una prenda de vestir)* could you take this skirt in? (d) *(comprender, abacar todos los aspectos)* he reeled off so many facts and figures that I couldn't take them all in (e) *(abarcar, comprender)* the Prime Minister's tour will take in a number of urban renewal projects (f) *(ir a ver)* do you want to take in a movie?; let's take in a few of the sights first (g) *(timar, engañar)* he took the old lady in by telling her he had known her son; don't be taken in by appearances (es decir, *las apariencias engañan*)

take off 1 VI (a) *(despegar, hablando de un avion)* we took off an hour late **(b)** **FAM.** *(despegar, desarrollarse)* the company's sales really took off last month **(c)** **FAM.** *(irse, marcharse)* they're taking off for France next week; *(salir del trabajo)* he's taking off early tonight
2 VT SEP (a) *(quitar)* take your hat off; *(retirar)* the policeman was taken off the murder enquiry because he knew the people involved **(b)** *(amputar)* they had to take her leg off below the knee **(c)** *(reducir)* he needs to take a few pound off (es decir, *debe perder* peso); the saleswoman took a couple off because of this stain (es decir, *ha rebajado el precio de los libros*) **(d)** *(coger un permiso)* why don't you take the rest of the day off? **(e)** *(imitar)* he takes off the president extremely well

take on VT SEP (a) *(hacerse cargo de)* when I married you I didn't realize I'd be taking on your whole family too; she's exhausted with all the extra work she's been taking on recently **(b)** *(contratar)* that new electronics firm took on 200 people this week **(c)** *(pelearse con)* why did you agree to take him on? – he's twice your size; *(enfrentarse a)* it was a mistake to take on the best snooker player in the club **(d)** *(adquirir)* his face took on a cunning look; life has taken on a whole new meaning since I met you **(e)** *(recoger)* the train made an unscheduled stop to take on passengers

take out VT SEP (a) *(sacar)* if you want to work in the garage, you'll have to take the car out; *(quitar)* washing won't take that stain out, the dress will have to be dry cleaned **(b)** *(quitar, arrancar)* I'm having two teeth taken out tomorrow **(c)** *(retirar, sacar, hablando de dinero)* how much do you think we need to take out of our account? **(d)** *(llevar, invitar)* he took her out to dinner at a lovely restaurant **(e)** *(contratar)* have you taken out insurance on the new car?; *(suscribirse a)* how about taking out a subscription to this computer magazine? **(f)** *(descargar, hablando de la ira, etc.)* why should he take his anger out on us? **(g)** **FAM.** *(locución) (cansar)* kids take a lot out of you; that really took it out of me **(h)** **FAM.** *(destruir)* our men took out three enemy encampments

take over 1 **VI** *(tomar el poder, la dirección, etc.)* the new chairman will take over next week; *(invadir)* we ought to do something about the garden – the weeds are taking over
2 **VT SEP** (a) *(tomar la dirección o el poder de)* she will be taking over the running of the hotel (b) *(absorber, adquirir)* they were taken over by a Japanese firm

take round **VT SEP** (a) *(llevar)* take this cake round to your grandmother's for me (b) *(hacer visitar)* the supervisor was asked to take the trade delegates round the factory

take to **VT INSEP** (a) *(hacer amistad con)* I've never really taken to the people next door (b) *(adquirir la costumbre de, ponerse a)* he has taken to treating me like an enemy (c) *(huir a)* the outlaws took to the hills

take up 1 **VI** *(continuar, retomar el hilo)* anyway, to take up where I left off, she's been fired
2 **VT SEP** (a) *(levantar)* during their search, the policemen even took up the floorboards (b) *(subir a un piso superior)* take this tray up to your mother (c) *(acortar)* these curtains need to be taken up a couple of inches (d) *(ocupar)* I've taken up too much of your time; the bed is so large it just about takes up the entire room (e) *(discutir sobre, hablar de)* I think you should take up the question of training with the personnel manager (f) *(ponerse a, hablando de un pasatiempo)* he must be mad taking up jogging at his age!; *(aceptar, coger, hablando de un empleo)* when she first took up the appointment she had very little marketing experience (g) *(aceptar)* I'm going to take up that offer of a weekend in the country (h) *(continuar, retomar)* her sister took up the thread of the conversation

take up on **VT SEP** (a) *(retomar, hablando de un tema en un debate, etc.)* the Leader of the Opposition took the Prime Minister up on that last point (b) *(aceptar, hablando de una oferta, etc.)* if they don't take me up on this offer it's their loss not mine; *(hacer cumplir, hablando de una promesa)* have you taken him up on his promise of a lift to work every morning?; I'll take you up on that sometime (es decir, *otra vez será*)

take upon **VT SEP** *(encargarse de)* you took that task upon yourself; why did she take it upon herself to call the police?

take up with **vt insep** *(hacer amistad con, frecuentar)* he's taken up with a bad crowd recently

talk away 1 **vi** *(hablar sin parar)* the old lady was talking away about her youth
2 **vt sep** *(pasar el tiempo hablando)* we talked half the night away

talk back **vi** *(contestar con insolencia, sobre todo los niños)* don't talk back to your father

talk down **vt sep** (a) *(convencer para que baje, hablando de una persona que pretende suicidarse tirándose desde un lugar elevado)* the police officers managed to talk her down (b) *(dar instrucciones para aterrizar por radiocontrol)* the fog was so thick at the airport that several planes had to be talked down

talk down to **vt insep** *(hablar con aires de superioridad)* I wish she wouldn't talk down to me –I'm not stupid

talk over **vt sep** *(hablar de)* they've decided to talk things over and see if they can reach some kind of agreement

talk round 1 **vt sep** *(hacer cambiar de opinión a)* Dad won't let me go to the concert – could you try talking him round?
2 **vt insep** *(dar vueltas a)* they seemed nervous about tackling the problem directly and just talked round it

tamper with **vt insep** *(manipular)* after the car accident, he claimed that the brakes had been tampered with

tangle up **vt sep** (a) *(enredar, enmarañar)* the kitten tangled all the wool up (b) *normalmente en voz pasiva (enredarse)* he got tangled up in the barbed wire when he tried to climb the fence (c) *(estar involucrado en)* I'm sure she's tangled up in something dishonest

tangle with **vt insep** **fam.** *(pelearse con)* he tangled with a drunk about some stupid football game

tear apart **vt sep** (a) *(destruir, destrozar)* the country is being torn apart by civil war (b) *(registrar, poner patas arriba)* the police tore the place apart looking for drugs

tear away **vt sep** (a) *(arrancar)* I tore away the wrapping paper (b) *(alejarse, despegarse)* if you can tear yourself away from that television for a minute, we could actually have a conversation

tear into vt insep (a) *(abalanzarse sobre)* the lion tore into the flesh of the deer it had killed (b) fam. *(echar una bronca a)* the boss tore into me for being late for the meeting

tear off vt sep *(arrancar)* she tore the label off the suitcase

tear up vt sep (a) *(romper en trocitos)* his letter made her so angry she tore it up and threw it in the bin (b) fig. *(anular, romper)* the football player threatened to tear up his contract if the club didn't pay him more

tell off vt sep *(reñir)* I told him off for his cheek

tell on vt insep (a) *(denunciar)* Mum knows about the practical joke we were planning – someone must have told on us (b) *(tener un efecto negativo sobre)* the strain of waiting for news is telling on her

thaw out vi (a) *(descongelarse)* leave the meat to thaw out (b) fig. *(entrar en calor)* have a cup ot tea and thaw out; *(soltarse, coger confianza)* he's pretty unsociable but he does thaw out sometimes

thin out 1 vi *(perder el cabello)* he's thinning out on top; *(mermar)* audiences are thinning out; his hair is thinning out 2 vt sep *(entresacar, aclarar)* thin the plants out in autumn

think about vt insep (a) *(pensar en)* it's strange that you should have phoned just when I was thinking about you (b) *(pensar, tener previsto)* I'm thinking about going to the cinema tonight – do you want to come?

think back vi *(intentar recordar)* think back and try to remember what had happened; thinking back, I don't believe we did send them a Christmas card (es decir, *ahora que lo pienso...*)

think of 2 vt insep (a) *(pensar en)* it's about time she started thinking of herself instead of other people all the (b) *(recordar, acordarse de)* I can't think of his telephone number at the moment (c) *(imaginar)* just think of it, a holiday in the Caribbean! (d) *(tener una opinión sobre)* what do you think of the latest fashions?; she thinks very highly of him (es decir, *ella tiene una muy buena opinión de él*) (e) *(considerar)* we wouldn't think of letting our daughter go to Thailand on her own (f) *(tener la idea de, encontrar)* who thought of coming to this restaurant?; I've thought of a solution to the problem think out/through **vt sep** *(meditar)* I don't think you've thought out your plan very thoroughly; let's think things through before we make any firm decision

think over **vt sep** *(reflexionar sobre)* I told him I would think his offer over

think up **vt sep** *(tener, hablando de una idea, etc.)* they've thought up a brilliant idea

throw away **vt sep** (a) *(tirar)* throw those old papers away (b) *(malgastar)* she threw away her chance of a place at university; you're just throwing your money away buying all those computer games and DVDs

throw back **vt sep** (a) *(volver a tirar)* the fish was so small that the angler threw it back (b) *(echar hacia atrás)* she threw her head back

throw in **vt sep** *(regalar)* we took the bed and they threw in the mattress for nothing

throw off **vt sep** (a) *(quitarse rápidamente, hablando de una prenda de vestir)* he threw off his clothes and jumped into the river (b) *(deshacerse dede, hablando de una enfermedad, etc.)* I can't seem to throw off this virus

throw out **vt sep** (a) *(tirar, echar a la basura)* don't throw those photographs out (b) *(rechazar, hablando de una propuesta, etc.)* after discussion, the committee threw the proposal out (c) *(expulsar, echar)* the boys got thrown out of the cinema for misbehaving

throw together **vt sep** (a) **fam.** *(hacer algo deprisa y corriendo)* it's not very well made, it looks a bit thrown together (b) *(meter)* he threw some clothes together in a suitcase and raced to the airport (c) *(reunir, juntar, hablando de personas)* fate threw the two of them together; on such a small cruise ship, everyone is thrown together, like it or not

throw up 1 **vi fam.** *(vomitar)* no wonder you threw up, mixing your drinks like that
2 **vt sep** *(dejar escapar)* imagine throwing up a chance to go to the United States

tick off **vt sep** (a) *(marcar con una cruz)* will you tick people's names off as they come in to vote? (b) **BRIT. FAM.** *(echar la bronca a)* the teacher ticked him off for being late

tick over VI *(ir bien, funcionar, hablando de una máquina, un comercio, etc.)* the restaurant is ticking over quite well

tide over VT SEP *(llegar a, hablando de dinero)* could you lend me twenty pounds to tide me over until the end of the week?

tie down VT SEP *(atar)* children tie you down; I don't want to be tied down to any specific date

tie in VI *(concordar, encajar)* how does the suspect's story tie in with his wife's?

tie up   1 **VI** *(concordar, estar relacionado)* his debts, the robbery, and now a new car – it all ties up
2 **VT SEP** *normalmente en voz pasiva* (a) *(invertir, inmovilizar, hablando de)* my capital is tied up in stocks and shares; his money is tied up until he's 25 (b) *(estar ocupado)* she'll be tied up all afternoon

tighten up VT SEP (a) *(apretar)* he bent to tighten up his shoelaces (b) *(reforzar, intensificar)* they're tightening up the rules on tax shelters; the company has decided that security must be tightened up

tip off VT SEP FAM. *(advertir, dar un soplo a)* someone must have tipped him off that the police were on their way; the reporter was tipped off about an interesting story

tone down VT SEP (a) *(rebajar el tono de)* we toned our original colour scheme down (b) **FIG.** *(suavizar, moderar)* the reporter was told to tone his article down or the paper would be sued

top up VT SEP BRIT. *(llenar, hablando de un vaso, un depósito, etc.)* he kept topping my glass up; *(servir más, hablando de una bebida)* can I top you up?

touch down VI *(aterrizar, hablando de un avión, una nave espacial, etc.)* Concorde touched down exactly on schedule

touch up VT SEP (a) *(retocar)* this bit of the window frame needs to be touched up; she's just gone to touch up her make-up (b) **BRIT. FAM.** *(sobar, manosear)* if you don't stop touching me up I'll slap your face

touch (up)on vt insep *(abordar)* his speech didn't even touch on the pollution problem

toughen vt sep *(hacer más fuerte)* he's one of those parents who send their sons to boarding school to toughen them up

trail away/off vi *(debilitarse, hablando de una voz, un ruido, etc.)* his voice trailed away with embarrassment

trot out vt sep fam. *(salir con)* don't trot out the same old excuses; he's not going to trot that speech out again, is he?

try for vt insep *(intentar obtener)* she is trying for a place at music school; he's trying for the record (es decir, *intenta batir el récord*)

try on vt sep *(probarse, hablando de una prenda de vestir, de calzado, etc.)* I've been trying dresses on all morning

try out vt sep *(poner a prueba)* the football club is trying him out in goal; *(probar)* you can have the car for a day to try it out

turn against 1 vt insep *(volverse contra)* why have you turned against me?
2 vt sep *(volver contra)* she claims that her ex-husband is turning their children against her

turn back 1 vi *(dar media vuelta)* we turned back because the path had become too faint to follow
2 vt sep (a) *(negar la entrada a, hacer volver a)* the refugees were turned back at the border (b) *(abrir)* she reluctantly turned back the bedclothes and got up (c) *(atrasar, hablando de un reloj, etc.)* we turned our watches back an hour

turn down vt sep (a) *(bajarse)* since the rain had stopped, he turned his coat collar down (b) *(bajar, hablando de la calefacción, el sonido, etc.)* turn the heating down a bit; can you turn your music down a bit? (c) *(rechazar)* I've been turned down for that job I applied for; she turned down his offer of a weekend in Paris

turn in 1 vi fam. *(acostarse)* it's late, why don't we turn in?
2 vt sep (a) *(denunciar a la policía)* his former wife turned him in (b) *(devolver, entregar)* hundreds of weapons were turned in during the amnesty

turn off 1 **vi** *(girar, hablando de un vehículo, etc.)* you turn off at the second street on the left
2 **vt sep** (a) *(apagar, hablando de la radio, un motor, etc.)* be sure to turn the stove off; *(cerrar)* who didn't turn the tap off? (b) **fam.** *(asquear, dar asco, a menudo desde un punto de vista sexual)* smelly feet really turn me off

turn on 1 **vt sep** (a) *(encender, hablando de un aparato, etc.)* turn the gas on for me (b) **fam.** *(excitar, a menudo desde un punto de vista sexual)* rock music turns her on; he is turned on by her
2 **vt insep** (a) *(volverse contra)* one of her dogs turned on her; he turned on me when I suggested that he retire (b) *(depender de)* the company's success turns on the skills of its employees

turn out 1 **vi** (a) *(acudir, presentarse)* not many people turned out for his funeral (b) *(resultar ser)* it's one of those silly stories where the heroine turns out to be a lost heiress (c) *(quedar, salir)* how did the cake turn out?; *(acabar)* everything will turn out fine (es decir, *todo se arreglará, todo irá bien*)
2 **vt sep** (a) *(apagar)* it's time you turned the light out and went to sleep (b) *(vaciar)* I turned out my handbag to look for my keys (c) *(producir)* we're now turning out 100 computers a day (d) *(echar)* the old man was turned out of his cottage

turn over 1 **vi** *(darse la vuelta)* he turned over in bed; *(volcar)* the lifeboat turned over and sank in seconds
2 **vt sep** (a) *(entregar)* the suspect was turned over to the police; *(dar)* they have turned the running of the restaurant over to their son-in-law (b) *normalmente juntos (ganar alrededor de)* he must be turning over a good ten thousand a week

turn round 1 **vi** (a) *(volverse)* he turned round and looked at her (b) *(dar media vuelta)* he just turned round and punched the other guy
2 **vt insep** *(girar, dar la vuelta en)* turn round the next corner
3 **vt sep** (a) *(enderezar)* the company was headed for bankruptcy but the new management team turned it round (b) *(ejecutar)* how quickly can you turn this order round? (c) *(girar, dar la vuelta a)* she turned the chair round and sat down

turn up 1 **vi** (a) *(aparecer, presentarse)* he always turns up late; she turned up at the party with her new boyfriend (b) *(encontrar)* if you're sure that you lost it in the house, then it's bound to turn up one day (c) *(pasar, producirse)* things always have a habit of turning up when you least expect them to

2 **VT SEP** (a) *(subirse)* he turned his collar up in the wind (b) *(subir, hablando del volumen, la calefacción, etc.)* turn the television up, will you, I can hardly hear; turn the heat up a bit

urge on **VT SEP** *(animar)* the marathon runner said he managed to finish the race only because the crowd urged him on; *(incitar, alentar)* her family is urging her on to go to university

use up **VT SEP** *(acabar)* use up the last of the milk before it turns sour; *(agotar)* the children used up all their energy playing

verge on **VT INSEP** *(estar al borde de)* I was verging on tears; they are verging on bankruptcy; *(rozar)* his feeling was one of panic verging on hysteria; she's verging on forty

vote down **VT SEP** *(rechazar, hablando de una enmienda, etc.)* the amendment to the law was voted down

vote in **VT SEP** *(elegir)* the other members of the committee voted her in as chairperson

vote on **VT INSEP** *(votar)* union members will be asked to vote on management's latest offer; it was voted on last night

wade in **VI BRIT. FAM.** *(meterse en)* when the fight started, everybody waded in; our discussion wasn't really anything to do with her, but she waded in anyway

wade into **VT INSEP BRIT. FAM.** *(acometer)* he got up early and waded into the job of cleaning the windows; *(arremeter contra)* I'm sorry,

I shouldn't have waded into you for something so minor

wait behind vi *(quedarse atrás)* she volunteered to wait behind until the doctor came

wait in vi *(quedarse esperando en casa, en el despacho, etc.)* I was late because I had to wait in for the telephone engineer

wait on 1 vi *(esperar)* he waited on in the hope that she would eventually arrive
2 vt insep *(servir)* the waitress who was waiting on them seemed to have vanished

wait up vi *(esperar levantado, esperar despierto)* don't wait up, I'll be very late

wake up 1 vi (a) *(despertarse)* she woke up when the church bells started ringing (b) fig. *(abrir los ojos)* his mother never did wake up to the fact that he was a thief
2 vt sep (a) *(despertar)* don't wake me up too early tomorrow (b) fig. *(espabilar, despertar)* this country needs waking up

walk into vt insep (a) *(entrar en)* she walked into the room; *(caer en)* the suspect walked right into the trap the police had set for him (b) *(chocar con)* I almost walked into a lamp post

walk off 1 vi *(marcharse, irse)* he walked off and left us standing there
2 vt sep *(dar un paseo para bajar la comida)* let's go out and walk off our Christmas dinner

walk off with vt insep (a) *(alzarse)* she walked off with the first prize in the short-story competition (b) *(robar)* the bank manager has walked off with a million pounds (c) *(coger, llevarse)* who keeps walking off with the scissors?

walk out vi (a) *(salir)* she walked out of the room (b) *(declararse en huelga)* hundreds of workers walked out yesterday

walk out on vt insep *(abandonar, hablando de la familia, la pareja, etc.)* you can't just walk out on your wife and children!

walk over 1 vt insep *(dar una paliza a, vencer)* the champion walked all over another opponent today
2 vi *(ir)* I'll walk over to her place tomorrow

walk through vt insep *(conseguir fácilmente)* you'll walk through the job interview

walk up **vi** (a) *(subir andando)* the lift was out of order so we had to walk all the way up (b) *(acercarse)* a complete stranger walked up and started talking to me

warm up **1** **vi** (a) *(hacer más calor)* I hope it starts warming up now that spring is here (b) *(calentar)* tennis players get a couple of minutes to warm up before the match
2 **vt sep** (a) *(calentar)* warm up some soup for yourself (b) *(animar)* can't we do anything to warm this dinner party up?; *(calentar, preparar al público, etc.)* the star of the show doesn't appear until the other acts have warmed the audience up

warn off **vt sep** (a) *(desaconsejar)* I was going to buy it but someone warned me off (b) *(pedir insistentemente a alguien que se vaya)* he warned them off his land

wash down **vt sep** *(hacer bajar, hablando de una comida, un medicamento)* have a glass of water to wash your medicine down

wash off **1** **vi** *(quitarse, desaparecer)* do you think these stains will wash off?
2 **vt sep** *(lavar, quitar lavando)* just let me wash the oil off my hands

wash out **vt sep** (a) *(enjuagar)* wash your mouth out, please (b) *normalmente en voz pasiva (ser suspendido por la lluvia)* the women's tennis final has been washed out

wash over **vt insep** *(dejar indiferente)* anything I say just washes over her; his mother's death seems to have washed over him

wash up **1** **vi** (a) **Brit.** *(fregar la vajilla, lavar los platos)* whose turn is it to wash up? (b) **U.S.** *(lavarse)* don't serve supper until I've washed up
2 **vt sep** (a) **Brit.** *(fregar, lavar)* why I am always left with the greasy pots to wash up? (b) *(arrastrar hasta la costa)* a body was found washed up on the beach

watch out **vi** *(tener cuidado)* watch out for bones when you're eating the fish; watch out, you nearly broke the window

water down **vt sep** (a) *(aguar, rebajar una bebida alcohólica)* water this down with a drop of soda, will you? (b) **fig.** *(suavizar)* the theatre critic accused the editor of watering his review down

wave down **vt sep** *(hacer señas para detener)* he didn't see the policeman waving him down

wave on VT SEP *(hacer señas para seguir)* the border guard waved them on without looking at their passports

wear away VT SEP *(erosionar)* the sea is wearing the coastline away

wear down VT SEP (a) *(gastar, desgastar)* I've worn the heels of my shoes down (b) *(agotar, extenuar)* her busy schedule finally wore her down

wear off VI *(desaparecer)* the effect of the anaesthetic is wearing off

wear out 1 VT SEP (a) *(gastar)* that's the second pair of shoes he's worn out in six months (b) *(agotar, extenuar)* she's wearing herself out with the preparations for her daughter's wedding 2 VI *(desgastarse)* the carpet is wearing out

weed out VT SEP FIG. *(descartar)* we have weeded out the least promising candidates

weigh down VT SEP (a) *(doblar por el peso)* the branches were weighed down with snow; *(cargar)* don't weigh me down with anything more to carry (b) FIG. *(abrumar)* they are both weighed down with grief

weigh in VI (a) *(pesarse)* the champion weighed in at just under the limit; have you weighed in yet? (b) *(tomar parte)* I wish she wouldn't keep weighing in with comments that are totally irrelevant

weigh up VT SEP (a) *(examinar, sopesar)* weighing up the situation, she decided it was time to leave (b) *(juzgar)* he's very good at weighing people up quickly

while away VT SEP *(pasar el rato, hacer pasar el tiempo)* how did you while away all those hours you had to spend in the airport lounge?

whip away VT SEP (a) *(llevarse, hablando del viento, etc.)* a sudden gust whipped my hat away (b) FAM. *(quitar o llevarse bruscamente)* the waiter whipped our plates away before we'd finished eating

whip out 1 VS SEP *(sacar bruscamente de un bolso, de un bolsillo, etc.)* he whipped out his wallet 2 VI FAM. *(correr, salir pitando)* I'm just whipping out to the car for my briefcase

whip round VI (a) *(girarse o volverse bruscamente)* he whipped round and stared at me (b) **fam.** *(ir corriendo a)* whip round to the chemist's for me

whip up vt sep (a) *(entusiasmar)* such speeches are intended to whip an audience up (b) *(obtener)* what can we do to whip up support for the campaign? (c) *(batir)* whip up some cream for me, could you? (d) **fam.** *(improvisar, hablando de una comida)* I whipped up a meal for them

whisk away vt sep (a) *(apartar de un manotazo)* whisk the wasps away from the jam (b) **fam.** *(llevarse rápidamente)* the president was whisked away by helicopter

whittle away vt sep *(mermar)* she is whittling away her opponent's lead; support for the government is being whittled away by its evident failure to control inflation

whittle down vt sep *(reducir con esfuerzo)* we've whittled the number of candidates down

win back vt sep *(volver a ganar)* he won back all the money he had lost the previous week

win out/through vi *(triunfar)* he finally won out over his parents' objections; the strikers won through in the end (**es decir,** *los huelguistas acabaron por ver aceptadas sus reclamaciones*)

win over/round vt sep *(convencer)* they are trying to win me over to the idea of a camping holiday; *(seducir)* she is charming and has quite won us over

wind down 1 vt sep *(reducir la actividad de)* the company has decided to wind down its operations in that part of the world 2 **vi** *(tocar a su fin)* we went home since the party was winding down

wind up 1 vt sep (a) *(arreglar, hablando de un reloj, un despertador)* the clock needs to be wound up (b) *(acabar)* we wound up our holiday with a weekend in Paris (c) **brit. fam.** *(tomar el pelo a)* he really wound her up with those remarks about her dress; don't you know when you're being wound up? 2 **vi** = end up

winkle out vt sep fam. *(arrancar, lograr sacar)* I finally winkled the information out of him; it's no good trying to winkle any money out of me

wipe off **VT SEP** *(borrar)* the teacher wiped the equation off the board; *(quitar, limpiar)* wipe that grin off your face!

wipe out **VT SEP** (a) *(borrar)* she has completely wiped out the memory of the crash; *(hacer perder)* the power failure wiped out three weeks' work (b) *(dilapidar, hablando de dinero)* his gambling debts wiped out his entire fortune (c) *(destruir, exterminar)* enemy fire wiped out the village; whole families have been wiped out by the disease (d) **FAM.** *(agotar)* I feel wiped out

work in **VT SEP** *(mencionar en un discurso, etc.)* I think we should work something in about the help we received from other people; *(incorporar, agregar)* work the other ingredients in gradually

work off **VT SEP** *(descargar la ira, etc.)* she worked her anger off on the squash court; *(gastar energías)* I worked off my excess energy chopping wood

work on **VT INSEP** (a) *(buscar, trabajar en)* have you got any ideas? – I'm working on it; the police are working on who stole the jewels; *(intentar resolver)* he's been working on his emotional problems (b) *(partir de la base de)* we'll have to work on what we have (c) *(persuadir)* I've tried working on him but without much success

work out 1 **VI** (a) *(salir, resultar)* it depends on how things work out (b) *(funcionar)* that relationship will never work out (c) *(elevarse a)* how much do you make that work out at? (d) *(hacer ejercicio, entrenarse)* she's been working out all morning
2 **VT SEP** (a) *(resolver)* once you've worked out the exact problem, we can start to think about possible solutions; *(arreglar)* they'll have to work things out between themselves, I'm not getting involved (b) *(elaborar)* he's worked out a plan

work up **VT SEP** (a) *(desarrollar, experimentar, hablando de un sentimiento, etc.)* I can't work up any enthusiasm for this project (b) *(alterarse)* she was getting all worked up at the prospect of a holiday

work up to **VT INSEP** *(prepararse para)* he's working up to proposing to her; *(ir a parar)* it was easy to see what she was working up to

wriggle out of **VT INSEP** *(librarse de, hablando de una tarea, una obligación, etc.)* why did you let them wriggle out of doing their homework?; you can't wriggle out of this one

write away for VT INSP *(escribir para solicitar)* if you want to know more, write away for our free brochure

write in VI *(escribir cartas)* a great many viewers have written in with their comments about last week's programme

write off 1 VT SEP (a) *(condonar)* his debts have been written off (b) *(dejar por los suelos)* the critics wrote the play off (c) BRIT. *(cargarse)* she wrote her father's car off
2 VI *(solicitar por correo)* I've written off for tickets

write out VT SEP (a) *(redactar, pasar a limpio)* have you written out your essay? (b) *(hacer, hablando de un cheque, un recibo, etc.)* just write me out a cheque; the shop assistant wrote out the receipt (c) *(eliminar, hablando de un papel o un personaje en una serie de televisión, etc.)* her part has been written out

write up VT SEP *(preparar, redactar)* he's writing up a report on his business trip

zap up VT SEP FAM. *(hacer más vivo o más colorido)* the prose style could do with a bit of zapping up; *(realzar)* they've certainly zapped up the colour scheme

zero in on VT INSEP (a) *(dirigirse hacia)* the missile zeroes in on its target from a range of several kilometres (b) *(dar en el clavo)* they immediately zeroed in on the one weak point in the argument

zip up 1 VT SEP *(cerrar o subir la cremallera de)* she zipped her skirt up; zip me up, will you?
2 VI *(cerrarse con cremallera)* the dress zips up at the back

ÍNDICE DE VERBOS INGLESES

Las referencias alfanuméricas de este índice de verbos remiten a los modelos de verbos explicados en las páginas 16 a 18. El código M9 indica que el verbo es irregular (véanse las páginas 22 a 29).

Los verbos acabados en -ate y en -ize no figuran en este índice: estos se conjugan siempre según el modelo M4.

Los verbos que comienzan por los prefijos de-, dis-, mis-, out-, over-, re- y un- se pueden consultar a partir del segundo elemento de su construcción (por ejemplo, para misunderstand, véase understand).

La abreviatura *(U.S.)* indica la ortografía del inglés americano, que se explica en el modelo M5, en la página 17.

A

abase M4
abet M5
abhor M5
abide M4 o M4M9
abide by M4
abjure M4
abolish M2
abridge M4
absolve M4
abuse M4
abut M5
accede M4
access M2
accompany M6
accomplish M2
accrue M4
accuse M4
ache M4
achieve M4
acknowledge M4
acquiesce M4
acquire M4
acquit M5
ad-lib M5
address M2
adhere M4
adjudge M4
adjure M4
admire M4
admit M5
adore M4
advance M4
adventure M4
advertise M4
advise M4
age M4
agree M3
allege M4
allot M5
allude to M4
allure M4
ally M6

amass M2
amaze M4
amble M4
ambush M2
amplify M6
amuse M4
analyse M4
angle M4
announce M4
annul M5
appal M5
appease M4
apply M6
appraise M4
apprentice M4
apprise M4
approach M2
approve M4
arch M2
argue M4
arise M4M9
arouse M4
arrange M4
arrive M4
ascribe M4
assess M2
assuage M4
assume M4
assure M4
astonish M2
atone M4
attach M2
attribute M4
attune M4
avenge M4
aver M5
average M4
awake M4 o M4M9
axe M4

B

babble M4

baby M6
baby-sit M5M9
baffle M4
bag M5
bake M4
balance M4
bale out M4
ban M5
bandage M4
bandy M6
banish M2
bar M5
barbecue M4
bare M4
barge M4
barrel M5 *(U.S.)*
barricade in M4
base M4
bash M2
baste M4
bat M5
bathe M4
battle M4
beach M2
bear M1M9
beat M1M9
beatify M6
beautify M6
become M4M9
bed M5
bedazzle M4
bedevil M5 *(U.S.)*
beetle along M4
befall M1M9
befit M5
befog M5
befuddle M4
beg M5
beget M5M9
begin M5M9
begrudge M4
beguile M4
behave M4
behold M1M9

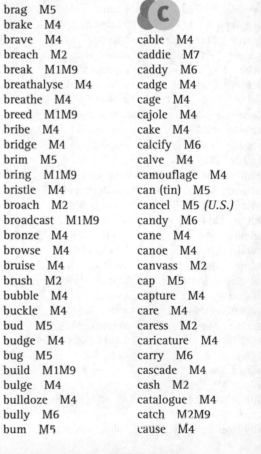

cave   M4
cavil   M5 *(U.S.)*
cease   M4
cede   M4
censure   M4
centre   M4
certify   M6
chafe   M4
challenge   M4
chance   M4
change   M4
channel   M5 *(U.S.)*
chap   M5
chaperone   M4
char   M5
charge   M4
chase   M4
chat   M5
cherish   M2
chide   M4M9
chime   M4
chip   M5
chisel   M5 *(U.S.)*
chivvy   M6
choke   M4
choose   M4M9
chop   M5
chortle   M4
chuckle   M4
chug   M5
chum up   M5
cinch   M2
circle   M4
circumscribe   M4
cite   M4
clam up   M5
clap   M5
clarify   M6
clash   M2
class   M2
classify   M6
cleanse   M4
cleave   M4 o M4M9
clench   M2

climax   M2
clinch   M2
cling   M1M9
clip   M5
clog   M5
clone   M4
close   M4
clot   M5
clothe   M4 o M4M9
club   M5
clue up   M4
clutch   M2
coach   M2
coalesce   M4
coax   M2
cobble   M4
code   M4
coerce   M4
cohere   M4
coincide   M4
collapse   M4
collide   M4
combine   M4
come   M4M9
commence   M4
commit   M5
commute   M4
compare   M4
compel   M5
compere   M4
compete   M4
compile   M4
complete   M4
comply   M6
compose   M4
compress   M2
comprise   M4
compromise   M4
con   M5
concede   M4
conceive   M4
conclude   M4
concur   M5
concuss   M2

condense   M4
condole   M4
condone   M4
confer   M5
confess   M2
confide   M4
confine   M4
confuse   M4
conjecture   M4
conjure away   M4
connive   M4
conserve   M4
console   M4
conspire   M4
constitute   M4
consume   M4
continue   M4
contravene   M4
contribute   M4
contrive   M4
control   M5
convalesce   M4
convene   M4
converge   M4
converse   M4
convince   M4
convulse   M4
cop   M5
cope   M4
copy   M6
core   M4
corpse   M4
corral   M5
corrode   M4
cosh   M2
cost   M1M9
counsel   M5 *(U.S.)*
couple   M4
course   M4
cox   M2
crackle   M4
cradle   M4
cram   M5
crane   M4

explode   M4
explore   M4
expose   M4
express   M2
extinguish   M2
extol   M5
extradite   M4
exude   M4
eye   M4

face   M4
facet   M1 o M5
fade   M4
fake   M4
fall   M1M9
falsify   M6
famish   M2
fan   M5
fancy   M6
fare   M4
fatigue   M4
fax   M2
faze   M4
feature   M4
feed   M1M9
feel   M1M9
fence   M4
ferry   M6
fetch   M2
fete   M4
fib   M5
fiddle   M4
fight   M1M9
figure   M4
filch   M2
file   M4
filigree   M3
finance   M4
find   M1M9
fine   M4
finish   M2

fire   M4
fish   M2
fit   M5 o M5M9
fix   M2
fizz   M2
fizzle   M4
flag   M5
flake   M4
flame   M4
flannel   M5 *(U.S.)*
flap   M5
flare   M4
flash   M2
flee   M3M9
fleece   M4
flesh out   M2
flex   M2
flinch   M2
fling   M1M9
flip   M5
flit   M5
flog   M5
flop   M5
flounce   M4
flourish   M2
flush   M2
fly   M6M9
fob   M5
focus   M2
fog   M5
fondle   M4
forage   M4
forbid   M5M9
force   M4
forecast   M1M9
forego   M2M9
foresee   M3M9
foretell   M1M9
forge   M4
forget   M5M9
forgive   M4M9
forgo   M2M9
format   M5
forsake   M4M9

forswear   M1M9
fortify   M6
fox   M2
fracture   M4
franchise   M4
free   M3
freeze   M4M9
fret   M5
fricassee   M3
fringe   M4
frolic   M8
fry   M6
fudge   M4
fuel   M5 *(U.S.)*
fulfil   M5
fumble   M4
fume   M4
funnel   M5 *(U.S.)*
fur up   M5
furnish   M2
fuse   M4
fuss   M2

gab   M5
gabble   M4
gad about   M5
gag   M5
gainsay   M1M9
gamble   M4
gambol   M5 *(U.S.)*
game   M4
gape   M4
garage   M4
garble   M4
gargle   M4
garnish   M2
garrotte   M4
gas   M5
gash   M2
gauge   M4
gaze   M4

gel   M5
gen up   M5
gesture   M4
get   M5M9
gibe   M4
giggle   M4
gild   M1 o M1M9
gird   M1 o M1M9
girdle   M4
give   M4M9
glance   M4
glare   M4
glass   M2
glaze   M4
glide   M4
glimpse   M4
glorify   M6
glory   M6
gloss over   M2
glue   M4
glut with   M5
gnash   M2
go   M2M9
gobble   M4
goggle   M4
gore   M4
gorge   M4
gouge   M4
grab   M5
grace   M4
grade   M4
grapple   M4
grass   M2
grate   M4
gratify   M6
gravel   M5 *(U.S.)*
graze   M4
grease   M4
grieve   M4
grin   M5
grind   M1M9
grip   M5
gripe   M4
grit   M5

grope   M4
gross   M2
grouch   M2
grovel   M5 *(U.S.)*
grow   M1M9
grub   M5
grudge   M4
grumble   M4
guarantee   M3
guess   M2
guide   M4
gum   M5
gun   M5
gurgle   M4
gush   M2
gut   M5
guzzle   M4

haemorrhage   M4
haggle   M4
halve   M4
ham   M5
handicap   M5
handle   M4
hang   M1 o M1M9
harangue   M4
harass   M2
hare   M4
harness   M2
harry   M6
hash   M2
hassle   M4
hatch   M2
hate   M4
have   M4M9
hear   M1M9
heave   M4 o M4M9
heckle   M4
hedge   M4
hem   M5
hew down   M1 o

M1M9
hiccup   M1 o M5
hide   M4M9
hike   M4
hinge   M4
hire   M4
hiss   M2
hit   M5M9
hitch   M2
hive   M4
hoax   M2
hobble   M4
hobnob   M5
hoe   M3
hog   M5
hold   M1M9
hole   M4
home   M4
hop   M5
hope   M4
hose   M4
hot up   M5
house   M4
huddle   M4
hug   M5
hum   M5
humble   M4
humidify   M6
hunch   M2
hurry   M6
hurt   M1M9
hurtle   M4
hush   M2
hustle   M4

ice   M4
identify   M6
idle   M4
ignite   M4
ignore   M4
imagine   M4

243

K

L

lead   M1M9
lean   M1 o M1M9
leap   M1 o M1M9
leapfrog   M5
learn   M1 o M1M9
lease   M4
leave   M4M9
lecture   M4
lend   M1M9
let   M5M9
level   M5 *(U.S.)*
levy   M6
liaise   M4
libel   M5 *(U.S.)*
license   M4
lie   M7M9
light   M1 o M1M9
like   M4
line   M4
liquefy   M6
live   M4
loathe   M4
lob   M5
lobby   M6
lodge   M4
log   M5
loose   M4
lop   M5
lope   M4
lose   M4M9
lounge   M4
louse   M4
love   M4
lug   M5
lunch   M2
lunge   M4
lurch   M2
lure   M4
lynch   M2

machine   M4

magnify   M6
make   M4M9
man   M5
manage   M4
mangle   M4
manicure   M4
manoeuvre   M4
manufacture   M4
map   M5
mar   M5
march   M2
marry   M6
marshal   M5 *(U.S.)*
marvel   M5 *(U.S.)*
mash   M2
masquerade   M4
mass   M2
massacre   M4
massage   M4
mat   M5
match   M2
mate   M4
mature   M4
mean   M1M9
measure   M4
meddle   M4
meet   M1M9
melt   M1 o M1M9
menace   M4
merge   M4
mesh   M2
mess   M2
mime   M4
mimic   M8
mince   M4
mine   M4
mingle   M4
mislay   M1M9
mislead   M1M9
misread   M1M9
miss   M2
mistake   M4M9
mix   M2
mob   M5

model   M5 *(U.S.)*
modify   M6
mop   M5
mope about o around   M4
mortgage   M4
mortify   M6
motivate   M4
move   M4
mow down   M1 o M1M9
muddle   M4
muddy   M6
muffle   M4
mug   M5
multiply   M6
mumble   M4
munch   M2
muscle in   M4
muse   M4
muss   M2
mute   M4
mutiny   M6
muzzle   M4
mystify   M6

nab   M5
nag   M5
name   M4
nap   M5
needle   M4
nerve   M4
nestle   M4
net   M5
nibble   M4
nip   M5
nobble   M4
nod   M5
nose   M4
nosh   M2
notch   M2

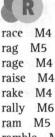

salvage M4
salve M4
sample M4
sanctify M6
sandwich M2
sap M5
satisfy M6
savage M4
save M4
saw M1M9
say M1M9
scab M5
scale M4
scan M5
scar M5
scare M4
scavenge M4
schedule M4
scheme M4
scorch M2
score M4
scrabble M4
scrag M5
scram M5
scramble M4
scrap M5
scrape M4
scratch M2
screech M2
scribble M4
scrounge M4
scrub M5
scrunch M2
scruple M4
scud M5
scuffle M4
sculpture M4
scurry M6
scuttle M4
scythe M4
search M2
secede M4
seclude M4
secrete M4

secure M4
seduce M4
see M1M9
seek M1M9
seethe M4
seize M4
sell M1M9
send M1M9
sense M4
sentence M4
serenade M4
serve M4
service M4
set M5M9
settle M4
sew M1M9
sex M2
shackle M4
shade M4
shag M5
shake M4M9
sham M5
shamble M4
shame M4
shape M4
share M4
shave M4
shear M1M9
sheathe M4
shed M5M9
shellac M8
shelve M4
shin M5
shine M4M9
shingle M4
ship M5
shit M5 o M5M9
shoe M4M9
shoot M1M9
shop M5
shore M4
shove M4
shovel M5 *(U.S.)*
show M1 o M1M9

shred M5
shrink M1M9
shrivel M5 *(U.S.)*
shrug M5
shuffle M4
shun M5
shush M2
shut M5M9
shuttle M4
shy M6
side M4
sidle M4
signal M5 *(U.S.)*
signify M6
silence M4
silhouette M4
simplify M6
sin M5
sing M1M9
singe M4
single out M4
sink M1M9
sip M5
sire M4
sit M5M9
site M4
size up M4
sizzle M4
skate M4
skedaddle M4
sketch M2
skid M5
skim M5
skin M5
skip M5
skive M4
slake M4
slam M5
slap M5
slash M2
slate M4
slave M4
sleep M1M9
slice M4

slide   M4M9
slim   M5
sling   M1M9
slink   M1M9
slip   M5
slit   M5M9
slog   M5
slop   M5
slope   M4
slosh   M2
slot   M5
slouch   M2
slug   M5
sluice   M4
slum   M5
slur   M5
smash   M2
smell   M1 o M1M9
smile   M4
smite   M4M9
smoke   M4
smooch   M2
smudge   M4
smuggle   M4
snaffle   M4
snafu   M2
snag   M5
snake   M4
snap   M5
snare   M4
snatch   M2
sneak   M1 o M1M9
sneeze   M4
sniffle   M4
snip   M5
snipe   M4
snitch   M2
snivel   M5 *(U.S.)*
snog   M5
snooze   M4
snore   M4
snub   M5
snuffle   M4
snuggle   M4

sob   M5
solace   M4
sole   M4
solidify   M6
solve   M4
soothe   M4
sow   M1M9
space   M4
span   M5
spangle   M4
spar   M5
spare   M4
sparkle   M4
speak   M1M9
specify   M6
speckle   M4
speechify   M6
speed   M1M9 o M1
spell   M1M9 o M1
spend   M1M9
spice   M4
spike   M4
spill   M1M9 o M1
spin   M5M9
spiral   M5 *(U.S.)*
spit   M5M9
spite   M4
splash   M2
splice   M4
split   M5M9
splurge   M4
spoil   M1 o M1M9
sponge   M4
spot   M5
spread   M1M9
spread-eagle   M4
spring   M1M9
sprinkle   M4
spruce up   M4
spur   M5
spy   M6
squabble   M4
square   M4
squash   M2

squat   M5
squeeze   M4
squelch   M2
squiggle   M4
squire   M4
stab   M5
stable   M4
stage   M4
stake   M4
stalemate   M4
stampede   M4
stand   M1M9
staple   M4
star   M5
starch   M2
stare   M4
startle   M4
starve   M4
stash   M2
state   M4
staunch   M2
steady   M6
steal   M1M9
stem   M5
stencil   M5 *(U.S.)*
step   M5
stereotype   M4
stet   M5
stick   M1M9
stifle   M4
sting   M1M9
stink   M1M9
stir   M5
stitch   M2
stoke   M4
stone   M4
stop   M5
store   M4
straddle   M4
strafe   M4
straggle   M4
strangle   M4
strap   M5
streamline   M4

stress M2	suppress M2	tap M5
stretch M2	surface M4	tape M4
strew M1 o M1M9	surge M4	tar M5
stride M4	surmise M4	tarnish M2
strike M4	surpass M2	tarry M6
string along M1M9	surprise M4	taste M4
strip M5	survive M4	tat M5
stroke M4	suss M2	tattle M4
strop M5	swab M5	tax M2
structure M4	swaddle M4	taxi M2
struggle M4	swan around M5	teach M2M9
strum M5	swap M5	tear M1M9
strut M5	swash M2	tease M4
stub M5	swat M5	tee M3
stucco M1 o M2	swathe M4	teethe M4
stud M5	swear M1M9	telecast M1M9
study M6	sweat M1 o M1M9	telephone M4
stultify M6	sweep M1M9	telescope M4
stumble M4	swell M1 o M1M9	televise M4
stun M5	swerve M4	telex M2
stupefy M6	swig M5	tell M1M9
style M4	swim M5M9	tense M4
subdue M4	swindle M4	terrace M4
sublease M4	swing M1M9	terrify M6
submerge M4	swipe M4	testify M6
submit M5	swish M2	thatch M2
subscribe M4	switch M2	thieve M4
subside M4	swivel M5 *(U.S.)*	thin M5
substitute M4	swoosh M2	think M1M9
subsume M4	swot M5	thrash M2
subtitle M4	syringe M4	thresh M2
suckle M4		thrive M4 o M4M9
sue M4		throb M5
suffice M4		throttle M4
suffuse M4	table M4	throw M1M9
sully M6	tackle M4	thrum M5
sum up M5	tag M5	thrust M1M9
sun M5	take M4M9	thud M5
sunbathe M4	talc M8 o M1	tickle M4
sup M5	tally M6	tide over M4
supersede M4	tame M4	tidy M6
supervise M4	tan M5	tie M7
supply M6	tangle M4	tile M4
suppose M4		time M4